1 1/5/-

D

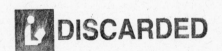

OXFORD HISTORICAL SERIES

Editors

R. W. SOUTHERN   J. S. WATSON   R. B. WERNHAM

SECOND SERIES

NOTE

This series comprises carefully selected studies which have been submitted,
or are based upon theses submitted, for higher degrees in this University.
The works listed below are those still in print

FROM JOSEPH II
TO THE
JACOBIN TRIALS

*Government Policy and Public Opinion
in the Habsburg Dominions in the
Period of the French Revolution*

By

ERNST WANGERMANN

OXFORD UNIVERSITY PRESS
1959

Oxford University Press, Amen House, London E.C.4

GLASGOW NEW YORK TORONTO MELBOURNE WELLINGTON
BOMBAY CALCUTTA MADRAS KARACHI KUALA LUMPUR
CAPE TOWN IBADAN NAIROBI ACCRA

PRINTED IN GREAT BRITAIN

TO
CHRISTOPHER HILL

PREFACE

JOSEPH II has attracted the attention of many historians. Yet no one has so far attempted to give us a comprehensive account of the reign of his successor Leopold II. Mitrofanov intended to do so, but got no farther than foreign policy. The subtlety of Leopold's policy and his early death have left many problems difficult of solution. The early years of Francis II's reign are the subject of many publications, but have remained remarkably obscure as far as internal policy is concerned. Wolfsgruber's biography stops at 1792. Bibl's work is incredibly superficial. Professor Langsam's new biography (if we may judge from Volume I which alone has so far appeared) is based on far too narrow a selection of original sources, and therefore sheds a distorting light. The important and interesting episode of the 'Jacobin trials' has been properly investigated only by Hungarian historians (Fraknoi, Mályusz, Benda), whose publications deal only with the Hungarian side of the affair.

The subject-matter of the present work is the interaction of government policy and public opinion in the Habsburg dominions in the period of the French Revolution. The material which I have examined has brought out sharply features of Joseph II's reign which have perhaps been insufficiently stressed by other writers. It has helped me to raise a number of important questions about the policies of Leopold II, though not to find complete answers to them. It has thrown much new light on the 'Jacobin trials', revealing the inadequacy and inaccuracies of the earlier accounts.

The *Justizpalast* fire of 1927 and a bombardment of 1945 have left painful gaps in the records of the Vienna archives. The records of the Ministry of Police and the Court Chancellery are now very incomplete, and those of the Council of State have perished altogether for the period under consideration. Of the two former, I have been able to find a few duplicate records in the provincial archives. For the latter, the brief summaries of the *Staatskanzleidirektor* Vogel which are preserved in the *Kaiser Franz Akten* are now indispensable substitutes. In the following pages, however, many questions are raised which, in the absence of the documents lost in 1927 and 1945, must for the present remain open.

It is a pleasure to acknowledge the numerous obligations which I have incurred in the course of my work. Dr. Albert Hollaender originally suggested the field of research. The generosity of the Fellows of Balliol College and the Ministry of Education made possible more than two years' work in the Austrian archives. The unfailing courtesy and energy of the staff of these archives enabled me to make the utmost use of the time at my disposal. In this connexion I should like to mention especially the staff of the *Haus-, Hof- und Staats-archiv* and the *Allgemeine Verwaltungsarchiv*, Vienna, where I found most of my material. For valuable and helpful criticism and suggestions I am indebted to Dr. Franz Pollack-Parnau, Dr. Hans Schenk, and to the editors of the Oxford Historical Series, especially Mr. J. Steven Watson. My debts to scholars in neighbouring fields of research are, I hope, adequately acknowledged in the footnotes and the bibliography. I take this opportunity of expressing my thanks to Dr. Muriel M. Edwards, Mr. Christopher Hill, and Mr. and Mrs. F. Dichter, without whose help in one way and another this work could not have been completed.

E. W.

Earls Colne
March 1958

CONTENTS

A NOTE ON THE REFERENCES

THE name of the repository is indicated where this is not the *Haus-, Hof- und Staatsarchiv* or the *Allgemeine Verwaltungsarchiv*, Vienna. To indicate these in each case would lead to unnecessary repetition. All documents whose repository is not indicated are kept in the *Haus-, Hof- und Staatsarchiv*, except the records of the *Hofkanzlei*, the *Polizeihofstelle*, and the *Pergen Akten*, which are in the *Allgemeine Verwaltungsarchiv*.

Recently, the staff of the *Haus-, Hof- und Staatsarchiv* have carried out some rearrangement with regard to the *Kaiser Franz Akten* and the *Vertrauliche Akten*. The *Faszikel* number quoted in this work refers to the old arrangement throughout, and strictly speaking the word *alt* should have been added in brackets after the number in each case.

The following abbreviations have been used:

Au.	Alleruntertänigste(r).
Ah.	Allerhöchste(s).
F.	Faszikel.
fol(s).	folio(s).
Vertr. Akten	*Vertrauliche Akten.*

In the quotations the original spelling has been preserved, though the punctuation has at times been altered to increase clarity.

INTRODUCTION

MANY philosophers wrote with the aim of converting rulers. Many philosophers of the eighteenth century believed that they had succeeded. Some lived to be disillusioned.

The apparent conversion was in fact due to purely practical considerations. Many governmental policies which have commonly been regarded as the fruits of the prevailing enlightened philosophy, may be interpreted more convincingly as the appropriate eighteenth-century form of the general policy of centralizing and strengthening the State, attempted by monarchs in western Europe since the thirteenth century.[1]

Since the development of the Atlantic trade routes, the countries sharing the Atlantic seaboards had been in the vanguard of economic advancement, and therefore of political centralization. The countries of central and eastern Europe, far away from the new trading centres and afflicted by invasion from primitive and savage nations, remained backward in comparison until the end of the seventeenth century. At about that time, able monarchs in Russia and Brandenburg-Prussia embarked on a policy of state centralization and expansion by importing artificially some at least of the economic development which had made England, Spain, and France powerful. The growing strength and the expansion of Russia and Prussia caused alarm and forced the pace in the Habsburg dominions. The loss of Silesia to Prussia in 1740 was a symptom of the ominous fact that the Habsburgs had fallen behind in the European rulers' race for strength. The greatness of the Empress Maria Theresa lies in the fact that she was prepared to take all necessary steps to remedy this situation, however strongly these might conflict with her personal inclinations.

The Empress was determined to regain Silesia in a new trial of strength. This determination was the starting-point

---

[1] G. Lefebvre, 'Le Despotisme éclairé', in *Annales historiques de la Révolution française*, xxi (1949), 98.

of the great series of reforms which is associated with her name and that of her son Joseph. A beginning was made with the reform of the armed forces. This implied reforms in other fields: the maintenance of the new armed forces required a substantial increase in taxation which, in turn, could be obtained only by constitutional, political, economic, and administrative reforms of the most far-reaching order. To put the reforms into effect, a new civil service was required, and to train the civil servants, a new educational system freed from clerical control and censorship had to be built up.

A policy of enlightened despotism thus appeared in Austria no less than elsewhere in response to certain practical and urgent necessities, and not as the fruit of philosophical persuasion.[1] The statement is as valid for the reign of Joseph II as it is for that of his mother. The 'revolutionary' Emperor undertook little that was entirely new in principle. But his obstinate consistency and enthusiasm has always provided historians with an additional temptation to impute philosophical motives to him, which has resulted in a long-standing and sterile controversy as to the theoretical origin of his reforms.[2]

It does not, of course, follow that the philosophy and political theory of the eighteenth century is irrelevant to the study of enlightened despotism. The philosophers and their disciples played a role in the practical application of the enlightened despots' policies which was neither insignificant nor without consequences. They were mistaken in their belief that they had converted the despots. But it was an

---

[1] O. Hinze, 'Der österreichische und der preußische Beamtenstaat im 17. and 18. Jahrhundert', in *Historische Zeitschrift*, Neue Folge, l (1901), 438. Also P. Müller, 'Der aufgeklärte Absolutismus in Österreich', in *International Bulletin of the Historical Sciences*, ix, *passim*.

[2] Among the disputants on the question of which set of theories was responsible for the Josephinian reforms may be mentioned A. Jäger, 'Das Eindringen des modernen kirchenfeindlichen Geistes in Österreich', in *Zeitschrift für katholische Theologie*, ii (1878); H. v. Voltelini, 'Die naturrechtlichen Lehren und die Reformen des 18. Jahrhunderts', in *Hist. Zeitschr.*, Dritte Folge, ix (1910); G. Holzknecht, 'Ursprung . . . der Reformideen Josephs II', in *Forschungen zur inneren Geschichte Österreichs*, xi (1914: Innsbruck); T. v. Borodajkevicz, 'Die Kirche in Österreich', in Nadler-Srbik, *Österreich, Erbe und Sendung im Deutschen Raum* (1936: Vienna); E. Winter, *Der Josephinismus und seine Geschichte* (1943: Vienna); F. Maass, 'Der Josephinismus, Quellen zu seiner Geschichte in Österreich 1760–1790', I, in *Fontes Rerum Austriacarum*, 2nd ser., lxxi (1951), Introduction.

unmistakable resemblance between many of the reforms and
the principles they were advocating that gave rise to their
illusion. The resemblance symptomized a certain limited
conformity of interest between the monarchy and the classes
for whom the philosophers of the Enlightenment were speaking. To increase its financial resources, the absolute monarchy needed a more numerous and prosperous capitalist
class. To combat the short-sighted opposition of aristocracy
and clergy against the curtailment of their privileges, it had
to bring up behind its lines the ideological cannon of middle-
class anti-aristocratic and anti-clerical philosophers, journalists, and university professors. To implement the vast
programme of far-reaching reforms, it had to rely on the
initiative and enthusiasm of the graduate civil servants
trained by the latter.[1]

In this way the reforms of enlightened despotism helped
to awaken the non-privileged classes in the Habsburg
dominions from their political slumber and to bring them,
for the first time since the Reformation, into the field of
political action. Not all the consequences of such a political
renaissance had, however, been foreseen by Joseph II, and
some of them alarmed him and his successors acutely. For
the political struggle of the Fourth Estate[2] transcended
fairly quickly the limits marked out by official instructions
and encouragement. By the end of Joseph II's reign, the
non-privileged classes had gained enough at the expense of
the privileged to desire more; enough, in fact, to envisage,
however vaguely, complete social and political emancipation.

So far was this from the intentions of Joseph II, that we
may regard it as among the decisive factors leading ultimately to the abandonment of enlightened despotism by the
Habsburg monarchy.[3] The more timid elements in the

[1] Lefebvre, pp. 108–9.

[2] As the Knights constituted a separate estate distinct from the Peers, the non-
privileged orders are referred to as the Fourth Estate in the Habsburg dominions.
The French division of society into three Estates obtained only in the Austrian
Netherlands.

[3] Cf. Lefebvre, pp. 110–15, where he contrasts the essentially conservative aims
of enlightened despotism with the revolutionary aims of the French Third Estate.
In the light of this, the abandonment by the monarchy of enlightened despotism is
a perfectly natural consequence of the unforeseen revolutionary impact of its own
reforms.

Fourth Estate relapsed into a disillusioned inactivity. The rest, encouraged by the news from France after 1789, found themselves inevitably driven into opposition to the monarchy itself. The monarchy, now thoroughly frightened, embarked on the political suppression of its former allies whom it had so recently strengthened and encouraged, but now found to be infected with the 'fever of freedom' and the poison of 'Jacobinism'.

I have tried in the pages which follow to examine the character of the political thought and activity of the Fourth Estate which developed in the wake of the great flood of reforms from above, to describe the growing estrangement between the monarchy and the non-privileged classes, and to estimate the influence of these two factors on the evolution of Habsburg internal policies from the last years of Joseph II's reign until the suppression of 'Jacobinism' in Austria.[1]

---

[1] I am not qualified to attempt a comprehensive account of developments in Hungary. Such accounts are already available, at least in the Hungarian language. I have, however, included material relating to Hungary whenever this has been necessary for my analysis of Habsburg policies.

I

CONFLICTS AND IDEAS ENGENDERED
BY THE POLICIES OF JOSEPH II

1. *The Fourth Estate in the Battle against the Clerical and*
Aristocratic Opposition

I<small>N</small> 1754 Maria Theresa founded the Chair of Natural Law
in the University of Vienna.[1] In 1781 Joseph II considerably relaxed the severity of the Austrian censorship
regulations.[2] In 1786 he commissioned the first Magyar
newspaper ever published in Vienna.[3] These measures
formed part of a series designed to strengthen the enlightened monarchy in its efforts to restrict the privileges of
clergy and nobility.

They did indeed strengthen the monarchy in this struggle.
Arguments from natural law were used to confute papal
claims, to demonstrate the anomalies of the old feudal con-
stitutions, and to frustrate Migazzi, Archbishop of Vienna, in
his tenacious defence of ecclesiastical independence and property.[4] The graduates of the reformed universities throughout the Habsburg dominions entered the service of the state,
where their training in the new political theories provided
the essential ideological basis for their task of imposing the
new laws and regulations upon a reluctant ruling class. The
relaxation of the censorship regulations opened the gates to
an unprecedented flood of tracts arguing the case against the
Papacy and against clerical and aristocratic privileges in
general.[5] The new Magyar newspaper, written and edited

[1] A. Menzel, 'Beiträge zur Geschichte der Staatslehre', in *Sitzungsberichte der
Akad. der Wissensch., Wien*, ccx. 451.

[2] H. Gnau, *Die Zensur unter Joseph II* (1911: Leipzig), pp. 43 ff.

[3] Grossing to Francis II, 29 Dec. 1792, *Kaiser Franz Akten*, F. 154, Konv. 1,
No. 23.

[4] P. v. Mitrofanov, *Joseph II, seine kulturelle und politische Tätigkeit* (1910:
Vienna), pp. 779–80. Cf. also F. Valjavec, *Die Entstehung der politischen Strömungen
in Deutschland 1770–1815* (1951: Vienna), p. 22.

[5] Mitrofanov, pp. 780–6, where a summary of their contents may be found.

by men from the ranks of the middle class, put forward the
government's case in accordance with the instructions of
Joseph II[1] against the ever more obstinate conservative-
nationalist opposition of the Hungarian magnates and gentry.

In this way the monarchy helped to bring certain sections
of the non-privileged classes into the turmoil of political and
religious controversy. This was soon followed by quite spontaneous political action on the part of the non-privileged,
who were after all no less interested than the monarchy in the
curtailment of aristocratic and clerical privileges.

There can be little doubt that many of Joseph II's civil
servants wanted to see a more radical ecclesiastical policy
than the Emperor, a faithful Roman Catholic, was willing to
countenance. When protests and remonstrances from the
bishops were addressed to the Emperor, the civil servants
through whose hands the documents had to pass, did all in
their power to prevent a weakening in the government's
determination to press on with their policies. Such government departments as the Commission for Ecclesiastical
Affairs (*Geistliche Hofkommission*) under Kressel,[2] and the
Commission for Education and Censorship (*Studien- und
Zensurshofkommission*) under Gottfried van Swieten[3] consistently attempted to give the widest possible interpretation
to their instructions if it was a matter of restraining clerical
influence or facilitating the expression of anti-clerical
opinions.[4]

Rebuffed by the government, the clergy appealed to public opinion. It could not do so in writing, because van
Swieten's censors refused to pass most publications expressing the views of the clerical opposition. Sermons, however, were not subject to government censorship. Zealous
preachers, therefore, frequently attacked the Emperor's

---

[1] Grossing to Francis II, 29 Dec. 1792, *Kaiser Franz Akten*, F. 154, Konv. 1,
No. 23.

[2] Franz Karl Freiherr Kressel v. Gualtenberg (1720–1801), Councillor of the
Court Chancellery, President of the Commission for Ecclesiastical Affairs, succeeded
Chotek as Court Chancellor on the latter's resignation in 1789; forced to retire 1792.

[3] Gottfried Freiherr van Swieten (1734–1803), son of Gerhard van Swieten;
Ambassador in Brussels, Paris, Berlin, and Warsaw; Custodian of the Imperial
Library 1777, President of the Commission for Education and Censorship 1781.

[4] C. Wolfsgruber, *Cristoph Anton Kardinal Migazzi* (1890: Saulgau), pp. 502–624,
Nachlaß Kollowrat, F. 13, No. 1169.

ecclesiastical policy in their sermons. This challenge was taken up in a way which provides one of the most significant examples of spontaneous political action on the part of the non-privileged.

Anti-clerical pamphlets had been in fashion since the relaxation of the censorship in 1781. To parry the onslaught of the pulpit against the Josephinian reforms, some of the more enterprising anti-clerical authors organized themselves in the so-called 'Institute of Sermon Critics'. The aim was to put some kind of check on the preachers by subjecting their sermons to searching criticism in the Institute's weekly publication, *Wöchentliche Wahrheiten über die Predigten in Wien*.[1]

This publication was strongly denounced by the clergy as one tending to impair the prestige of the word of God. Its influence was none the less considerable. Publications were cheap and the reading public was growing. The *Wöchentliche Wahrheiten* helped to stimulate popular interest in the great argument about religion. Congregations began to listen to their sermons with greater care, to think for themselves about the issues raised in them and so, at times, to take sides in the controversy. The scanty evidence available does not allow us to make any far-reaching generalizations concerning the trend of opinion in the congregations. But there is some evidence to show that preachers who dissociated themselves from strict traditionalist views and attempted to bring Catholic dogma and practice into some harmony with the philosophy of Enlightenment and the requirements of the State, had a considerable following in the populous new suburbs of Vienna.

The case of the Piarist preacher Wieser provides a vivid illustration of this. In accordance with the more modern trends in the theology of the time, Wieser insisted on the overriding importance of the moral element in Christianity, and denounced mechanical observation of ceremonies and 'superstitious' beliefs and practices. The consistory of Vienna tended to be suspicious of such attempts to compromise with

[1] Alois Blumauer, 'Beobachtungen über Österreichs Aufklärung und Literatur' (*c.* 1783), in *Sämtliche Werke und handschriftlicher Nachlaß* (1884: Vienna), iv. 239–48.

the fashionable philosophy of the time, and considered their worst apprehensions confirmed in 1786, when Wieser overstepped the bounds of doctrinal orthodoxy in his teaching concerning the devil. The Archbishop, Cardinal Migazzi, ordered the suspension of the unorthodox preacher and a consistorial investigation of his views and teaching.[1]

Wieser's congregation reacted with considerable vigour. A petition to the Emperor asserting that he had preached the true word of the gospel and demanding his reinstatement was signed by a hundred people.[2] A pamphlet refuting Wieser by Fast, apparently the most pugnacious of the traditionalist preachers whose sermons had often been criticized in the *Wöchentliche Wahrheiten*, was answered by one from the hand of a member of Wieser's congregation, Felberer, who was a cobbler by trade.[3]

The Emperor, presumably on the advice of Kressel, decided to grant the petition and ordered Wieser's reinstatement. This was evidently regarded by the congregation as a political victory for themselves. Felberer's account of the day of reinstatement illustrates the really wide interest aroused by the case, and seems curiously reminiscent of victory celebrations of middle-class political parties in the nineteenth century.

A large company of citizens and officials celebrated this day. A festive dinner was held at Dornbach[4] to which Wieser and I were invited. Among the guests was the master tailor Engel, a florist called Bichler, the auditor Kramer with his two sons, Wieser's two brothers, a [female] cook from the General Hospital who had also written a pamphlet against Fast, the upholsterer Storch from Neubau,[5] and many others, . . . all in all some fifty people.[6]

Felberer was rewarded for his part in the campaign by a collection taken on this occasion which enabled him to buy his citizenship of the city of Vienna and to become a master cobbler.[7]

---

[1] Lorenz Hübner, *Lebensgeschichte Josephs II* (1790: Salzburg), ii. 335.
[2] Ibid.
[3] Auszug aus dem Verhörsprotokoll Felberers, 1794, *Erzbischöfl. Ordinariatsarchiv, Regesten*, No. 773.   [4] At this time a village just outside Vienna.
[5] Suburb of Vienna.
[6] Auszug aus dem Verhörsprotokoll Felberers, 1794, quoted by Wolfsgruber, p. 827, n. 1.   [7] Ibid.

In Graz, capital of the Duchy of Styria, a similar battle of ideas was raging. At the head of the anti-clerical publicists stood Franz Xaver Neupauer, Professor of Canon Law at the University of Graz.[1] He had published a number of books on the problems of Church and State and one on the validity of monastic vows. Gradually he had been driven to the conclusion that individual learned works would not achieve lasting results, and had therefore embarked on the publication of a monthly periodical, *Der Weltpriester*, which was specifically designed to win the clergy for more enlightened views.[2]

Like the *Wöchentliche Wahrheiten* in Vienna, Neupauer's periodical helped to stimulate popular interest in the religious controversy. The citizens of Graz took Neupauer's side and gave expression to their support by arranging feasts in his honour.[3] Even in some of the smaller Styrian cities, the religious controversy was a favourite topic of conversation.[4] As late as 1793, when many people had become reluctant to express their opinions in public, a petition was sent to the Court Chancellery[5] signed by numerous male and female citizens of Graz, asking for the reinstatement of a suspended clergyman. In this case, however, the government's decree did not order the desired reinstatement, but instructed the governor of Styria to prevent such collections of signatures in future.[6]

The recalcitrant aristocracy found itself in difficulties similar to those of the clergy. Their remonstrances, too, had to pass through hostile government departments before reaching the Emperor. If we may trust the assertions of aggrieved landlords, the Commission for Commutation of

---

[1] For the career and views of Neupauer, cf. A. Posch, *Die kirchliche Aufklärung auf der Universität Graz* (1946: Graz), *passim*.

[2] Majestätsgesuch der grazer Bürgerschaft, 17 July 1791, *Kaiser Franz Akten*, F. 126.

[3] Posch, pp. 108 ff.

[4] Schriftliches Geständnis Dirnböcks, 2 Apr. 1795, *Vertrauliche Akten*, F. 29, fols. 9–10.

[5] The Court Chancellery was renamed *Directorium* in 1792 when it was once more amalgamated with the *Hofkammer*. It seems preferable, however, to keep to the old name in the English text.

[6] Hofdekret, 12 Oct. 1793, *Steiermärkisches Landesarchiv, Miszellen*, Kart. 225.

Labour Services (*Robotreluitionshofkommission*) under the Councillor of State Friedrich v. Eger,[1] was staffed exclusively with officials bitterly hostile to the cause of the aristocracy. Eger himself, like Kressel and Gottfried van Swieten in matters relating to the clergy, consistently tried to induce Joseph II to remain firm in face of the increasingly importunate representations of the nobility against the great feudal reforms of 1789.

The Hungarians were in the vanguard of the aristocratic opposition, and it is therefore in Hungary that the struggle of the non-privileged against it came into evidence most clearly.

Ever since Joseph had received information that some Hungarian magnates and gentry were intending to indulge in treasonable activity by getting in touch with the Prussian government (i.e. since July 1788),[2] the police officials in Hungary were in the forefront of the battle against the aristocratic opposition.

At the head of the police in Pest, one of the centres of the opposition, was Franz Gotthardi, one-time merchant of Pest who had been elected by his fellow citizens to the office of *Stadthauptmann*.[3] He was an enthusiastic supporter of the Josephinian reforms in Hungary. When the opposition began to assume disquieting proportions, he at once advocated a policy of severity against the malcontents who 'in their blindness failed to appreciate the noble, righteous, and generally useful measures of the monarch'.[4]

Gotthardi spared no effort himself to enable the government to pursue a policy of severity. He organized a wide network of correspondents recruited from elements hostile to the aristocratic agitation. He specialized in cultivating the friendship and confidence of middle-class freemasons who could furnish details of the efforts made by aristocratic masons to use the order for their political ends.[5] This enabled

---

[1] Friedrich Freiherr v. Eger (1734–1812), Councillor 1769, Councillor of State 1785; succeeded Zinzendorf as President of the Commission for Commutation of Labour Services 1789.

[2] E. Wertheimer, 'Baron Hompesch und Joseph II', in *Mitteilungen d. Instituts für öst. Geschichtsforschung*, Ergänzungsb. VI, pp. 656–7.

[3] Verhörsprotokoll Gotthardis, fols. 154 ff., *Vertr. Akten*, F. 4.

[4] Gotthardi to Beer, 24 July 1788, *Pergen Akten*, xi/B20, H2.

[5] *Pergen Akten*, x/A3, H75, 76, 79.

him to pass on to the Ministry of Police in Vienna a continuous stream of useful information.[1]

At times he exceeded the bounds of his official competence by venturing suggestions which required decisions at the highest level. Late in 1789, for example, he recommended to the government the publication of a counterblast to the strident conservative-nationalist propaganda of the Hungarian opposition, which was just then being spiced with allusions to the upheaval in France. The author of the manuscript he submitted was Leopold Alois Hoffmann, a former contributor to the *Wöchentliche Wahrheiten*, and now Professor of German at the University of Pest. Though Gotthardi's plan had originally been sanctioned, the Emperor finally refused to sponsor the publication of Hoffmann's manuscript, because he did not approve of the author's references to the French Revolution.[2]

The need for an effective reply to the growing output of aristocratic propaganda was widely felt. It was warmly advocated amongst others by the Piarist Gabelhofer, Professor of Moral Theology at the University of Pest.[3] A reply was eventually published by Molnár, the head of the Protestant community in Pest and a member of the *Illuminati* Sect.[4]

It would be easy to regard this spontaneous political activity of the non-privileged as a powerful factor strengthening the enlightened monarchy in its struggle against the clerical and aristocratic opposition. Joseph II, however, and his principal advisers, regarded it with very mixed feelings, because it became increasingly clear that the political motives of the non-privileged had little in common with those of the government. Public opinion in the Fourth Estate had overtaken enlightened despotism by which it had first been aroused. It was beginning to question the fundamental

---

[1] Only a fraction of Gotthardi's numerous reports to his superior at the *Polizeioberdirektion* in Vienna seems to have survived. They are to be found—some badly damaged by the fire of 1927—in various sections of the *Pergen Akten*.

[2] Ibid. xi/B24, H32; x/A3, H74, 77, 80, 81.

[3] Gabelhofer to Gotthardi, 28 Nov. 1789, *Pergen Akten*, x/A3, H75.

[4] (Anon.), *Politisch-kirchlicher Manch-Hermaeon* (1790: Leipzig). Gotthardi revealed Molnár's authorship to Francis II in Gotthardi to Francis II, 6 Mar. 1792, *Vertr. Akten*, F. 57, fol. 414.

assumptions of aristocratic privilege, of Christianity, and of despotism itself.

2. *Public Opinion in the Fourth Estate overtakes Enlightened Despotism*

The case of Professor Hoffmann's proposed publication against the Hungarian nobility shows that Joseph II's ministers were aware of the difference in approach to the aristocratic problem as between themselves and their would-be supporters of the Fourth Estate. The Minister of Police, Count Pergen,[1] advised the Emperor not to sanction pub-lication, precisely because he had detected unmistakable signs of this difference in Hoffmann's arguments. The word-ing of Pergen's Note indicates this clearly:

In view of the delicate and complicated state of affairs in Hungary, where the opinions of so many malcontents have taken such a danger-ous turn; in view, moreover, of the various references to the present revolution in France, which are open to different sorts of interpretation by people of differing political outlook, I will not venture to advise that this manuscript be printed with official sanction. . . .[2]

What was this difference in political outlook to which Pergen refers? Put briefly, it was this. While Joseph II was merely developing his mother's policy of restricting aristo-cratic privileges which impeded the full unfolding of the power of the State, public opinion in the Fourth Estate was beginning to deny the justification of aristocratic privilege as such.

When in 1781 the commoner Wolfgang Amadeus Mozart came into conflict with the archiepiscopal Chamberlain Count Arco, and finally severed his connexion with the Archbishop of Salzburg, he became fully conscious of his own claim to equality of status with the privileged. In justi-fication of his action he wrote to his father: 'It is his heart which ennobles a man. I may not be a Count, but I have more honour within myself than many a Count.'[3]

---

[1] Johann Anton Graf v. Pergen (1725–1814), in charge of various commissions in the Empire 1751–63; Plenipotentiary in Galicia 1772–4; President of the Lower Austrian Government 1782.

[2] Au. Note Pergens, 8 Dec. 1789, *Pergen Akten*, x/A3, H80.

[3] L. Schiedermair (ed.), *Briefe Mozarts u. seiner Familie* (1914: Munich), ii. 91.

It was an attitude which Mozart's father utterly failed to understand. But in the years which followed, this attitude became an integral aspect of his own art. He was attracted to the subject-matter of Beaumarchais's *The Marriage of Figaro*, because it expressed his own feelings in this matter. 'Parce que vous êtes un grand Seigneur, vous vous croyez un grand génie! Noblesse, fortune, un rang, des places: tout cela rend si fier! Qu'avez-vous fait pour tant de biens! Vous vous êtes donné la peine de naître, et rien de plus; du reste, homme assez ordinaire'.[1]

Figaro's words had to be omitted in da Ponte's libretto before the Emperor would agree to lift the ban he had imposed on Beaumarchais's play.[2]

Under the treatment of Mozart and da Ponte, however, the underlying political message of the play survived the enforced textual changes.

The sentiments of Beaumarchais's Figaro are clearly reflected also in the words of Andreas Riedel, one-time tutor of the Archduke Francis. Riedel, who was sentenced to sixty years imprisonment in 1795 as head of the 'Jacobin Conspiracy' in Austria, desired the abolition of a nobility,

who ruthlessly exploited the most useful and indispensable section of the population only to squander the wealth so hardly produced; . . . for the sake of whose frivolity countless people have to labour more than the slaves of Asia; . . . for whose younger sons, whatever their abilities, new offices, foundations and institutions must ever be invented and maintained by the labour of poor men . . .

For Riedel the true noble was he

who goes forth into the wild plains of the Banat . . . and of Podolia to teach its primitive inhabitants the blessings of civilisation . . . and how to till their soil; he who helps to populate the uninhabited regions of this vast monarchy; he who leaves the cities in order to free the peasants from the intolerable yoke of subordinate officials; he who knows the value of the really useful people who alone produce what we enjoy.[3]

The case against aristocratic privilege as such was given

---

[1] Beaumarchais, *Le Mariage de Figaro*, Act V, Scene III.
[2] L. da Ponte, *Denkwürdigkeiten*, ed. Gugitz (1924: Dresden), i. 233–4.
[3] Schriftliche Aussage Riedels, *Vertr. Akten*, F. 8, fols. 292–3.

its theoretical formulation by Ignaz Joseph v. Martinovics
who was executed in 1795 as head of the 'Jacobin Conspiracy' in Hungary. According to Martinovics, 'the [social]
contract binding members of society grants equal justice to
all members of society, so that they may equally enjoy the
fruits of security and liberty'.[1]

Privileges and immunities of any kind he considered
incompatible with this principle.[2]

In matters of religion, too, the measures and intentions
of enlightened despotism were soon overtaken by public
opinion in the Fourth Estate.

Joseph II's celebrated Edict of Toleration of 1781 was
regarded as inadequate by all who saw in toleration something more than a device for attracting foreign skilled crafts-
men to the new industries of Austria and settlers to the wastes
of Hungary.[3]

A poem on toleration by the leading poet of the Austrian
Enlightenment, Johann Baptist v. Alxinger, was suppressed
by the Josephinian censorship[4] and had to be published in
Leipzig.

> Nur dort, wo man in jedem guten Mann
> Der Gottheit heil'gen Abdruck ehret,
> Von jenem, der nicht glauben kann,
> Nie, daß er glauben soll, begehret,
> Den züchtiget, der als Tyrann
> Die Menschen mit der Geißel lehret,
> Unglauben nicht bestraft, und Glauben nicht belohnt,
> Dort ist es, wo die Duldung wohnt.[5]

By this standard, Joseph could not claim to have bestowed
the blessings of toleration on his dominions. The ruthless
persecution of the Bohemian Deists was not interrupted by
the 'Toleration' Edict, and served as a vivid illustration of
the wide chasm which separated the principle of toleration
from the principles of Joseph II.[6]

---

[1] (Anon.), *Oratio pro Leopoldo Secundo* (1792: Germania), p. 14.
[2] Ibid., pp. 17–19.   [3] Mitrofanov, p. 787.
[4] E. Probst, 'Johann B. v. Alxinger', in *Jahrb. d. Grillparzergesellschaft*, vii
(1897), 180.
[5] *Alxingers sämtl. poetische Schriften* (1784: Leipzig), Anhang, p. 4.
[6] (Anon.), *Freimüthige Betrachtungen eines philosophischen Weltbürgers über
wichtige Gegenstände* . . . (s.l.: 1793), ch. 5.

Many supporters of the Emperor's ecclesiastical reforms advocated the abolition of clerical celibacy as a logical corollary of these reforms, until Joseph finally prohibited further discussion of this topic.[1]

Joseph was throughout his life a believing and practising Roman Catholic.[2] He desired to strengthen and enrich the State by reducing the independent power and the wealth of the Church,[3] but it was never his intention to weaken the paramount authority of the Catholic faith over his subjects.

Nevertheless such a weakening was the result of Joseph's ecclesiastical reforms. The educated urban middle class had begun by discarding the superstitious trimmings of baroque Catholicism which had been suppressed by government decree. And in the end many discarded all revealed religion as well.[4] The Josephinian reforms of the Church had made scepticism and irreligion fashionable in educated middle-class circles.

The new trends of thought seem to have been particularly prominent among the students. According to the Hungarian public prosecutor, one generation of students had been irrevocably ruined, and the next was going the same way already.[5] A similar opinion was expressed by the Supreme Chancellor, Count Kollowrat. He reported that contempt for religion had become 'almost universal' among students.[6] Candidates for the priesthood were very few.[7]

It is interesting to note that Kollowrat echoes the repeated assertion of Cardinal Migazzi,[8] that the blame for this state of affairs rested on the shoulders of Gottfried van Swieten and his Commission for Education and Censorship, who, he alleged, had paid insufficient attention to the religious principles of the professors they had appointed. At the University of Graz, Professor Neupauer was openly advocating a union of the Catholic and Protestant Churches.[9] If this was at all typical of opinion among the Josephinian professors,

---

[1] Ibid.   [2] Mitrofanov, pp. 673–5.   [3] Ibid., pp. 676–7.
[4] Ibid., p. 776, where the memoires of Caroline Pichler are cited.
[5] Memorandum Johann v. Némeths, 25 July 1795, in S. Domanovszky, *József Nádor iratai* (1925: Budapest), No. 2.
[6] Au. Note Kollowrats, 5 Mar. 1794, *Nachlaß Kollowrats*, F. 14, No. 1284.
[7] Wolfsgruber, pp. 568–72.
[8] Ibid., pp. 511–19.   [9] Posch, pp. 117–18.

we may well conclude that Migazzi and Kollowrat were not exaggerating.

The mental nourishment, which sustained the new outlook gained in the universities, was provided by a brisk black market in uncensored books. The continuous search for illegal publications containing atheist tenets and 'calculated to undermine all revealed religion' kept the new Josephinian police very busy.[1]

Though middle-class rationalists and atheists agreed that religion was indispensable for the maintenance of morality and good order among the lower classes,[2] the prevailing intellectual ferment helped to diffuse an attitude of critical inquiry and scepticism also among some of the common order of men. The enlightened Catholicism encouraged by the government and preached by its clerical supporters gave rise to very lively speculations and discussions in some congregations, discussions in which the preachers did not always have the last word, and which therefore often led to conclusions which must have caused them some anxiety.

We are lucky in having some evidence[3] concerning the developing religious opinion of some members of Wieser's congregation who had been so active in securing his reinstatement as their preacher.[4]

---

[1] Cf., e.g. Au. Note Pergens, 24 Feb. 1791, *Pergen Akten*, ix/B5, H26.

[2] Cf. J. B. v. Alxinger, *Bliomberis* (1791: Leipzig), p. 136:
> Der Knab', ein starker Geist mit sechzehn Jahren schon,
> Belächelt die Religion,
> Legt aber bald darauf die Stirn in Falten,
> Und heißt sie gut, das Volk in Ordnung zu erhalten.

[3] In view of Mitrofanov's categorical assertion (pp. 776–7) that the lower classes in the town remained uninfluenced by the new ways of thought, it may be as well to set out this evidence in some detail. The following exposition is based on the records of police investigations into the religious views of a number of people accused of atheism (1794). They are to be found—very badly damaged—in the police records: *Polizeihofstelle*, 1794/197, 262, and 308–9. The accused answered all questions freely, as they were under the illusion that the Patent of Toleration of 1781 had given them the right to hold any opinion they liked in matters of religion. Their answers were recorded with care, read to the accused at the end of every investigating session, so that they could raise any objections they might have to the written rendering of what they had said. When these had been dealt with, they signed the protocol. Where the *Verhörsprotokoll* is no longer available, the very exact indirect rendering of it in the police officer's reports (*Referat*) has been used. The significance of the case as a whole and its results are discussed in a later chapter.

[4] Cf. *supra*, pp. 7–8.

The cobbler Felberer who had taken a leading part in the campaign for reinstatement, eventually went well beyond the position of Wieser in his views. He had begun to take an interest in theological questions as a result of the public controversy between the anti-Josephinian preachers and the Institute of Sermon Critics.[1] At first he had taken the preachers' side, and had even taken up the pen in their cause, but his manuscripts had been rejected by the censor on account of numerous orthographic errors.

After becoming a regular attender of Wieser's sermons, Felberer began to see the whole question in a different light. The former's emphasis on the New Testament and its ethical implications stimulated him to read the Bible and some of the current commentaries on it which were coming into Austria from Germany, e.g. those of Lessing and Bahrdt. These led him to the conclusion that Jesus had been 'a man just like ourselves, who through his teachings had become an eminent reformer and improver of the human heart', and obedience to whose precepts was necessary for the attainment of human happiness. Hence he endeavoured always to act in accordance with these precepts which, in his view, coincided with the laws of nature and the dictates of human reason.

In order to avoid giving unnecessary offence to his less enlightened fellow citizens, he continued to conform to the practices of the Catholic Church, though he could not, of course, believe in their efficacy.

As regards the creation of the world, he had not yet reached any definite conclusions. He was, he said, unable to believe in the biblical version, because other nations, e.g. the Chinese, had books containing quite different 'calculations'. Natural science seemed to him to point to a much longer process of creation than was indicated by the Books of Moses, while the law of the conservation of matter appeared to make any theory of creation in the accepted sense of the term improbable.[2]

Another regular attender of Wieser's sermons, Johann Ignatz Hermele, who was also a cobbler, was particularly

[1] Cf. *supra*, pp. 6-7.
[2] Verhörsprotokoll Felberers, 24 Jan. 1794 and ff.

struck by the preacher's insistent demand that Christians must study the Bible, that they should not be satisfied with a superficial reading, but try to get at its inner meaning. Hermele therefore bought himself an old German Bible, and, unable to read it himself, asked one of his literate friends to read it to him. Together they looked up the passages commented on by Wieser, and tried to recall what the preacher had said about them. As a result, Hermele became, in the words of his own testimony, 'not a little shaken in [his] religious convictions'.

He now asked his friend to read Lessing and Bahrdt to him. Lessing made him doubt the existence of God, and Bahrdt the divinity of Christ. His doubts were not resolved by the preachers, whose sermons he had attended ever since Wieser's appointment to the university. For Anton Kick, vicar of Penzing (then a village just outside Vienna), and the Benedictines André Wenzel and Benedikt Liechtensteiner, who had been recommended to him as preaching in the same spirit as Wieser, also encouraged a more critical attitude among their congregations, and urged them not to take the truth of their sermons for granted.[1]

Yet another cobbler, Niklas Mest, gives the following account of his change of belief. He had been introduced to the religious controversy by a friend, a tailor called Wilhelm, who praised the teachings of Christ but denied his divinity. The tailor's advanced years gave weight to his opinions in Mest's eyes. Accordingly, when the former had recommended the sermons of Kick and Wenzel, the latter had agreed to attend them. At these sermons he had been surprised to find a large number of his fellow cobblers as well as many other citizens, all of whom were as enthusiastic in their praise of the sermons as they were unanimous in their denial of the divinity of Christ.

After studying the New Testament himself, Mest gradually adopted their views. And, like them, he went on to even more radical conclusions. For as a child, he had been taught that God was everywhere, and this childhood belief had helped him to a conception of nature as a manifestation of a

[1] Vortrag der Untersuchungskommission über Hermele, *Polizeihofstelle*, 1794/262.

universal creative power. He could not now believe in a god apart from nature.

Mest admitted that his loss of faith had caused him a good deal of trouble. At first he had gone 'nearly mad' at the 'grim' thought that there was nothing to expect after death. However, he had slowly found consolation in the consideration that every human action, according as it was good or bad, brought with it good or bad consequences, i.e. reward or punishment. Once he had realized this, he had recovered his peace of mind.[1]

These are only the most striking examples of a development resulting from the joint impact of the ecclesiastical reforms of Joseph II and the popularization of rationalist ideas on the minds of a not inconsiderable number of people from the lower strata of Vienna's population.[2]

It is not possible to say with any certainty whether Vienna constituted a single exception in this respect, or whether similar developments were taking place also in other towns. The evidence is too scanty. One slight indication is provided by the depositions of Professor Neupauer's student Georg Dirnböck, who was arrested by the police as a Jacobin in 1795. Dirnböck had been an enthusiastic adherent of his teacher's advanced views on religion, and the latter's party[3] in Graz therefore took him under their wing when he had finished his studies in 1788. This circumstance secured his election as secretary to the magistrates of Knittelfeld.[4] In this capacity he had to move much in the burgher and petty-bourgeois circles of the Upper Styrian towns, where, according to his testimony, the Catholic faith was certainly losing ground. He described one of his acquaintances (a scythe manufacturer) as having no faith at all, and all the others (including himself) as adherents of 'natural religion'.[5]

Many reforms attempted by enlightened despotism were

[1] Vortrag der Untersuchungskommission über Mest, *Polizeihofstelle*, 1794/197.
[2] About twenty people were actually involved in the police investigations into atheism. The evidence deposited shows that many more people were affected by the ideas under investigation, who were not, however, brought before the police.
[3] Cf. *supra*, p. 9.
[4] Schriftliches Geständnis Dirnböcks, 2 Apr. 1795, *Vertr. Akten*, F. 29, fols. 9–10.
[5] Verhörsprotokoll Dirnböcks, ibid., fol. 526.

given theoretical justification by arguments based on the principles of the school of natural law. But despotism itself, the concept of the unlimited sovereignty of the ruler, was decisively rejected by the exponents of the theory of natural law.

According to Martini,[1] the most distinguished exponent of this theory in Austria, men enter upon the social contract after long experience for the sake of increased security. The contract is not an act of violence, but a voluntary agreement among the heads of families to submit to the decisions of the community. In this way, a democratic society comes into being, but the community is free to choose between the continuation of democracy and the institution of monarchy. Thus the right of the monarch derives from the right of the people who have decided to confer their power on him. The 'contract of submission' (*Unterwerfungsvertrag*) does not entail a surrender of innate rights. On this point Martini insists with some emphasis:

> The subjects retain their innate rights as well as those social rights which they have obtained through the contract of submission, by which each individual has promised society and society has promised each individual to promote their mutual welfare. The contract of submission does not confer on the ruler any more power than is necessary for the attainment of the social purpose. He cannot transcend this limitation of his power without violating the rights of his subjects.[2]

Christian August Beck, who had been a tutor of Joseph II, propagated ideas similar to those of Martini.

> Sovereigns must consider, [he wrote], that it is their task to promote the security and welfare of their subjects. As true fathers of the fatherland they must never lose sight of the laws of justice and righteousness. . . . As God's lieutenants on earth they must imitate humanity's lawgiver and never demand from us but what will be conducive to our own happiness.

Beck goes on to say that sovereigns will be truly successful only when their subjects are also convinced of the justice of their laws, since compulsory obedience is unsafe.[3]

---

[1] Karl Anton Freiherr v. Martini (1726-1800), Professor of Natural Law at Vienna University 1754; Councillor of the Supreme Judiciary 1764, Vice-President 1787. President of the Commission on Legislation.

[2] Quoted by Menzel, pp. 454-5.   [3] Ibid., pp. 467-8.

From the political theorists these ideas were taken over by the pamphleteers who helped to popularize them, and gave them a significantly sharper formulation. Martinovics, for instance, after outlining the theory of the social contract, demands that 'the contract by which the members of society promise each other security and the essentials of natural liberty, ought to be so firmly established that nothing can be introduced into society which might undermine or destroy it without the commission of a serious crime'.[1]

Stated merely in the form of pious aspirations, however sharply worded, these political theories would be interesting rather than important. However, the practical implications were not neglected. Public opinion in the Fourth Estate strongly resented all manifestations of arbitrary rule.[2] The need was widely felt for a practical remedy, for an effective safeguard against the ruler's tendency to exceed his legitimate powers.

One remedy which was strongly and frequently advocated was the publication of a set of fundamental laws, based on commonly agreed principles, to which the ruler would have to conform. This was in fact the demand for the State based on right and law, the *Rechtsstaat*.

It is important to distinguish clearly between the appearance of this demand as an up-to-date façade concealing the age-old pretensions of the privileged orders, and its emergence among the political aspirations of the Fourth Estate. For the idea of sovereignty limited by law had long been exclusively associated with unpopular feudal pretensions and aristocratic oppression.[3] Now, however, it was beginning to be realized that monarchy could be limited by the representatives and interests of the non-privileged classes no less than by those of the aristocracy.[4]

The demand for a monarchy thus limited seems to have

---

[1] *Oratio pro Leopoldo Secondo*, p. 5.

[2] Mitrofanov, p. 568; Alxinger, *Prosaische Schriften* (1812: Vienna), p. 208; *Vertr. Akten*, F. 2, Verhörsprotokoll Gilovskys.

[3] Though Mitrofanov admits (pp. 298–9) that the philosophy of the Enlightenment tended to reject absolutism, he quotes only statements in favour of absolutism from this side (pp. 291–2). His description of the reasoned case against absolutism is based exclusively on the statements of the privileged opposition (pp. 293–311).

[4] Alxinger, *Prosaische Schriften*, p. 167.

received its fullest formulation in a memorandum submitted
to Maria Theresa by Joseph von Sonnenfels,[1] a disciple of
Martini, who was both Professor of Political Science at
Vienna University and a Councillor at the Court Chancellery.

The memorandum was drawn up in connexion with a project for the compilation of all political legislation, which was
being considered towards the end of Maria Theresa's reign.[2]
The Court Chancellery envisaged the task as a purely
mechanical one of mere collection. Not so Sonnenfels.

Starting from the theoretical premises of the natural law
school, Sonnenfels laid down certain principles of government, i.e. generally agreed aims the attainment of which was
the only legitimate purpose of legislation. In his formulation
of these agreed aims, Sonnenfels tried to give concrete sub-
stance to the rather nebulous 'general welfare' which it was
the ruler's duty to promote.

[General welfare] means security and livelihood. Security must
be maintained against external and internal enemies. Livelihood
(*Leichtigkeit der Erwerbung*) depends on the expansion of employment,
and this, in turn, depends on [the growth of] internal and external
trade.[3]

Here, then, was the basis for the new compilation. Laws
and regulations not calculated to promote the above agreed
aims were to be discarded. New legislation, in so far as required for the furtherance of these aims, was to be enacted.[4]
By proclaiming these aims, in Sonnenfels's own words,

the government would have deprived itself of the power in future to
act indiscriminately and in contravention of those principles which it
had already acknowledged as valid, which by its own decision it had

---

[1] Joseph Edler v. Sonnenfels (1732–1817), son of a Rabbi of Nikolsburg; studied
under Martini; Professor of Political Sciences at Vienna University 1763; Councillor
of the Lower Austrian Government 1769; Councillor of the Court Chancellery and
member of the Board of Education 1779.

[2] For the history of this project, cf. S. Adler, 'Die politische Gesetzgebung in
ihren geschichtlichen Beziehungen zum Allgemeinen Bürgerlichen Gesetzbuche',
in *Festschrift zur Jahrhundertfeier des Allgemeinen Bürgerlichen Gesetzbuches*
(1911: Vienna), pp. 87–145.

[3] Quoted by Adler, p. 103.

[4] Elsewhere Sonnenfels demands that all new laws should have a preamble stating
the reasons for their promulgation, so that their relation to the agreed aims should
be clearly apparent: *Uiber Liebe des Vaterlandes* (1785: Vienna), pp. 69–70.

raised to the status of fundamental laws, and by means of which all arbitrary measures . . . could be prevented.[1]

To attain complete security of the subjects against arbitrary interference by the government, Sonnenfels proposed to include in the published compilation all the laws and regulations governing the relations of various public authorities to one another and to the subject. 'Civil liberty demands', he wrote, 'that every citizen be informed concerning the powers of each official and of each department of government. The best way to forestall arbitrary measures and oppression is to make publicly known the duties and rights of each public authority.'[2]

It is clear that in Sonnenfels's hands the projected codification of Austrian public law would have become an instrument for the transformation of the far-flung and despotically governed Habsburg dominions into one great *Rechtsstaat*, where the authority and jurisdiction of every department of government would be clearly circumscribed by law, and where every citizen would live securely in the knowledge that he enjoyed the protection of the law under all circumstances. Sonnenfels did not hesitate to give to this kind of code the name of 'State Constitution'. Without it, there could be no lawful government.

Without a State Constitution, lawful government cannot even be thought of, because the lack of a Constitution is too akin to arbitrary power; and arbitrary power is not government but anarchy. . . .[3]

The idea of a monarchy limited by law had thus ceased to be a monopoly of the feudal interest in Josephinian Austria. Public opinion in the Fourth Estate as expressed in the political literature of the time equated the tyrant with the ruler who was free from the law (*Princeps legibus solutus*) and accepted as lawful only the ruler who was himself under the law. We find the case admirably stated by Martinovics:

Sovereignty must steer a middle course between despotism and anarchy; and the Law must carefully keep it equidistant from both. . . .

---

[1] Quoted by Adler, p. 94.
[2] *Hofkanzlei*, III A 3, Kart. 310, Einleitung zum Plan einer vollständigen politischen Gesetzessammlung.
[3] Quoted by Adler, p. 100.

A monarch has full power over his subjects; but the laws have full power over him. He has an absolute power to do good, but when he is about to do evil, his hands are tied.[1]

The fashionable poet Lorenz Leopold Haschka incurred the grave displeasure of Joseph II by his 'Ode to Kings', in which he reserved grudging homage exclusively for kings yoked to the written law:

> Gut ist keiner. Doch ist der minder Böse
> Von den Königen der, den seines Volkes
> Majestät bei der Krone
> Faßt und unters Gesetzbuch beugt.[2]

When despotism was crumbling in France with the meeting of the Estates General, Conrad Dominik Bartsch, the editor of the *Wiener Zeitung*, wrote enthusiastically:

In France a light is beginning to shine which will benefit the whole of humanity. Necker has persuaded the King to leave the throne of despotism, and to set an unprecedented example which is of such a nature that all countries will have to follow it sooner or later. For this he deserves a golden column of honour.[3]

Franz Xaver Huber, the journalist and author, concluded his history of Joseph II's reign with a significant reproach:

[It was the cardinal mistake of Joseph II] that he . . . brought in his . . . beneficial measures in an arbitrary manner, and not with the consent of the whole nation. No sovereign has ever had such a splendid opportunity of giving to his country a good and stable constitution without violent convulsions. . . . Assured of the love and devotion of the largest and strongest section of the people, he could have restored to the nation its original rights by the stroke of a pen, and he could have written these rights into 'Fundamental Laws' totally binding on his successors.[4]

The fact that public opinion in the Fourth Estate so quickly overtook enlightened despotism even to the point

---

[1] *Testament politique de l'Empereur Joseph II* (1791: Vienna), pp. 6–7. The work appeared anonymously; Martinovics claims its authorship in his petition for mercy, 5 May 1795, in K. Benda, *A magyar jakobinusok iratai* (1952: Budapest), ii, No. 103.
[2] Quoted by Gugitz in his notes to da Ponte's Memoires, i. 395.
[3] Bartsch to Hajnóczy, 12 May 1789, *Vertrauliche Akten*, F. 71, fol. 193.
[4] *Beiträge zur Charakteristik und Regierungsgeschichte Josephs II., Leopolds II., u. Franz' II.* (1800: Paris), pp. 64–65.

of criticizing absolutism itself, reflects a discrepancy between
the aspirations of the non-privileged and the policies of
Joseph II which has not, so far, received adequate attention
from historians. The opposition of the privileged orders
towards the end of Joseph's reign has stolen the limelight.
Yet if we are to attain a full understanding of the crisis of
enlightened despotism in Austria, it will be necessary to
examine also the opposition of the non-privileged, which
was the more significant in that it was sustained by a high
and rising level of political consciousness.

3. Discontent and Opposition in the Fourth Estate

Joseph II's arbitrary and despotic methods of government
aroused universal resentment, even among those who acclaimed the aims of the policy he was pursuing in this way.[1]
The Emperor's 'unlimited passion for despotism' antagonized opponents and adherents of the Enlightenment alike.[2]
Moreover, by no means all the policies of Joseph II won
the approval of the Fourth Estate. Many of them were subjected to severe and bitter criticism; some led even to unrest
and rebellion in that quarter.

The writers, of course, complained above all of Joseph's
utter lack of respect for learning and letters. They con-
trasted their earlier vision of Josephinian Vienna as the
Empire's cultural metropolis with the actual situation in
which they were held in contempt by the government and
deprived of access to the Court. Alxinger, the leading poet
of the Austrian Enlightenment, found himself unable to
preface the first published collection of his poems with a
dedication to an Emperor who refused to honour the Muses:

> Wer nicht die Musen liebt und ehrt, dem sey
> Auch ihre Leyer lautlos wie ein Fisch.[3]

Resentment against the government's contempt for the
fine arts was not confined to men of letters. Joseph Richter,

[1] F. Engel-Jánosi, 'Der Tod Josephs II. im Urteil seiner Zeitgenossen' in
Mitteilungen d. Inst. f. öst. Geschichtsforschung, xliv (1930), 327.

[2] Bartsch to Hajnóczy, 24 Feb. 1786, *Vertrauliche Akten*, F. 71, fol. 141.

[3] Dedication in Verse: 'An mein Buch', *Alxingers Sämtliche Gedichte* (1784:
Leipzig), p. 12.

who was probably a shrewd observer of public opinion, mentions it among the causes of Joseph's unpopularity with the common people: 'All who care for their country (*Die Edlen im Volke*) desire that Joseph should have more respect for the arts and sciences, because a nation ought to be ashamed if its artists have to go begging and its writers starve. . . .'[1] Prince Kaunitz, Chancellor of State and himself a generous patron of the arts, fully confirmed Richter's observation, and held that Joseph's openly expressed contempt for science and letters fostered the 'general development of a sometimes very harmful spirit of opposition' against his government.[2]

The money which might have been used for patronage of learning and letters remained in the coffers of the State. The financial needs of the State, which made necessary many of the reforms enthusiastically welcomed by the Fourth Estate, also made necessary numerous measures which aroused criticism and serious discontent in all classes.

They were responsible, in the first place, for a large and constant demand on the capital market which resulted in a chronic shortage of credit and inflation of the interest rate for private would-be borrowers. Financiers preferred to lend to the capital-hungry State rather than invest in rickety new industrial or commercial enterprises.

Joseph II's decree (1786) stipulating the immediate transfer of all capital assets in private foundations to state funds, at once transformed a situation of chronic shortage into one of acute crisis. For considerable sums from these private assets had been advanced to peasants and entrepreneurs of all kinds for repairs and other necessary investments. The decree in question not only put a stop to such investments for the future, it also saddled the debtors with the burden of immediate repayment of their loans. For most of them the only way out led into the clutches of the moneylenders.

But Joseph II had two more blows in store for them. Pursuing another settled line of policy without reference to

[1] *Warum wird Kaiser Joseph von seinem Volke nicht geliebt?* (1787: Vienna), reprinted in Gräffer, *Josephinische Curiosa* (1848: Vienna) i. 64–65.
[2] Nachtrag zum Votum Kaunitz', *Kaunitz Voten*, 5987 ex 1792.

the interests involved, he decided at this precise juncture (January 1787) to repeal the existing usury laws, thereby taking the lid off the interest rate altogether at the very time when his own policy had helped to create an exceptionally inflated demand for loans.[1] Secondly, in order to raise money for the disastrous Turkish War, he added insult to the debtors' injury by demanding extraordinary taxation and supplies.

When, on top of all that, a sharp economic depression spread over most of the Habsburg provinces, the debtors' endurance reached breaking-point. In the Tyrol, where the flood disasters of 1789 aggravated the effect of war and crisis, their exasperation helped considerably to bring about the ensuing revolutionary situation.[2] The indebted peasants and burghers of this province compelled the dying Emperor to concede to them an indefinite deferment of capital-repayments due to the State.[3] Leopold II abandoned Joseph's policy altogether.[4]

Acute discontent arose also as a result of the dissolution of the 'brotherhoods' (*Bruderschaften*). Originally associations of a purely religious character, these had eventually become mutual friendly societies in which a very large number of poor people had invested their meagre savings. The decree of dissolution contained a clause expressly providing for the repayment of contributions to all who filed a formal petition for this purpose. By the spring of 1789, however, the government's financial plight was so serious, the number of petitions so unexpectedly large, that Joseph issued a further decree, fixing retrospectively a time-limit for filing the petitions (2 May 1785). Thus, by a stroke of his pen, the Emperor had declared the greater part of the petitions null and void. For most people had been reluctant to incur the considerable expense involved in filing a petition until they

---

[1] Sonnenfels, *Uiber Wucher u. Wuchergesetze* (1789: Vienna), pp. 65–75; J. Pezzl, *Charakteristik Josephs II* (1790: Vienna), pp. 201 ff.; Au. Note Pergens, 13 Jan. 1790, *Staatskanzlei, Noten von der Polizei*, F. 29.

[2] Sauer an Pergen, 11 Jan. 1790, *Pergen Akten*, x/A6, H5.

[3] Ah. Resolution über Vortrag der Vereinigten Hofstelle, 22 Jan. 1790, *Hofkanzlei*, IV M 3, Kart. 1351.

[4] F. Kropatschek, *Sammlung aller unt. d. Reg. Kaiser Leopolds II.... ergangenen Verordnungen u. Gesetze*, ii, N. 301; iii, N. 443, 545, 567; iv, N. 658.

had seen the first repayments actually taking place, i.e. until 1788. Thereupon, within a period of only three months some 23,000 of them had handed their petitions in to the appropriate authority (incidentally paying some 2,000–3,000 florins into the state coffers by way of petition dues). For many of the 23,000, this had meant incurring debts against the security of the money due to them from the State.

Their reaction to Joseph's breach of faith was one of intense indignation, the brunt of which descended on the heads of the innocent officials dealing with this matter. In the spring of 1789, the government of Lower Austria considered it necessary to warn the Court Chancellery of the serious danger of trouble from the numerous aggrieved petitioners. And though no outbreaks actually occurred, Count Pergen referred to this as late as January 1790, as one item of the general discontent and unrest which he considered to have become a serious danger to the stability of the monarchy.[1]

The decision to stop repayment of the brotherhood contributions was only one of many hardships to which the inhabitants of the towns and the peasants were subjected as a result of the enormous expenditure on the Turkish War. In preparation for, and as a result of, this war, Joseph II introduced a great many measures which were bound to arouse their hostility and antagonism.

Since the Seven Years War, the philosophers of the Enlightenment had done much to create a generally anti-militarist climate of public opinion in Austria no less than in other European countries.[2] Joseph II's patent partiality for the military estate,[3] therefore, was not calculated to increase his popularity with his subjects, nor were his military innovations likely to meet with their approval. Under the new system of recruitment to the regiments, nearly all non-privileged subjects and especially the peasants, lived under the constant threat of having to spend the rest of their lives

[1] The foregoing details are taken from the report of the government of Lower Austria to the Court Chancellery, 2 Apr. 1789, *Archiv für N. Öst., Präsidialakten,* 1789/21, and on section 8 of Pergen's Note, 13 Jan. 1790, *Staatskanzlei, Noten v.d. Polizei,* F. 29.

[2] Mitrofanov, pp. 370–1.

[3] Ibid., pp. 347–8.

in the army. This system was universally condemned.[1] Austrians protested against this 'Prussian' innovation, which subordinated all else to military considerations, thereby destroying the foundations on which alone the arts and sciences could flourish.[2] They protested against the Emperor's 'lust for conquest' (*Eroberungsschwindel*), of which it seemed to them the result.[3] By rising in rebellion against this system, the Tyroleans finally compelled Joseph to withdraw it from their province.[4]

To many Austrians there seemed to be little doubt that the Turkish War was the outcome of their sovereign's *Eroberungsschwindel*, cleverly exploited for her own selfish ends by Catherine II.[5] The general reaction to the declaration of war was, therefore, one of indignation.[6] Peasants, burghers, officials, and artisans had to foot the mounting bills as the war dragged on and brought in its wake a severe economic depression.

The bills were indeed heavy. Peasants, especially those in the provinces behind the battlefront, suffered greatly from requisitions and from the imposition of extraordinary labour services for the maintenance of the army.[7] The burghers (and the badly-paid officials) were subjected to the new war tax at the very time when rapidly rising prices had already forced them to tighten their belts a good deal. The rapid rise in prices had originally been caused by the diversion of supplies to the armies.[8] It was aggravated by the fact that the Emperor, undeterred by the extraordinary situation created by the war, remained faithful to his policy of abolishing governmental regulation of internal trade,[9] and simultaneously reducing imports. Thus the Viennese poor man's diet

---

[1] Ibid., pp. 373–90.
[2] Richter, pp. 59–60.
[3] *Freimüthige Betrachtungen* . . ., ch. 1.
[4] Mitrofanov, pp. 376–81.
[5] *Freimüthige Betrachtungen* . . ., pp. 124–5.
[6] L. A. Hoffmann, *Patriotische Bemerkungen über die gegenwärtige Theuerung in Wien* (1791: Vienna), p. 9; Mitrofanov, pp. 212–13.
[7] Mitrofanov, pp. 215–16.
[8] Ibid., pp. 217–21.
[9] Au. Note Pergens, 6 Aug. 1788 (copy), *Staatskanzlei, Notenwechsel mit der n.ö. Regierung*, F. 2; Au. Note Pergens, 16 Dec. 1789, *Pergen Akten*, x/A3, H83, according to which the price of bread, meat, and wood had been mainly affected.

of imported fish disappeared from the market at the same time as bread and meat were rising in price.[1]

The chief sufferers were, of course, the artisans and factory workers of Vienna, whose population had greatly increased during the preceding few years. And it was they who finally compelled the government to modify its policy. It so happened that a number of populous Viennese suburbs were without bread altogether on the last day of July 1788. Only the more expensive white rolls were available which the mass of people could not afford. The reason was that millers and bakers were holding back their supplies of rye-flour in expectation of the day on which the maximum price on black bread was to be lifted. But on the last day of July 1788 hungry and angry crowds stormed and plundered the shops of all the Viennese bakers who had refused to sell bread. The government was alarmed at this outburst of popular fury, ordered an inquiry, punished the offending bakers, and— reimposed the maximum price on black bread.[2] The general price-level, however, continued to rise, causing serious discontent in the large towns. Joseph set up a committee to propose measures for reducing prices, but no relief came during his reign.

All police reports of the years 1788 and 1789 agree as to the increasing unpopularity of the war and the growing desire for peace. When Joseph returned to Vienna late in 1788, he returned to a hostile city. The Turkish War had wiped out the last remnants of the popularity he had enjoyed in the earlier part of his reign.[3] There is a report of a mass demonstration against the war tax in front of the palace gates in 1789.[4] Leopold II's conclusion of peace with the Turks was popularly acclaimed with joy and relief.[5]

Even the peasants, who had benefited more than any other

[1] K. Příbram, *Geschichte der österreichischen Gewerbepolitik* (1907: Leipzig), I, 465 ff.

[2] Au. Noten Pergens, 31 July and 6 Aug. 1788 (copies), *Staatskanzlei, Notenwechsel mit der n.ö. Regierung*, F. 2. Extracts are quoted by W. Ernst, 'Die Preissenkungsaktion Kaiser Josefs II.', in *Österreichische Volksstimme*, 30 Dec. 1951.

[3] Mitrofanov, p. 222.

[4] A. J. Gross-Hoffinger, *Joseph II als Regent u. Mensch* (s.d.: Strassfurt), p. 193.

[5] F. Hegrad, *Versuch einer kurzen Lebensgeschichte Leopolds II bis zu dessen Absterben* (Prague: 1792), p. 148; J. Mrázek, *Rede an Österreichs Völker* (1792: Vienna), p. 11. Cf. also the anti-war play *Die Kriegssteuer* (1789: Vienna).

class from Joseph's reforms, were in a rebellious mood towards the end of the reign. We have already noted the unrest
called forth by the new system of recruitment and by the
hardships due to the Turkish War. The peasants also strongly
resented some of the religious innovations of the reign. A
good deal of money passed from the hands of the pious
peasantry into those of the Church in the course of the multi-
farious traditional ceremonies which seemed grossly superstitious to the philosophers and to people influenced by the
Enlightenment. Joseph II and the party of the Enlightenment therefore agreed on the desirability of reducing and
simplifying these ceremonies and diverting the money involved into more useful channels.[1] But these ceremonies
constituted an important aspect of the social and spiritual
life of the peasants who firmly resisted interference in it. In
some areas, the attempts of the local authorities to comply
with decrees on religious matters led to local peasant rebellions, which compelled a restoration of the *status quo*. In
Carinthia, for instance, the peasants from a large area organized themselves for the defence of statues and plaques
which the government had earmarked for removal. Officials,
in some cases in military uniform, were driven out of the
villages. Priests, who attempted to comply with orders, were
maltreated, even injured. Others were compelled to sign
declarations that they would keep to all the traditional usages.
In view of the Turkish War, the government was unable to
gather sufficient military strength in the province to deal
with the disorders, which continued for some ten months.
The peasants were finally allowed to have their own way.[2]
This was in 1788. In the summer of 1789 exactly the same
was happening in Vorarlberg.[3] There, too, the government
was forced to yield. Encouraged by this, the Tyrolean
peasants extorted a similar concession by similar methods.[4]

Paradoxical though it may seem, the great reform of 1789,
which was intended to put an end to all labour services and

[1] Mitrofanov, pp. 776, 779-81.
[2] O'Donnel's report to the Court Chancellery (copy), 18 Jan. 1793, *Polizeihofstelle*, 1793/197.
[3] Mitrofanov, p. 779.
[4] Au. Vortrag der Vereinigten Hofstellen u. Ah. Resolution, 22 Jan. 1790,
Hofkanzlei, IV M 3, Kart. 1351.

to limit definitely the peasants' financial obligations to their
lords and to the State, became itself the most important
source of unrest among the peasantry. The peasants objected
no less than the lords to the calculation of their tax-obliga-
tions on the basis of gross income, and where this calculation
signified an increase in the traditional amount of taxes paid,
payment of the increased obligation was not infrequently
refused.[1]

Standardization of feudal dues inevitably imposed new
burdens in a number of areas where traditional dues had been
light, while universal commutation of labour services and
dues in kind was not welcomed by the peasants of the
more backward areas, where money was hard to come
by.[2]

This resentment against various aspects of the reform was
the more serious in that it came from a peasantry who were
just then awakening politically as a result of the recent improvement in their economic position and their social elevation to the status of citizenship. The peasants who now
retained a little more of the wealth they produced, used it
to buy not only better food and clothes, but also newspapers.[3]
Enterprising journalists were not slow to exploit to the full
the new market for their products, and in nearly every province of the Habsburg dominions new popular and cheap
newspapers appeared which addressed themselves to the
peasants in their own language. And their peasant readers
soon formed their own ideas of the rights to which they were
entitled by their new status of citizenship.

Existing legislation regulating the status and obligations
of the peasants fell far short of the peasants' new ideas of the
rights they ought to enjoy. This was a situation fraught with
troublesome consequences for the government and the ruling classes. To remove this potential danger was one of
Joseph II's aims in introducing the reform of 1789. But he
was caught in a vicious circle: the preparations for the great
reform, in which peasants were called upon to take an active
part, served only to give a further stimulus to the new

[1] Mitrofanov, pp. 477-8.
[2] Ibid., p. 649.
[3] Ibid., pp. 657-8.

political consciousness that was abroad in the country-
side.¹ When the reform came into force in the autumn of
1789, it provoked discontent and unrest not only among
those peasants who anticipated heavier material burdens
as a result of its provisions, but among all those—and
their number was rapidly increasing—who looked to
the Emperor to abolish feudal dues and feudal lordship
altogether.²

This was the solid basis of the numerous reports and
rumours which reached the central government from many
areas in the autumn of 1789, that the peasants were quite
determined not to pay any more dues and tithes at all regard-
less of the provisions of the new law.³ The government was
disposed to take such reports and rumours all the more
seriously at a time when the news from France told of an
agrarian revolution sweeping across the entire French countryside. For the peasants in the Austrian dominions were
showing a particularly keen interest in the news of the risings
in France which figured prominently in their peasant news-
papers.⁴

Indeed it was not very long before the French example
was imitated in various parts of Joseph II's dominions, in
defiance of the Patent issued especially to impress on the
peasants their continued obligations. From October 1789
onwards, serious cases of refusals to discharge feudal obligations occurred. Attempts by manorial officials to enforce payment usually led to outbreaks of violence which could be
quelled only by calling in the military.⁵

Bohemia was the main centre of the trouble. There the
peasants were everywhere 'loud in their praise of the Men
of their own rank in France', and, like the latter, many

¹ O'Donnel's report to the Court Chancellery (copy), 18 Jan. 1793, *Polizeihofstelle*, 1793/197.
² Mitrofanov, pp. 647–50; also Au. Note Pergens, 13 Jan. 1790, *Staatskanzlei,
Noten v.d. Polizei*, F. 29.
³ Cf. the provincial police reports of this period, e.g. Ambschell to Beer from
Prague, 29 Aug. 1789, *Pergen Akten*, xi/B24, H18; d'Herbel to Beer from Troppau,
4 Sept. 1789, ibid. H23; Okacz to Beer from Brünn, 6 Oct. 1789, ibid. x/B7, H2.
⁴ Mitrofanov, p. 658.
⁵ Eighty soldiers on foot and horse were sent to quell one such riot in Moravia
according to Okacz's reports, 3 and 4 Nov. 1789, *Pergen Akten*, x/B7, H3,
H4.

refused 'to fulfil the duty of their Station as Labourers to their Masters'.[1]

The provincial government of Bohemia had to remain on the alert for a considerable time. As late as the middle of November 1789, Joseph had to abandon his plan of sending some German regiments from Bohemia to put down the Netherlands revolt: the governor of Bohemia insisted on the retention of the troops in his troubled province.[2]

These unlooked for consequences of the Josephinian peasant reforms greatly alarmed the ruling classes and members of the government. They saw in these manifestations a challenge not only to the enforcement of a particular law, but to the entire social order, with all its ties subordinating *Untertan* to *Obrigkeit*; not merely the symptoms of local unrest, but the first storm-signals of revolution.[3]

By the end of 1789, when the opposition of the privileged orders in the Habsburg dominions entered the stage of open rebellion, the time for purely aristocratic revolts had already passed. The numerous grievances and the far-reaching political aspirations of the non-privileged helped to drive them into the ranks of the constitutional and nationalist movements which they transformed, though they did not as yet (as in France) assume the leadership.

In Belgium all classes openly co-operated in the opposition: 'Catholic priests embraced atheist lawyers, the nobles offered their fulsome compliments to the middle-class Vonckists in the Constitutional Party.'[4] According to the Belgian councillors, the new doctrine had become the creed of all classes—merchants, nobles, peasants, and soldiers.[5]

The political pattern in Hungary was very similar. Magyar nationalism was not the monopoly of the magnates and gentry. The lawyers of the Hungarian capital unanimously protested against the use of German as the official language

---

[1] Sir R. M. Keith to the Duke of Leeds, 24 Oct. 1789, *Public Record Office*, FO.7/18, fol. 74.

[2] Keith to the Duke of Leeds, 14 Nov. 1789, ibid., fol. 114.

[3] Mitrofanov, pp. 630–1. The anxiety of the Estates was fully shared by Pergen: Au. Note Pergens, 13 Jan. 1790 (copy), *Staatskanzlei, Noten v.d. Polizei*, F. 29: '. . . zumalen der Nexus zwischen Herren und Unterthanen beynahe gänzlich aufgehoben . . .'.

[4] F. Fejtő, *Un Habsbourg révolutionnaire—Joseph II* (1953: Paris), p. 297.

[5] Ibid., p. 290.

in their country.[1] Not even the most enthusiastic opponent
of aristocratic and clerical pretensions could remain unmoved
by the great wave of nationalist enthusiasm which swept over
Hungary in 1789 and 1790, or banish the hope that the
recalled diet would bring about a great national regeneration
rather than a purely feudal reaction.[2] Hungarian Protestants,
disappointed by the limitations of Josephinian toleration,
were easily cajoled by flattery and promises into taking a
vigorous part in the opposition.[3] The peasants, driven to
despair by famine and merciless war-requisitions, and spurred
on by hopes of complete emancipation, could be incited to
rebellion even by the gentry, who quickly realized their
opportunity.[4]

The ruling classes and the government were aware that
the prevailing popular discontent amounted to something
more than mere grumbling at the hardships resulting from
one or other of the government's measures. They were aware
of a new tone, a new propensity to discuss and criticize all
governmental actions, a new sense of equality. Expressing
his deep concern at the change, Friedrich Schilling, secretary
at the Ministry of Police, wrote:

> Your Majesty . . . will have noticed how greatly the tone in the
> capital has changed in the last few years. They are no longer the long-
> suffering (*gutmüthig*) people they used to be, who blindly obeyed the
> laws without arguing, looked up to their superiors with respect, and
> were proud of the honour to be subjects of the German Emperor. . . .
> One looks in vain now for these . . . loyal and contented people.[5]

This, then, was the ultimate outcome of enlightened
despotism. It was as unforeseen as it was alarming. And in
its alarm, the government of Joseph II abandoned enlightened despotism.

---

[1] Gotthardi to Beer, 4 Oct. 1789, *Pergen Akten*, x/A3, H63.
[2] Cf. letters of Bartsch to Hajnóczy, 29 Jan., 27 Feb., 9, 16, and 25 Mar. 1790.
Vertr. Akten, F. 71, fols. 201–12.
[3] J. Molnár, *Politisch-kirchlicher Manch-Hermaeon*, pp. 18, 243–6; Projekt
Kélers, 15 Sept. 1790, *Ungarische Akten, Allgemeines*, F. 261, Konv. 5, fols. 303–8.
[4] Au. Note Pergens, 13 Jan. 1790 (copy), *Staatskanzlei, Noten v.d. Polizei*, F. 29.
[5] Projekt des Sekretär Schilling die Stimmung des Publikums zu leiten, s.d.
(probably 1791), *Kaiser Franz Akten*, F. 150, No. 19; cf. also Au. Note Sauers,
12 Aug. 1791, *Archiv für N. Öst., Präsidialakten*, 1791/2.

4. *Retreat from Enlightened Despotism*

Joseph II's ministers were acutely alarmed by all these developments and referred with increasing anxiety to 'the prevailing highly critical situation' (*die dermaligen äußerst kritischen Zeitumstände*).

It was indeed dangerous for the government to have incurred the hostility of the popular classes just when these had been able to make some remarkable economic, social, and political progress. Joseph II was compelled to recognize that enlightened despotism had reached the stage of crisis in which it was beginning to contradict its own purposes.

To safeguard these purposes, the Emperor devised and executed new policies with his habitual determination. While thus preoccupied, he would no doubt have welcomed a relaxation of the struggle against the privileged orders. But the latter chose rather to profit from his additional difficulties, and to exploit his internal isolation no less than his unfortunate foreign entanglements to enforce a far-reaching restoration of those rights and privileges which had been suppressed, because they were incompatible with the full development of the monarchy's strength.

Thus the crisis of enlightened despotism imposed upon Joseph II three main lines of policy:

(i) The reorganization of the police into an effective machinery for the supervision and control of public opinion, and the prevention of sedition and revolt among the lower classes.

(ii) The modification or abandonment of all those enlightened policies which had helped to bring about the dissemination of ideas calculated, in the Emperor's own words, to 'undermine all religion, morality, and social order', contrary to the original intention.

(iii) The far-reaching restoration of rights and privileges to the Estates, in the hope that they would in future provide voluntarily the minimum requirements of the state, which enlightened despotism had tried to extract from them by force.

All three lines of policy marked a retreat from enlightened

despotism and an advance along the road which led to the
Jacobin trials, the *Vormärz*, and, ultimately, to the débâcle
of 1848.

(i) *Police reorganization*

According to the political theorists of the eighteenth century, the State must organize a police in order to supersede
the out-dated feudal and municipal administrations, and to
secure to the citizens of the state their newly-won rights.[1]
The province of the police was wide, but its role was the
subordinate one of enforcing the laws.

In view of the disturbing developments in public opinion,
Joseph II considered it essential to extend the scope of the
police in such a way that it could be used as an organ for the
control of public opinion and for the detection of popular
discontent and unrest. Hence the far-reaching reorganization of the police which Count Pergen, the President of the
Lower Austrian government, effected so much to the Emperor's satisfaction and to the dismay of the adherents of the
Enlightenment.

The first step in the new direction had undoubtedly been
taken in December 1785, with the 'Patent concerning Freemasons' which empowered the police to supervise the
activities of all masonic lodges and required their official
registration.[2]

Subsequent extensions of the scope of police activity in
this direction were not, however, embodied in published
Patents, but remained shrouded in the secrecy of cabinet
decrees and instructions based upon them.

In 1786 the police received most elaborately formulated
but highly secret instructions:

... unobtrusively to investigate what the general public is saying about
the Emperor and his government, how public opinion is developing in
this respect, whether among the upper or the lower classes there are
any malcontents or perhaps even agitators (*Aufwickler*) coming to the

---

[1] For a full discussion of the idea of police in eighteenth-century political theory,
cf. Anna Hedwig Benna, *Die Polizeihofstelle*, unpubl. thesis submitted to the phil.
faculty of Vienna University 1942, chs. 1–2.

[2] L. Abafi, *Geschichte der Freimaurerei in Österreich-Ungarn* (1823: Budapest),
iv. 146–507.

fore; all of which is to be consistently reported to headquarters according to the prescribed procedure.[1]

This kind of duty quickly assumed increasing importance as compared to the many others specified in the 'Secret Instruction' of 1786. From 1789 onwards, the police reports deal almost exclusively with the state of public opinion, with 'agitators', and with the danger of unrest among the peasantry. The new emphasis is reflected in the summary of the tasks of the secret police which Pergen drew up for the information of Leopold II on 1 March 1790, and which is concerned almost entirely with the problem of subversion. According to this document, the main duties of the secret police are

. . . to discover all persons who are or might be dangerous to the State . . .;

to discover any discontent arising among the people, all dangerous thoughts (*üble Gesinnung*) and especially any incipient rebellion (*aufkeimende Meuterei*), and to nip these in the bud where possible . . .;

. . . secretly and unnoticeably to influence public opinion in favour of any government measure for which Your Majesty desires such a preparation . . .;

. . . to protect the person and family of Your Majesty, and to discover all hostile designs against them. . . .[2]

Apart from these, only one other duty, that of watching the movements of foreign diplomats, was specified in the summary. From this it was a far cry indeed to the duties of the police as envisaged by the adherents of the Enlightenment—the duties of a hand-maiden of the law.

If the men of the Enlightenment had good reason to condemn the aims of the Josephinian police, they had even better reason to condemn its methods.

Sonnenfels claimed, as we have seen,[3] that every citizen had the right to know the powers and competence of each official and of each public authority. Joseph's police, how-

---

[1] Geheime Instruktion (1786), pt. i, para. 2, quoted by A. Fournier, 'Kaiser Joseph II. und der "geheime Dienst" ', in *Historische Studien und Skizzen*, Dritte Reihe (1912: Vienna and Leipzig), p. 11.

[2] Quoted by Fournier, pp. 5–6.

[3] *Supra*, p. 23.

ever, was a secret police, not only because it employed secret
agents and spies,[1] but more especially because the character
and scope of its duties were deliberately withheld from the
public.

Sonnenfels demanded that the organization and jurisdiction of all public authorities be based on agreed principles
embodied in public law. In 1789, however, Joseph II yielded
to Pergen's repeated request and transferred the administration of the police from the jurisdiction of the Court Chancellery to that of Pergen's police department which was based
on cabinet decrees unknown even to the other ministers.[2]
The public was merely informed of the fact that the Vienna
police department had been raised to the status of a ministry.

Sonnenfels demanded that the procedure of the police
conform to publicly known regulations.[3] In fact, Joseph II
and Pergen kept these a jealously guarded secret. Sonnenfels
claimed for every citizen the right to the protection of the
law, even if he was arrested by the police.[4] But according to
Pergen's account of the duties of the secret police, submitted
to Leopold II in 1790, the summary investigation of arrested
persons provided the basis for the Emperor's decision
'whether they are to be handed over to the Criminal Court,
or whether there is to be a secret police investigation'.[5]
Clearly, in the latter case, the prisoner would be deprived
of the protection of the law, for there were no published
regulations governing 'secret police investigations' regarding
methods of investigation, witnesses, or proof of guilt. In all
these respects the prisoner was to be at the mercy of Pergen
or his deputy, Hofrat Beer, and of the Emperor.

This was no mere theoretical matter. It was liable to affect
crucially the security, liberty, and welfare of Joseph II's
subjects, as will be shown by two *causes célèbres* which
occurred during the great crisis marking the end of Joseph's
reign.

[1] Secret Instruction (1786), pt. ii, paras. 4–7, quoted by Fournier, pp. 14–15.
[2] F. Walter, 'Die Organisierung der staatlichen Polizei unter Kaiser Joseph II.',
in *Mitteilungen d. Vereins für Geschichte der Stadt Wien*, vii (1927), 38–40.
[3] Ausarbeitung Sonnenfels' über die Polizeigesetze (s.d.: 1795), paras. 18–40,
Polizeihofstelle, 1795/809.
[4] Ibid., para. 157.
[5] Quoted by Fournier, p. 5.

In view of the treasonable contact established between the disaffected Hungarians and the Prussian government, the police had orders to watch closely the movements of the Prussian resident Jacobi and of the people who called on him. In the course of this observation the police discovered that a certain Josepha Willias,[1] who had rather a bad reputation as a habituée frequenting the company of officers stationed along the Croatian frontier, had taken a packet containing sketches of Austrian military dispositions into Jacobi's house. She was arrested and taken into the custody of the police. Under the circumstances, Joseph thought it desirable that Jacobi should be kept in some uncertainty as to the cause of Willias's arrest by making it appear that she had merely been imprisoned for debt[2] (debtors being normally confined in the *Polizeihaus*). This appearance was effected by not proceeding with any investigation whatsoever for about six months. All this time the unfortunate woman was suspended in complete uncertainty as to her fate and subjected to all the rigours and hardships of police arrest, which had been aggravated by the circumstance that her impassioned protests against this treatment had made the police officials in charge lose their heads and their tempers. After six months, a joint secret police and military investigation was held, at the end of which Joseph resolved not to hand the prisoner over to the criminal court, but to keep her in precautionary police custody until the end of the Turkish War. Willias had pleaded in her defence that she had been unaware of the contents of the packet she had taken to Jacobi and that the officer who had asked her to take it had abused her trust. The investigating commission had been unable to invalidate this plea, which, had it been upheld by an ordinary criminal court, would have been taken into consideration as an important extenuating circumstance. When Joseph II died, Josepha Willias was still languishing in the custody of Pergen's police, exposed to the insults and execrations of Pergen's subordinates, whose patience and temper had given way under the strain imposed upon them as a result of the

---

[1] The records relating to the Willias case are to be found in *Pergen Akten*, vii/4.
[2] Kommentar Schillings über die Ausarbeitung Sonnenfels', 31 Dec. 1795, *Polizeihofstelle*, 1795/809.

prisoner's nervous breakdown. In the course of Leopold II's reign, she was to emerge from obscurity as the symbol of the late Emperor's supreme disregard for the ideals of the school of natural law.

The dire results of this disregard were also experienced by the well-known publisher and bookseller Georg Philipp Wucherer, who had called upon his own head the wrath of the literary world by his persistent and (for himself) lucrative exploitation of the circumstance that there were as yet no copyright laws in existence. It was for another reason, however, that he had incurred the wrath of Joseph II and the watchful eye of the secret police. The Emperor's displeasure had been aroused by the fact that Wucherer, astute business man that he was, specialized in cheap pamphlets criticizing the government (*Schmähschriften*) which sold like hot cakes in the latter years of the reign, when the wave of general discontent was rising. And this, in turn, had led Joseph and Count Pergen to suspect that Wucherer must be at least partly responsible for the flourishing black market in uncensored books the contents of which were becoming increasingly alarming in their eyes. The police spies, therefore, received strict orders to do their utmost to obtain a *corpus delicti* on the basis of which the police could proceed against him. But Wucherer shrewdly refused to be caught out.[1]

Unfortunately for himself he was not quite cautious enough. For when he heard in 1788 that the well-known German radical Karl Friedrich Bahrdt had founded a new secret society called the German Union, he rushed to become its chief (*Diözesan*) for the Habsburg dominions in the hope of adding the new society's literary output to his business interests. Commercially it was no doubt a promising proposition; there was an eager and expanding market for the literary products of the Enlightenment—and the more radical the content, the keener the appetite for the publication. But Wucherer had failed to take into account the extent of the political reaction which was setting in. Joseph II and his Minister of Police were now quite unwilling to tolerate the setting up in the Habsburg dominions of a new middle-class secret society directed by a prominent and advanced

[1] Au. Note Pergens, 24 Feb. 1791, *Pergen Akten*, ix/B5, H26.

radical in Germany, and designed to counteract the new religious reaction which had set in in a number of German states. The Emperor gave the order to proceed against the Austrian 'diocesan' of the German Union. Hofrat Beer (Pergen had gone on holiday) therefore instructed one of the police agents to act as *agent provocateur* by inducing Wucherer to sell him a prohibited book which the police knew him to have printed.[1] After two fruitless attempts the agent succeeded the third time in the disguise of a stranger about to leave the country.[2]

Wucherer was immediately hauled before the police. Unfortunately for Hofrat Beer, he could not be persuaded to admit to anything but the single offence provoked by the police agent, and no other offence could be proved. According to the law, therefore, he was liable only to a fine of 50 florins. Joseph II, however, considering that he could ignore the law when he thought fit, ordered the police to search Wucherer's papers and books for possible incriminating *corpora delicti*.[3] There was no pretence that from the legal point of view, Wucherer had ever done anything at all to justify such a search.

The Emperor and Hofrat Beer were aghast at the large stock of uncensored or prohibited books in Wucherer's storeroom, but as for *corpora delicti*, the search yielded only a paltry copy of a printed 'Introduction to a Plan' containing, it was alleged, seventeen 'objectionable' maxims and principles. Nevertheless, a summary police investigation was held on the basis of this exhibit. After prolonged and harassing questioning, this, too, failed to lead to any discoveries which would have enabled the criminal court to deal with the 'diocesan'.[4]

[1] It must be remembered that in 1787 Gottfried van Swieten had persuaded the Emperor to withdraw his earlier decision that the sale of prohibited books abroad should be an offence: Au. Note Swietens, 10 Mar. 1787 mit Ah. Resolution, quoted by Gnau, pp. 185–6. The information that Wucherer had printed a prohibited manuscript was therefore insufficient in itself to justify proceedings against him.

[2] Au. Note Beers, 25 July 1789, *Pergen Akten*, ix/B5, H1.

[3] Ah. Resolution über Au. Note Beers, 29 July 1789, *Pergen Akten*, ix/B5, H2: '. . . jedoch sind vorher noch sein Verlag u. Schriften zu durchsuchen, ob man nicht hieraus auf weitere Spuren gelangen könne'.

[4] Vortrag der Voruntersuchungskommission (signed by Beer and two councillors of the Criminal Department of the Vienna Municipality), 24 Sept. 1789, *Pergen Akten*, ix/B5, H6.

Accordingly, Joseph proceeded to disregard the law even more flagrantly than he had already done in this case. He ordered Wucherer's expulsion from all his dominions (Wucherer was not Austrian-born), the pulping of his stock of uncensored and prohibited books, and a fine of 1,000 florins for having sold some of the latter in Germany.[1] The fine was unlawful, because according to the law at the time of Wucherer's arrest, it was definitely not a punishable offence to sell uncensored or prohibited books abroad. It was justified in Joseph's eyes, presumably, as a necessary deterrent to the black market in uncensored books, and in order to diminish the vast quantity of radical books circulating in Germany. The pulping was an unlawful infringement of Wucherer's property, because according to the law at the time of his arrest, it was explicitly permitted to print manuscripts before submitting them to the Board of Censorship, in accordance with the principle that the laws of censorship were concerned only with books in circulation.[2] In the eyes of the Emperor and of his Minister of Police, however, it was justified, because the state of public opinion made the complete suppression of these books an absolute political necessity.[3] The banishment was unlawful, because Wucherer had not been convicted of any crime for which the law provided such a severe sentence. The police advocated and Joseph II sanctioned violation of the law in this case, because in Beer's opinion Wucherer was 'a chief of the German Union and generally a thoroughly obnoxious and dangerous man in every respect'.[4]

When the Supreme Chancellor, Count Kollowrat, received notification of Wucherer's banishment from the Ministry of Police, he was apparently surprised to find that no reasons were given. He therefore dispatched a note to Count Pergen asking for the omitted information, so that it could be

---

[1] Ah. Resolution über Au. Note Beers, 2 Oct. 1789, *Archiv für N. Öst.*, *Präsidialakten*, 1792/56.

[2] Gnau, pp. 181-3.

[3] Au. Note Pergens. 24 Feb. 1791. *Pergen Akten*. ix/B5. H26: '. . . daß die vorhandenen Exemplare von den gefährlichen u. verbotenen Büchern ihm um so mehr haben abgenommen werden müssen, als dem Staate allzuviel daran gelegen war, selbe zu unterdrücken . . .'.

[4] Au. Note Beers. 29 July 1789. *Pergen Akten* ix/B5, H2.

included, according to the usual practice, in the necessary
instructions for the provincial governors. Pergen replied:

... I have the honour to inform Your Excellency that Georg Philipp
Wucherer has been banished from all His Majesty's hereditary
dominions, on the orders of His Majesty personally, for selling prohibited or even uncensored books, and for another extremely important
secret reason known to His Majesty.

The *princeps legibus solutus* had spoken. . . .[1]

(ii) *New policies for old*

The discovery of Wucherer's large stocks of 'dangerous'
books and of his practice of selling in Germany whatever he
failed to get past the Austrian censorship, seemed to Joseph II
to provide the clue to the secret of the increasing circulation
both in his own dominions and throughout Germany of
books, the contents of which were 'calculated to undermine
all religion, morality and the social order', and convinced
him of the necessity for a fundamental modification of the
policy he had hitherto pursued in relation to censorship,[2]
i.e. for a tightening-up such as was taking place in a number
of German states at this time.

The concrete proposals for the required change came from
the Minister of Police. Pergen evidently assumed that his
responsibility for the maintenance of public order against the
threat of social disturbances entitled him to make proposals
in relation to all departments of government affecting public
opinion and internal security. Joseph II's admission of this
claim was symptomatic of the change in the balance of power

[1] Pergen to Kollowrat, 29 Jan. 1790 (draft). The important phrase is: 'wegen
einer anderen Sr. M. bekannten höchst wichtigen geheimen Ursache', which was
apparently coined by Pergen personally, because it appears in place of the crossed
out 'bey ihm unter seinen Schriften gefundenen äußerst staatsgefährlichen Schrift'
in the original draft of his secretary.

[2] The later censorship regulations of Joseph II have confused Mitrofanov so
much that the section of his last chapter dealing with them is hopelessly confused
and unreliable. He deals with a mere fragment of the decrees issued on the subject, and
reads quite wrong meanings into them. Gnau, pp. 179 ff., gives a much fuller
and more reliable account, but as he had investigated only the documents of the
Board of Censorship and had not looked into the simultaneous police records, he
was puzzled by the new regulations, and thought that someone must have 'forgotten'
the earlier ones. It is hoped that what follows will help to close some of the gaps left
open by the above-mentioned historians.

and influence inside the imperial counsels in favour of the highest aristocratic ministers at the expense of those less exalted, who were the principal supporters and executors of the levelling reforms, a change which was an inevitable consequence of the gradual retreat from enlightened despotism. It encouraged Pergen to embark on a prolonged and determined effort to secure for his ministry a predominant influence in the shaping of Habsburg internal policy. During the short span of time which still remained to Joseph, this effort was crowned with success.

Joseph endorsed Pergen's proposals on a subject which had hitherto been exclusively within the province of the Court Chancellery, and which the minister had submitted as a matter arising out of the punishment of Wucherer.[1] Ignoring van Swieten's appeal not to punish all publishers for the offences committed by one of their number, he went back on his permission for printing manuscripts before submission to the censor, providing a fine of 50 florins for the first and forfeiture of the trading-licence for the second offence against the new prohibition, and made it illegal, moreover, to sell prohibited books abroad on pain of corporal punishment for all convicted offenders.[2]

This decision was embodied in a Patent published on 20 January 1790, just one month before the Emperor's death, which gave an unequivocal indication as to the political considerations which had motivated it. The sale of prohibited books abroad had to be made illegal, because, in the words of the Patent,

It is generally recognised that books, the contents of which are calculated to undermine the principles of all religion, morality, and social order, to promote the disintegration of all ties uniting states and nations, are in fact dangerous in their effects, and it is therefore a duty towards humanity to prevent, as far as possible, the circulation of such books.[3]

The meaning of this could not be misconstrued by the

---

[1] I have been unable to find this note, and have had to rely on the indirect evidence of Au. Note Pergens. 17 Oct. 1789, *Pergen Akten*, ix/B5, H7.

[2] Gnau, pp. 189–92.

[3] Patent, 20 Jan. 1790, F. Kropatschek. *Handbuch aller unter . . . Joseph II . . . ergangenen Verordnungen u. Gesetze*, xviii. 571–2, N. 13.

public. It was seen for what it was, as part of Joseph II's
determined effort to restrict a freedom of the press such as
he had himself formerly allowed, and which he now considered to have done a great deal of harm to his dominions.[1]

One result of the former extension of press freedom which
the governing classes considered more and more 'harmful'
towards the end of Joseph II's reign, was the importation
of ever-increasing numbers of papers and periodicals from
Germany and Salzburg, and the foundation of local newspapers in Vienna and the provincial capitals, many of which
were only copies of news items and articles appearing in the
foreign press. Most of these papers were cheap, and therefore enjoyed a wide circulation even among the poor. The
phenomenon of an eager and numerous newspaper-reading
public drawn from the ranks of the 'lowest classes' in town
and country would not have been calculated to arouse the
enthusiasm of Joseph II and his ministers and governors in
any circumstances. But when in 1789 the newspapers were
bristling with accounts of opposition movements and revolutionary manifestations in various countries, and especially
in those of which he was himself sovereign and in which his
favourite sister was Queen,[2] Joseph decided to take action
with a view to reducing the number of popular papers and
their circulation, and preventing the insertion of anything
'harmful' in those which survived.

In May of that year an order appeared imposing a stamp
duty on all newspapers and periodicals sold in the Emperor's
dominions, 'in order to hold back the rising flood of pamphlets and newspapers which, without contributing in any way
to national enlightenment, exercise a harmful influence on
public opinion and civil obedience'.[3]

Some two months later, Count Auersperg, the acting
governor of Lower Austria, received an order to suspend the
publication of the Viennese newspaper *Wiener Bothe* and to

---

[1] F. X. Huber, *Geschichte Josephs II.* (1790: Vienna), ii. 231.

[2] The British Chargé d'Affaires in Vienna reports that Joseph was thrown into
'transports of passion' and uttered the 'most violent Menaces of Vengeance' when
he was informed of the July events in France: Hammond to the Duke of Leeds,
29 July 1789, *Public Record Office*, FO. 7/17, fol. 232.

[3] Hofdekret, 11 May 1789, Kropatschek, *Handbuch*, xvii. 630–4, Schrift-
gießerei, N. 10; Huber, *Joseph II*, ii. 228–9.

close its premises because of the editor's 'very unsuitable selection of news items'. The governor, moreover, was 'to proceed with equal severity against all other editors who might venture to include similarly unsuitable news items', as this was 'the best way eventually to put an end to this senseless lust for writing'.[1]

Some of Joseph's ministers and governors were not satisfied with the scope of these repressive measures. Most papers survived the stamp duties, and the contents of the provincial papers were apparently but little affected by the Emperor's rough handling of the papers in the capital which came to his immediate notice. These sporadic outbursts could not conceal the fact that existing censorship regulations had not really provided for such new developments as the emergence of a popular provincial press, and did not include any instructions for the systematic supervision of its contents. The matter was left to the initiative of the individual governors. And some of the governors were alarmed by the contents of newspapers in 1789 and 1790, and felt that more needed to be done urgently about them than had been done by the central government.

Count Sauer, governor of the Tyrol, complained that the popular papers all concentrated on just those events which were most damaging and inconvenient to the government. All his efforts to secure a wide circulation for a 'loyal' paper had failed.[2]

Count Rottenhan, governor of Upper Austria, was dismayed to see the good results of his own consistent supervision of the Linz paper being dissipated by papers coming in from the provinces whose governors had regrettably failed to make it their duty to scrutinize the press. He branded the *Grätzer Zeitung* and the Styrian *Bauern Zeitung* as conspicuous by their lack of moderation and their audacity:

> In recent issues of both these papers, I have frequently come across reports both of political developments in countries which are not exactly on friendly terms with Austria, and of excesses against sovereign

[1] Ah. Handbillet an Auersperg, 23 July 1789, and Ah. Resolution, 26 July 1789 (copy), *Archiv für N. Öst., Präsidialakten*, 1789/31.
[2] Mitrofanov, pp. 824–5, n. 6.

authority indulged in by the mob in those countries where freedom is mistaken to mean unbridled licence; and, what is more, these reports are couched in terms giving no hint of critical disapproval, or even implicitly suggesting approbation.[1]

Count Rottenhan raised these points in a report to Count Pergen, for since the elevation of the Vienna police department to the status of an imperial ministry (*Hofstelle*), governors were instructed to report on all matters relating to the state of public opinion and internal security, not to the Court Chancellery, but to the Ministry of Police. Rottenham concluded:

I have taken the liberty of mentioning these details to draw Your Excellency's attention to the problem in general, in the hope that the governors concerned may perhaps be instructed to pay more careful attention to the contents of the Grätzer, Brünner, and Prager Zeitungen, at least in the present critical situation.

He had not mentioned these details in vain. For Count Pergen had himself become convinced on the basis of all the reports he had received, that 'The unsuitable material presented in various newspapers, which are so cheap that even the lowest classes are buying them, is having a very mischievous effect on their readers, induces them to draw ominous analogies, and stirs up a rebellious mood.' He therefore fully endorsed the governor's observations and recommendations, and asked for the Emperor's permission to instruct all governors to scrutinize with the greatest care all newspapers published in their provinces, and to cut out all news items and comments likely to lead some people to 'wrong-headed conclusions' or to 'spread a spirit of rebellion among those who are already inclined to unruliness'.[2]

This request fully accorded with Joseph II's views on this subject and received the imperial 'placet' without delay. On 23 January 1790 Pergen instructed all governors to examine the contents of all newspapers published in their provinces before publication.[3] In this way, a regular system of newspaper censorship was introduced in the Habsburg dominions

---

[1] Rottenhan to Pergen, 16 Jan. 1790, *Pergen Akten*, xvii/8, H1.

[2] Au. Note Pergens, (21 ?) Jan. 1790, *Pergen Akten*, xvii/8, H2.

[3] The text of this *Circulare* is quoted by Mitrofanov, p. 822, n. 3, but altogether out of its context and wrongly dated.

not only at the instance of the new Ministry of Police, but as part of its jurisdictional sphere which was expanding so rapidly during the last months of Joseph II's reign.

Pergen had necessarily gained his new influence in the field of censorship at the expense of Gottfried van Swieten, who, as a convinced adherent of the Enlightenment, looked upon censorship as a purely temporary expedient which would ultimately be rendered superfluous by human progress.[1] In the course of the retreat from enlightened despotism, van Swieten inevitably lost ground to his other conservative adversaries as well. By 1788, Cardinal Migazzi (who must have been encouraged at this time by Wöllner's growing influence over Prussian policy) strongly supported by the Supreme Chancellor, Count Kollowrat, had succeeded in convincing the Emperor of the necessity of active intervention in the field of educational policy, where van Swieten had hitherto been given more or less a free hand. The latter found that he was no longer able to defend the professors he had appointed (many of them were *Illuminati* expelled from Bavaria) or the 'philosophical' plan to which he worked, from the Archbishop's attacks. A number of professors, among them Dannenmayer and Watteroth, were subjected to the indignity of being summoned into the Emperor's presence to be charged with the dissemination of principles at variance with Catholic dogma, and threatened with immediate dismissal unless they mended their ways.[2] Migazzi and Kollowrat had a little more difficulty in convincing Joseph that his educational system as a whole was in need of fundamental revision. For van Swieten 'made it his principal concern to contradict (the Cardinal's) representations', and succeeded for a time in preventing the remedial actions to which Joseph himself strongly inclined.[3] However, as actual circumstances increasingly confirmed the Cardinal's dismal prophecies concerning the results of van Swieten's policy, the Emperor overruled the latter's objections and demanded from the Chancellery proposals for a fundamental revision of the existing system of education.[4] The order was dated 9 February

---

[1] Au. Note Swietens, 10 Mar. 1787, quoted by Gnau, pp. 185–6.
[2] Au. Note Kollowrats, s.d. (? Mar. 1790), *Nachlaß Kollowrat*, F. 13, No. 1169.
[3] Ibid.   [4] E. Benedikt, *Kaiser Joseph II.* (1936: Vienna), pp. 182–3.

1790. A few days later the Emperor was dead, and Leopold II had other ideas on education.

(iii) *Feudal restoration*

The highest dignitaries of state serving under Joseph II, men like Count Leopold Kollowrat (Supreme Chancellor), Prince Kaunitz-Rietberg (Chancellor of State), Count Rudolf Chotek (Court Chancellor), and Count Johann Anton Pergen (Minister of Police), all of whom belonged to the foremost landowning families of the realm, had been from the very beginning reluctant allies in the levelling crusade of enlightened despotism. As the reforming Emperor's reign proceeded on its venturesome course, they urged with increasing frequency that it was time to call a halt, and that it would be dangerous to alienate the Estates further.

Kaunitz warned Joseph against the perils of pursuing a 'tough' policy in the Netherlands. In 1787 he urged concessions.[1] Kollowrat consistently pleaded against the new land tax because of the hardships it would impose on the landowners.[2] Chotek finally resigned because the Emperor refused to listen to the Chancellor's representations.[3] While the police commandant of Pest, Gotthardi, advocated a policy of severity towards the Hungarian malcontents, the Minister of Police, Pergen, suggested (as early as November 1788!) that their 'enthusiasm seems to have reached such a pitch, that force and compulsion will scarcely suffice to constrain these people'.[4]

If we may believe his own testimony, Count Pergen was the most persistent and outspoken of the ministers, both in his advocacy of reconciliation with the Estates, and in his criticism of the supporters and executors of the levelling reforms inside the government (Swieten, Kressel, Eger, &c.). Joseph, he thought, had allowed himself to be duped:

Des ignorans et hypocrites, toujours prêts à rendre faciles les changements les plus délicats et épineux dans un gouvernement, se sont emparé de Sa confiance, ont abusé de Sa fermeté louable dans le fond, et, en lui

---

[1] Au. Note Kaunitz', 28 Jan. 1790, *Staatskanzlei, Vorträge,* F. 220.
[2] Mitrofanov, pp. 467–70.
[3] Ibid., pp. 470–1.
[4] Au. Note Pergens, 8 Nov. 1788, R. Gragger, *Preußen, Weimar u. die ungarische Königs Krone* (1923: Berlin), pp. 23–24.

représentant les choses dans un faux jour, ont sû eloigner les serviteurs fidèles et entrainer insensiblement ce Souverain bienfaisant dans son cœur à des actes de violence contre les proprietés, les privilèges, et droits de presque toutes les classes de ses sujets; démarches qui ont occasionné dans toutes les provinces de la Monarchie . . . une fermentation si générale, que le mécontentement et la méfiance ont pris la place du patriotisme et de l'attachement pour le Souverain.

Pergen felt that it was his moral duty to speak out:

Sa Majesté, convaincue de mon honnêteté et de ma franchise, a daigné écouter avec bonté les avis, que je lui ai donnés de l'aliénation successive des esprits.

But the adherents of the Enlightenment, whose indispensable services in the cause of the reforms had brought them into positions of some influence in the government, were formidable adversaries:

Mes remontrances, aussi sincères qu'isolées, et restraintes au départment, qui m'a été confié, ont dû céder aux insinuations du parti, qui a sû, je ne sais comment, faire goûter au Monarque des principes, qui par leur exécution odieuse ne pourront avoir que des suites dangereuses.[1]

The venerable Chancellor of State, to whom this plaintive account of frustrated efforts was addressed, must have smiled at his colleague's naïve conception of the motive power behind the reforms of Joseph II, his apparent ignorance of the compelling considerations which had induced the Emperor to go as far as he had done. But he must have realized at the same time, that the Emperor's capacity to reject the 'remonstrances' of his Minister of Police was at an end.

As it had been neither the aim nor, indeed, the result of the reform programme to oust the privileged Estates from their position of social supremacy in the State, or to compel them to share this position with any other class, Joseph II had to face the fact that the continuing functioning of his monarchy, 'enlightened' or otherwise, fundamentally depended on the co-operation or at least on the acquiescence of the privileged classes organized in the Estates. Without this co-operation or acquiescence, the Emperor was powerless

[1] Pergen to Kaunitz, 16 Jan. 1790, *Staatskanzlei, Noten v.d. Polizei*, F. 29.

to do anything except to preside over the disintegration of his monarchy.

The privileged classes withdrew their co-operation from, and ceased to acquiesce in the government of Joseph II, because they feared both material ruin and the loss of their position of social supremacy as a result of some of his innovations.

Joseph, impulsive and self-willed as he was, found it very difficult to face the facts. His first impulse was to fly in their face, and this lost him the Netherlands late in 1789. It made Kaunitz apprehend that, old though he was, he might yet be young enough to see the destruction of the monarchy.[1]

But Joseph II was not incapable of facing the facts. The very day on which the Chancellor had expressed his apprehension, a conciliatory reply was sent off to the Hungarian Estates, holding out the prospect of a coronation diet, the terms of which Joseph had sanctioned just before he received a note from Pergen insisting on this course as absolutely imperative.[2]

When Joseph saw that his reply had failed to appease the Hungarian Estates and to secure their renewed acquiescence in his government, he turned to his chief ministers for support without which any further action on his part would have been futile—for he was now a dying man. But these ministers, as we have seen, had been viewing the Emperor's despotic obstinacy in persevering with his levelling reforms with mounting disfavour for some time. Their sympathy was not entirely on the Emperor's side, and they were persuaded of the 'justice' of many of the Estates' grievances.[3] Moreover, by January 1790, they regarded the disintegration of the monarchy as imminent because of the probable war with Prussia and Poland, and the eventual suppression of the revolt impossible because of the participation in it of the Fourth Estate.[4]

---

[1] Entry in Count Zinzendorf's diary, 18 Dec. 1789, in Benedikt, p. 309.

[2] Ah. Resolution über Au. Note Pergens, 16 Dec. 1789, *Pergen Akten*, x/A3, H83.

[3] Cf., e.g., Au. Note Pergens, 13 Jan. 1790 (copy), *Staatskanzlei, Noten v.d. Polizei*, F. 29: 'Der Adel ist mit Rechte unzufrieden, weil derselbe durch die bürgerliche sowohl als Kriminalgesetzgebung u. durch die neue Steuerrectification in seinem Eigenthum ohne Verschulden äußerst gekränket und . . . erniedriget worden. . . .'   [4] Au. Note Pergens, 28 Jan. 1790, *Pergen Akten*, x/A3, H97.

With these powerful apprehensions uppermost in their minds, the ministers shut their eyes for the time being to the potential damage to the vital interests of the monarchy inherent in a far-reaching restoration of privileges and rights such as the Estates demanded. How were the most essential material requirements of the state to be met after a wholesale revocation of the reforms which were vital to their adequate fulfilment?

Kaunitz, who had such a clear appreciation of the practical needs of the time, and who had been largely responsible for the introduction of many of these reforms, did not say one word on this aspect of the question in January 1790. Count Pergen, who so naïvely misunderstood the motivation behind Joseph II's obstinacy, tried to bemuse the Emperor with vague prophecies of a return to the halcyon days of 1741 when the Magyar magnates and gentry so flamboyantly rose to the defence of their sovereign. An assurance of concessions 'is bound to produce a most salutary effect in this proud nation, which . . . once its . . . genuine confidence has been regained, is qualified by its excellent national character to prove itself the monarchy's most powerful support.'[1] He added the comforting assurance that, if Joseph could only see his way to revoking the measures he had introduced without the Estates' consent, the latter would be more likely to see reason, and would willingly co-operate in the substitution of the out-dated *Insurrection* (feudal levy) by a more up-to-date system of taxation and recruitment.[2]

Joseph II, who was more detached in his assessment of aristocratic sense of realities, duty and responsibility at the end of the 'Glittering Century' than most of his peers (except perhaps Kaunitz), was, we may be sure, less sanguine on the point than his Minister of Police, who was unable to transcend the political and mental horizons of his own class.[3]

---

[1] Au. Note Pergens, 16 Dec. 1789, *Pergen Akten*, x/A3, H83.

[2] Au. Note Pergens, 28 Jan. 1790, *Pergen Akten*, x/A3, H97. Pergen's rather unsupported hypothesis anticipates by 160 years the parallel hypothesis of the Jesuit historian F. Maaß (*Josephinismus*, i. 9–10) that Joseph might have achieved an 'honest compromise of interests' with the Church, had he not given way to extremists.

[3] It is perhaps not irrelevant to note at this point that despite all the concessions Francis II was able to continue the war against France beyond 1795 only with the help of English subsidies.

However, the rapid denouement of events left the harassed Emperor no time to secure ministerial consideration for this type of apprehension. Pergen already insisted quite specifically that the new system of land taxation be considerably modified in favour of the landowners in the German provinces and abandoned altogether in Hungary; that a definite date be fixed for the convocation of the Hungarian diet, without whose consent there were to be no further constitutional or legal innovations; and that concrete preparations be commenced for the convocation of a diet in Galicia to discuss all the grievances of the Polish nobility.[1]

For this far-reaching programme of restoration, Pergen was careful to enlist the vital support of Kaunitz.[2] The move was the more certain to succeed in that the Chancellor's profound appreciation of the motives behind Joseph II's reforms in no way lessened his apprehensions of the calamities for the monarchy which perseverance with them would now entail.

Thus there was every likelihood that the interview for which Pergen asked Kaunitz would result in a mutual and full understanding between the two ministers whose position in the government was such that their joint efforts could not but be decisive.

Full understanding was evidently achieved, for the interview galvanized the aged Chancellor into action. He decided to send his assistant, the Councillor Spielmann, on a mission to acquaint the Emperor with his views on the imperative need of very far-reaching concessions.[3]

By now Joseph was too ill to retain in his own hands all the reins of a government that had become so beset with vast difficulties. He therefore ordered his Hungarian Chancellery to sit in joint conference with the State Chancellery with a view to making recommendations for the solution of the Hungarian crisis.[4]

Kaunitz took this opportunity to send a note to the

[1] Au. Noten Pergens, 13 and 28 Jan. 1790, *Staatskanzlei, Noten v.d. Polizei,* F. 29, and *Pergen Akten,* x/A3, H97.
[2] Pergen to Kaunitz, 16 Jan. 1790, *Staatskanzlei, Noten v.d. Polizei,* F. 29.
[3] Au. Note Kaunitz', 25 Jan. 1790 (draft), *Staatskanzlei, Vorträge,* F. 220.
[4] Palffy to Kaunitz, 25 Jan. 1790, *Staatskanzlei, Noten v.d. Ungarischen Hofkanzlei,* F. 7.

Emperor which, despite its traditional 'most humble' introduction, was nothing less than an ultimatum demanding the
immediate implementation of the Kaunitz-Pergen policy as
the price of his participation in the conference.[1] The imperial
resolution to the protocol of the joint conference thus was,
in its essentials, a foregone conclusion.

Joseph recognized that there was now for him 'no stop-
ping half way' in respect of the Hungarian demands. The
ministers' attitude precluded any calculations as to the maximum which could be salvaged from the wreck, or as to the
tactics by which the opposition could be split. All he could
do was to try and circumvent the demand for fixing the date
of the diet by making more concessions on the spot than
even his ministers were stipulating.[2]

This manœuvre, so very characteristic of Joseph II, was
a desperate attempt to retain the political initiative which the
Estates and the ministers were wresting from his hands, a
desperate attempt to prevent the burning of the reform-boats.

But the Hungarian Estates burnt the records of the Josephinian government and expelled the Josephinian bureaucracy from their country, while the body of Joseph II
succumbed to multiple disease and was carried down into
the crypt of the Capuchins.

And so the political initiative passed altogether into the
hands of the Estates throughout the monarchy, and to
the great ministers in the government. The Estates staked the
claims; Kaunitz and Pergen set the pace of the retreat, and
prescribed the character and the extent of the concessions
with which the renewed acquiescence of the Estates in the
government was to be bought. The concessions which
Joseph II had still tried to elude were exacted from his
brother Leopold II as soon as he set foot in his inheritance.

In order to regain the political initiative for himself,
Leopold had to have recourse to some very extraordinary
devices.

[1] Au. Note Kaunitz', 25 Jan. 1790, *Staatskanzlei, Vorträge*, F. 220.
[2] Ah. Resolution über das Concertationsprotokoll, 28 Jan. 1790 (copy), *Staatskanzlei, Vorträge*, F. 220. Joseph hoped that in view of the sweeping character of his
immediate concessions 'werden die Stände einen Landtag nicht so dringend ver-
langen, welcher bei jetzigen Umständen u. Stimmung der Gemüther . . . zu halten
unmöglich ist'.

II

LEOPOLD II: ONE STEP BACK, TWO STEPS FORWARD

1. *Continuation of the Retreat from Enlightened Despotism*

I T was inevitable that Joseph II's successor should, for the time being, continue the retreat from enlightened despotism. Encouraged by the success of the Belgian and Hungarian rebellions, the Estates in all the Habsburg provinces had seized the initiative and now assumed a menacing attitude. As a new-comer to an inheritance threatened also by foreign invasion, Leopold II had to appease the privileged orders speedily by far-reaching concessions.

The impact of the French Revolution caused the government to watch with ever-increasing anxiety the development of public opinion in the Fourth Estate, and therefore to continue and develop Joseph's later repressive measures.

Louis XVI's attempted flight to Varennes brought about a significant *rapprochement* between Leopold and the emigrant leaders of the French aristocracy, and seemed to extend the principle of feudal restoration even to Habsburg foreign policy.

(i) *Appeasement of the privileged orders*

While Joseph II was making his death-bed concessions to the Hungarian opposition, the Estates in the other Habsburg provinces mobilized for action to exact for themselves similar concessions.[1]

As soon as the news of the Emperor's death had reached them, the Estates everywhere met openly to discuss their grievances and to put forward their claims for a restoration of all the privileges of which Joseph had deprived them. Most prominent and most insistent was the demand for the revocation of the Patent of 10 February 1789, by which Joseph had imposed both the new land tax and uniformly

[1] R. J. Kerner, *Bohemia in the Eighteenth Century* (1932: New York), pp. 86–87.

limited and commuted feudal dues. The bishops, too, submitted memoranda in which they demanded the restoration
of the former clerical authority in the field of theological
training, marriage, censorship, and education.[1]

Prince Kaunitz frankly told the new sovereign that if he
wished to restore order in his dominions, 'it will be necessary
to concede, *mutatis mutandis* . . ., to the Estates of all the
provinces of the Monarchy without exception, all that His
late Majesty has so wisely conceded to the Kingdom of
Hungary . . .'.

Kaunitz went on to prescribe even the manner in which
these concessions should be effected:

> Permission should be granted to all provinces in turn, beginning
> with the Kingdom of Bohemia, to send three deputies from the
> Estates to Court for the purpose of submitting their demands. These
> demands should be conceded as far as possible . . ., and the concessions
> put into effect with the utmost celerity.

In conclusion, the Chancellor advised Leopold to desist for
the time being from any further far-reaching innovations
likely to disturb the smooth running of the administration.[2]

Leopold had little choice but to acquiesce in the initiative
of the Estates. But, as he was aware of the incompatibility
of many of the aristocratic claims with the interests of a
strong monarchy, he was concerned to keep immediate concessions to a minimum, and to refer as many claims as
possible for later consideration, when he would be able to
negotiate from a position of greater strength.

The Patent of 10 February 1789 was of necessity sacrificed to win that minimum confidence of the Estates which
was essential to the continued existence of the monarchy.[3] It
would be difficult to exaggerate the significance of this concession for the subsequent fortunes of the monarchy; both
as a considerable limitation on its strength in future trials,
and as a fundamental impediment to the development of its
economic resources.

[1] Wolfsgruber, *Migazzi*, pp. 745-54.
[2] Au. Noten Kaunitz', 17 May 1790 (drafts), *Staatskanzlei, Vorträge*, F. 220,
fols. 133-60.
[3] E. Murr Link, *The Emancipation of the Austrian Peasant, 1740-1798* (1949:
New York), pp. 149-51.

The full significance of the other immediate concession to which Leopold was forced, the convocation of the diets in all provinces of the monarchy,[1] was, at the outset, uncertain. That would depend on the extent to which the diets and their spokesmen at Court would be able to exact further concessions from the Emperor and to assert their influence generally in the shaping of government policy. At the time of the Patent of Convocation, these were open questions.

(ii) *Continuation of Joseph II's later repressive policy*

The concessions to the Estates reduced the immediate danger of an aristocratic revolt. They helped to blunt the edge of the opposition of an aristocracy now confident that it would obtain further important concessions in time; that it was on the threshold of a new and, for itself, more propitious period.

However, the threat of aristocratic revolt had been but one of the apprehensions worrying Austrian ministers towards the end of Joseph II's reign. Although this threat was receding, the 'highly critical situation' resulting from the widespread discontent and ferment among the non-privileged classes still remained to worry them.

Indeed, it worried them more seriously as time went on. Not only did they fear that the established success of the popular revolution in France would help to make the Fourth Estate in the Habsburg dominions more impatient of their grievances. They also regarded the very fact of the Revolution itself and the positive response it called forth among the adherents of the Enlightenment in the other countries of Europe as the final confirmation of all their worst fears concerning enlightened opinions.

In Austria, a number of peculiar circumstances made the situation appear especially 'critical' in the eyes of the government.

They were worried about the influence on public opinion exerted by the fairly large French population which had come into Austria as a result of the economic inducements

---

[1] Ah. Handbillet an Kollowrat, 29 Apr. 1790, in H. I. Bidermann, 'Die Verfassungskrise in der Steiermark zur Zeit der ersten französischen Revolution', in *Mitteilungen des Historischen Vereins für Steiermark*, xxi (1873), 70–71.

offered by Joseph II. Most of these people still had many
contacts with France and must inevitably have contributed
to the popularization of the French Revolution in Austria.[1]

And then there was the continued unprecedented rise in
the cost of living, for which the government was generally
blamed. The consequent resentment gave rise to an unceasing stream of abuse and criticism of the government.[2]

Under the circumstances, many members of the government were naturally convinced of the necessity to continue
and to develop the policies which Joseph II had inaugurated
to deal with the earlier manifestations of this problem.

Presumably on the advice of the Supreme Chancellor,
Count Kollowrat,[3] and the insistence of Cardinal Migazzi,
Leopold II issued new regulations for university students
designed to ensure that their education should not in future
result in a loss of faith such as was the case so frequently at
the time.[4] Similarly, an attack by the Cardinal against van
Swieten's Board of Censorship, alleging that the latter's
practice was at variance with Joseph II's instructions, induced the Emperor to issue to the Board a formal reminder
'never to pass any books or pamphlets which cast ridicule
upon the teachings of religion, the constitution of the
Church, and the Clergy'.[5] Although this order merely confirmed what Joseph II had been insisting on for some time,
it was widely regarded as a further restriction of the freedom
of the press.

Newspapers continued to give rise to misgivings and concern. As the Revolution developed in France, and a revolutionary spirit infected more and more areas of Germany, the
existing policy in relation to the censorship of newspapers
appeared ever more inadequate.

Count Pergen was the first minister to draw Leopold II's
attention to the matter. If earlier he had been concerned
mainly with the comments and favourable insinuations with

[1] Report of L. A. Hoffmann, 23 July 1791, *Vertr. Akten*, F. 58, fol. 192.
[2] L. A. Hoffmann, *Patriotische Bemerkungen über die gegenwärtige Theuerung in Wien*, pp. 16–22.
[3] Au. Note Kollowrats, s.d. (? Mar. 1790), *Nachlaß Kollowrat*, F. 13, No. 1169.
[4] Hofdekret, 20 Dec. 1790, Kropatschek, *Sammlung*, ii. 292–4, N. 309.
[5] Wolfsgruber, pp. 776–7. The order was published as a Hofdekret, 1 Sept. 1790, Kropatschek, *Sammlung*, iii. 37–38, N. 379.

which the editors of Austrian original newspapers appeared
to adorn their news reports, he was now convinced that the
unadorned factual reports which made up the entire contents
of the numerous digests of foreign newspapers printed and
circulating in Austria, might well be no less mischievous in
their effect. Sober, factual reports of the proceedings in the
French National Assembly, for instance, could easily, in
Pergen's view, be exploited by revolutionary agitators for
their own ends and create very undesirable impressions on
the minds of newspaper readers. He therefore submitted
that 'it would be highly desirable to print alongside the very
dry . . . reports of the developments in France appearing in
the cheap popular papers at the moment, comments . . .
pointing out the dangers to public security inherent [in these
developments]'. Governors would have to choose someone
duly qualified to write such comments, as this could not
possibly be left to the editors of the digests. Leopold gave
his assent to Pergen's proposal.[1]

Whatever the success of this device may have been, voices
continued to be raised drawing attention to the danger
inherent in the dissemination of detailed reports on the developments in France. Not least among them was that of the
Crown Prince, Archduke Francis.[2] A variety of proposals
were submitted as to ways and means of disposing of the
newspaper problem, including, apparently, the simple remedy of a general prohibition of all digests of foreign papers.

The Emperor finally demanded a full report from the
Lower Austrian government, which was duly submitted
with a covering note from its President, Count Sauer, dated
4 August 1791.[3]

Sauer strongly opposed the idea of prohibition. This, he
thought, would be both inconsistent and useless so long as
the importation of the original editions of the foreign newspapers was still permitted. These would be subscribed to in
groups where they could not be afforded by individuals.
Prohibition, moreover, was dangerous in Sauer's view,

---

[1] Au. Note Pergens (? 20) Oct. 1790, *Pergen Akten*, xvii/9, H2.
[2] C. Wolfsgruber, *Franz I., Kaiser von Österreich* (1899: Vienna), ii. 179–80.
[3] The report, unfortunately, has disappeared. Sauer's covering note may be
found in Schilling's draft in *Archiv für N. Öst., Präsidialakten*, 1791/46.

because of the resentment it would arouse among the very large number of people for whom newspaper reading had become the favourite pastime ever since political developments in certain countries had taken such a dramatic and spectacular turn. 'They would all complain of government oppression and suspect the motives of the government. The mischievous ideas which it had been intended to obliterate would only gain further ground. The appetite for news would probably be stimulated rather than suppressed.'

Count Sauer therefore went on to consider ways and means of improving the censorship of these newspapers. To this end he proposed that four men from the staff of the government should be entrusted with the task of examining the contents of all newspapers before publication and cutting out all such items as might create an undesirable impression on the minds of readers. Developing Pergen's earlier proposal, Sauer further suggested that the four censors should exert pressure on editors to give prominence to those news items which tended to illustrate the 'dire consequences of political fanaticism in all their enormity' on the one hand, or the 'blessings of a monarchical constitution' on the other.

If this were done, Sauer concluded his note, newspapers, so far from being a source of anxiety to the government, might well become a means through which it could influence public opinion in its own favour and dispense an antidote to the vicious revolutionary poison.

Leopold II fully endorsed the President's proposals, adding the rider that the censors must be specifically instructed to cut out 'all . . . references to the French principles, so fraught with danger at the present time, as well as all expositions of, or favourable comments on, the French system, which in the present state of public opinion might well create a most mischievous and pernicious impression on the people'.[1]

Newspaper censorship thus became an important branch of the provincial governments.

(iii) *Police supervision*

Under Joseph II the detection of political agitators had become one of the principal tasks of the state police. Regula-

---

[1] Ah. Resolution über Au. Note Sauers, 4 Aug. 1791, *Kabinettsprotokoll*, 1791/9.

tions and instructions on this point were considerably elaborated under his successor.

The reason for the additional emphasis on this aspect of police duties lay in numerous ambassadorial and other reports reaching the government, to the effect that the 'democratic party' in Paris, headed by Mirabeau and the Duke of Orléans, had set up an organization with the specific aim of sending agents to all the countries of Europe to stir up revolution. The chief source of these and similar reports, of course, were the French *émigrés*; it was part of their vigorous campaign to induce the European monarchs to intervene actively on the side of counter-revolution in France.

The extent to which these reports were taken seriously by the ruling classes in the countries of Europe and were a source of considerable anxiety to them, may perhaps be taken as a measure of their alarm at the state of public opinion in their own respective countries. The 'French agents' theory provided them at once with an apparently plausible explanation of the intensity of popular discontent, and with a pretext for vigorous repressive action against its articulate manifestations. In the ruling class mind, the association between the ideas of 'discontent' and 'treason' was distinctly emerging.

The first official report on French agents reached the Austrian government in June 1790. It came from Coblentz, the French *émigré* headquarters; its author was Count Metternich.[1]

According to this report, the 'democratic party' in Paris had set up a *club de propagande* which aimed at engineering revolutions in other countries through correspondence and personal contacts.[2] A little later, similar information was forwarded to Vienna by Chiarardini, the Austrian ambassador in Turin.[3]

Prince Kaunitz, to whom these reports were addressed, was too level-headed to be unduly alarmed by them. In fact, he was inclined to discount them altogether, as he shrewdly

[1] Franz Georg Karl Graf v. Metternich-Winneburg (1746–1818), Imperial Minister Plenipotentiary, father of the later Austrian Chancellor of State.

[2] Metternich to Kaunitz, 19 June 1790, *Staatskanzlei, Diplomatische Correspondenz, Reich*, F. 223.

[3] Kaunitz to Kollowrat, 15 July 1790, *Hofkanzlei*, IV M 3, Tirol, Kart. 1351.

suspected their source.[1] But not every member of the government shared his equanimity.

The Archduke Francis, who had to go through the ambassadorial reports as part of his training for the throne, considered Metternich's report from Coblentz to be worthy of particular notice.[2]

It must have been the Archduke who informed the Supreme Chancellor, Count Kollowrat, that there were reports concerning French emissaries. The latter was evidently apprehensive about the possible implications of these reports for internal security and asked Kaunitz to supply him with all the relevant details.[3]

Kollowrat thought that the matter was urgent enough to warrant immediate action, which he took without hesitation: it was the beginning of a prolonged effort on the part of the government to deal with the supposed menace of French revolutionary agitation.

All provincial governors were informed of the ambassadorial reports concerning French agents, and instructed to keep a careful check on all foreigners entering their respective provinces or staying there without actually transacting any definite business. Should this vigilance bring to light seditious activities, governors were to arrest the culprits and to report the matter to the Court Chancellery.[4] Kollowrat also notified Pergen of the matter, as it would be the duty of the Ministry of Police to work out whatever detailed instructions might become necessary in this connexion.[5]

Apparently, Leopold II himself took the allegations concerning French agents seriously.

In November of 1790 Count Pergen received an order from Leopold to organize constant police supervision of all foreigners, especially Frenchmen and Italians, who were not staying in his dominions for any definite transaction of busi-

[1] Cf. Kaunitz to Kollowrat, 18 Feb. 1891 (draft), *Staatskanzlei, Noten an die Hofkanzlei,* F. 15.

[2] Wolfsgruber, *Franz,* ii. 160.

[3] Kollowrat to Kaunitz, 9 July 1790, *Staatskanzlei, Noten v.d. Hofkanzlei,* F. 39.

[4] Circulare an sämtliche Länderchefs, 25 Sept. 1790 (draft), *Hofkanzlei,* IV M 3, Kart. 1342.

[5] Kollowrat to Pergen, 9 Sept. 1790 (draft), *Hofkanzlei,* IV M 3, Tirol, Kart. 1351.

ness, as well as of coffee-houses and inns frequented by foreigners. All governors therefore received a further set of instructions on the supervision of foreigners based on the Emperor's order, this time from the Minister of Police.[1]

This order marked the beginning of the end of that period, in which foreigners felt more at ease in Vienna than anywhere else, thanks to the relative freedom and security they enjoyed in the Austrian capital.[2] Their security was now at an end. A number of Frenchmen and Italians who had been careless enough to incur Leopold's suspicion, were banished from all his dominions, without ever being informed of their offence.[3] Among them was the Italian Abbé da Ponte, the director of the Italian theatre in Vienna and librettist of the *Nozze di Figaro* and *Don Giovanni*.[4]

The weak link in these new defences against agitators was Hungary, where there was still plenty of inflammable material, but where the state police had fallen victim to the restoration of the old constitutional administration. There was now no organ in the kingdom for the control of foreigners residing there or travelling through.

Count Pergen, convinced as he was of the validity of the allegations that French agents were busy stirring up revolutions in other countries, set out to remedy this situation. If he could not keep a check on the movements of foreigners inside the kingdom, he wished at least to control their entry into it.[5]

Under the existing procedure, the issue of permits to foreigners to enter the kingdom of Hungary was a matter for the Chancellery of State or for the provincial governments. Pergen submitted to Leopold reports he had received alleging that disguised French and Polish agents had managed to slip into Hungary with permits, and used them to

---

[1] Au. Note Pergens, 25 Nov. 1790, *Pergen Akten*, ix/B11, H2. The Ah. Handbillet of 23 Nov. 1790 is here only mentioned. An undated and unsigned document in the hand of one of Leopold's cabinet officials in *Archiv für N. Öst., Präsidialakten*, 1791/2, is probably a copy of it.

[2] Cf. Mitrofanov, p. 272.

[3] e.g. Au. Note Pergens, 21 Dec. 1790, and Ah. Resolution, *Pergen Akten*, ix/B11, H7; Au. Note Sauers, 5 Feb. 1792, and Ah. Resolution, *Kabinettsprotokoll*, 1792/301.   [4] Da Ponte, ii. 28 ff.

[5] Cf. Pergen to Auersperg, 22 Nov. 1790, *Archiv für N. Öst., Präsidialakten*, 1790/40.

support his contention that police control over the issue of permits to enter Hungary was essential to the security of the State.

Pergen's reports and arguments evidently impressed the Emperor. Already at the end of November 1790, a decree to the provincial governments enjoined the most scrupulous care in the issue of permits; applicants now had to supply proofs of their identity and business.[1] The following January, Leopold II endorsed Pergen's proposals on permits to Hungary in their entirety. Henceforward all applicants for permits to enter Hungary had to be screened by the police before their application could be considered even by the Chancellery of State.[2] The jurisdiction of the police was thereby allowed to penetrate into an important new field.

(iv) *Pillnitz*

Eventually, the belief that the 'democratic party' in France was sending emissaries abroad to foster discontent and stir up revolution, was bound to become a factor in foreign policy as well as in internal policy.

The weakening of the central government in France which had resulted from the earlier legislation of the National Assembly, had been welcomed by the governments of the other European countries: they were looking forward to the extinction of France as a powerful factor in international diplomacy. However, their optimism was a little shaken as they gradually became aware of the danger that the progressive decline of the central government might conduce to the strengthening of the 'democratic party' and with it of its supposed campaign to sow the seeds of revolution all over Europe.

To reduce this danger was the chief aim of the secret negotiations which Leopold II carried on with his sister, the Queen of France.[3] The Emperor's plan was to organize a 'Concert' of the European powers to check the trend towards full democracy in France without endangering the personal safety of the French royal family.

[1] Hofdekret, 29 Nov. 1790, ibid.
[2] Pergen to Kaunitz, 12 Jan. 1791, *Staatskanzlei, Notenwechsel m.d. n.ö. Regierung*, F. 2.
[3] H. Schlitter, 'Zur Geschichte der französischen Politik Leopolds II', in *Fontes Rerum Austriacarum*, 2. Abt., xlviii/1 (1896), xii–xiii.

The flight to Varennes in June 1791 rather cut across
Leopold's carefully considered plans. But when the Emperor
heard that the royal family had been detected and brought
back to Paris virtually as prisoners, he feared that the danger
which he had been trying to ward off had fully materialized.
Nothing, it seemed to him, could now prevent the 'democratic party' from assuming full power in France and estab-
lishing unlimited democracy. And if this was to happen,
then surely no European sovereign could ever again be confident 'that he was bequeathing an undamaged crown to his
successors'.[1]

Leopold II took so serious a view of the potential consequences of Varennes, that he abandoned the rather hesitant
policy he had pursued hitherto with regard to the French
affairs. From Italy, where he was staying at this time, he
sent out urgent calls to the European governments to co-
operate in a Concert aimed at restraining the democratic
forces in France which would presently assume full control
of the country.[2]

Frederick William II of Prussia who himself had been
sounding the Austrian government on the question of intervention in France for some time,[3] was the first to respond
positively to Leopold's overtures, and agreed to meet the
Emperor at Pillnitz.

The Austrian diplomatic initiative augured well for the
French emigrant nobility headed by the Comte d'Artois,
whose advances had up to this time been rather cold-
shouldered in Vienna. If the project of a European Concert
against France were to materialize, the French nobility and
the forces it offered to raise would represent a considerable
constituent part of the armed strength giving weight to the
concerted policy.

After Varennes, Artois could look forward to a somewhat
warmer reception in Vienna. He was not disappointed.
Leopold now yielded to his persistent entreaties and allowed
him to come to Pillnitz together with his political adviser
Calonne.[4] And this was not an empty gesture. The presence

[1] Kaunitz to Reuss, 20 July 1791, quoted by Schlitter, p. liii.
[2] Schlitter, pp. li–lii.
[3] Ibid., p. xxii.   [4] Ibid., p. lxiv.

of the French *émigré* leaders at Pillnitz had a definite bearing
on the outcome of the negotiations taking place there. In
drawing up the Declaration of Pillnitz, the monarchs of
Prussia and Austria, yielding to the pressure of Calonne and
Artois, assumed a more threatening tone than they had
originally intended.[1]

At Pillnitz, the *rapprochement* between the monarchy and
the nobility in the Habsburg dominions was thus supplemented by a *rapprochement* with the French nobility striving
to regain its lost privileges and wealth. In each case, such a
course had become necessary in view of a 'highly critical
situation' created by the political opinions and actions of the
non-privileged classes in Austria and in France respectively.

The *rapprochement* with the nobility of the Habsburg
dominions had resulted in the revocation of numerous important reforms obnoxious to the privileged. Equally far-
reaching results were generally expected from Pillnitz. The
Declaration was enthusiastically received by the French
nobility, but it alarmed the non-privileged classes in France
and Austria. They all assumed that it was the prelude to a
counter-revolutionary war of intervention in which the armies
of the Habsburg Empire would fight for the restoration of
lost feudal rights and privileges to the French aristocracy
and to the feudal lords of Alsace and Lorraine.

2. *The Fourth Estate in the Battle against the Feudal Reaction*

While Leopold II's concessions to the privileged orders
healed the open breach between them and the monarchy,
they inevitably aroused bitter resentment in the Fourth
Estate.

The peasants were most unwilling to submit to burdens
which had once been abolished, and struggled more fiercely
than ever for the reduction of their obligations.

The extravagant demands submitted by the recalled diets
were roundly condemned by the publicists, and strenuously
resisted by the 'Josephinian' civil servants.

The prospect of a war of intervention against revolutionary France was regarded with no less indignation than had
been Joseph II's war of aggression against the Turks.

[1] Ibid., p. lxvi.

As in the previous reign, the struggle against the privileged orders helped to raise the level of political consciousness in the Fourth Estate. The Fourth Estate, in fact, submitted to Leopold a political programme of its own.

(i) *The struggle against the reimposition of labour services*

However intense the peasants' dislike for some provisions of the February Patent, few desired a reimposition of labour services on the old scale. The peasants' main criticism of the Patent was that it had not abolished feudal burdens altogether. The lords hoped that the repeal of the Patent was only the first step towards the re-establishment of their gravely weakened feudal dominion.[1]

The bland assurances in the preamble that the repeal had been decided on in the interest of the peasants, could not, under these circumstances, appear very convincing.

The Estates soon realized that there would be trouble. Khevenhüller from Styria submitted proposals on the severe measures which would obviously have to be adopted if the repeal was to be enforced. In accordance with these proposals, the Court Chancellery empowered provincial governors to proclaim a state of emergency, so that, if necessary, recalcitrant peasants could be flogged or taken into the army without undue formalities.[2]

The first signs of trouble appeared in Lower Austria where the Patent of repeal had first been published. Officials charged with the execution of the Patent were subjected to insults and attacks. From the end of April onwards large deputations were sent to Vienna—between three and four hundred peasants arrived every day according to a councillor who interviewed them. He found them 'obstinate and very determined' and anticipated more trouble.[3]

In Lower Austria, however, where the burden of labour services had been comparatively light, the rapid dispatch of cavalry reinforcements and the personal intervention of the acting governor seems to have prevented serious disorders.

---

[1] Kerner, pp. 288–93.
[2] Khevenhüller to Kollowrat, 7 May 1790, *Hofkanzlei*, IV M 3, Kart. 1342, 12 ex Maio 1790; Expeditionsentwurf an Länderchefs, 16 May 1790, ibid.
[3] Saurau to Colloredo, s.d. (Apr.–May 1790), *Sammelbände*, F. 347, fols. 524–5.

Elsewhere, notably in Bohemia, Hungary, and Inner Austria, there was active resistance.[1]

The pattern of revolt was fairly uniform in all these areas. The peasants assembled in or near their villages. Their mood was such that few officials dared to address them without the backing of a military escort, and fewer still managed to pacify them and persuade them to return home. From their assemblies, the angry peasants flocked to their respective manors, many of them armed with clubs and other weapons. They entered the manor houses, demanded from the lords of the manor (or from their manorial officials if the lords had fled) the surrender of the forms on which their obligations under the Josephinian law had been recorded, and exacted a solemn promise that no dues or services in excess of this should ever be imposed.

The provincial governments (at this time very much under the sway of the Estates) reacted to these events by applying—often hastily and indiscriminately—the recently revived power to put suspected 'ringleaders' into the army without prior conviction and to inflict corporal punishment. But such measures were not quite as effective in 1790, after the Theresian and Josephinian peasant legislation and the destruction of feudalism by the peasants in France, as they might have been half a century earlier. So far from effecting a resumption of labour services, they served only to aggravate the situation. For the peasants would congregate once more to devise some form of concerted action for the liberation of the recruits, and to demand compensation in cash for all those who had been flogged. In some areas troops were called in by panicky officials to disperse the peasants with bullets and bayonets.

By the autumn of 1790, open rebellion had been put down in most areas.[2] But a strong undercurrent of unrest and discontent remained to alarm lords and government. Discharge of labour services was sporadic, refusals were frequent. In the spring of 1791, Archduke Francis was still

[1] For Bohemia, cf. Kerner, pp. 286–7; for Hungary, cf. S. Adler, *Ungarn nach dem Tode Josephs II.* (1910: Vienna), p. 20; for Inner Austria, cf. *Hofkanzlei*, IV M 3, Kart. 1342, 205 ex Julio 1790.

[2] C. Grünberg, *Die Bauernbefreiung ... in Böhmen, Mähren u. Schlesien* (1893: Leipzig), ii. 465.

being overwhelmed in his audiences by large numbers of
Austrian peasants demanding a reduction of their obligations.[1] Throughout Leopold's reign, an uninterrupted flow
of complaints and petitions on the subject of labour services
continued to reach the authorities from the aggrieved peasants of all provinces.[2]

Late in 1790, a book was published which argued the
peasants' case and contained a strong attack on the repeal of
the Josephinian law.[3] It appeared anonymously, and despite
repeated efforts, the police were unable to discover the
author,[4] who had successfully evaded the censorship regulations.

The book is an interesting indication of the fact that in
their struggle against the repeal, the peasants had support
from the educated middle classes. This support was given in
various forms. Lawyers drew up their petitions, local officials
supported their suits, burgher deputies voted for dues reform
in the diets, and in Vienna influential councillors devised and
pleaded for legislation to restore the work impaired by the
repeal. There is nothing surprising in this. The struggle of
the peasants was, after all, part of the general struggle
against the wholesale feudal restoration to which the Estates
aspired, but the prospect of which was viewed with the
utmost dismay by all sections of the non-privileged.

(ii) *The struggle against the feudal pretensions of the Estates*

Joseph II's universal unpopularity had helped to obscure
the selfish character of the Estates' opposition at the end of
his reign. When the diets met spontaneously to express the
grievances and resentment against the Emperor's government, they seemed for a moment to represent more than
the privileged minorities who alone enjoyed the right of
representation.[5]

The diets' claim to represent the people as a whole was,
however, forfeited as soon as they submitted a definite list

[1] Wolfsgruber, *Franz*, ii. 185.
[2] Kropatschek, *Sammlung*, iv. 553, N.924.
[3] *Klagen der Unterthanen der österreichischen Monarchie wegen Aufhebung des neuen Steuersystems*, s.l. 1790; its contents are summarized in Link, pp. 152–5.
[4] Au. Note Pergens, Jan. 1790 with enclosures, *Pergen Akten*, xvii/10, H1–3.
[5] Cf. *supra*, pp. 34–35.

of demands. These made it clear that a majority of the nobility and clergy were seriously striving for a restoration of nearly all privileges lost or reduced during the last two reigns, and for the establishment of their own influence over future legislation.[1]

The feudal exclusiveness of the diets brought disappointment and disillusionment to the non-privileged, particularly in Belgium and Hungary where the united 'national' opposition had been so successful.

The spokesmen of the non-privileged were compelled to point out that the 'liberty' they had helped to win from the foreign oppressor, had been meekly surrendered to the native ruling classes.[2] 'Le peuple a anéanti le joug étranger par sa bravoure; les moines s'en sont aussitot prévalu.'[3]

In Hungary a whole flood of publications appeared in 1790 and 1791 restating the case against aristocratic privilege and condemning the extreme feudal claims contained in the diet's first draft of a new coronation charter.[4]

A number of these publications deserve individual mention at this point. Perhaps the most influential was the outspoken *Ad Amicam Aurem*, whose author, Alajos Batthyány, was, paradoxically, a member of one of the foremost aristocratic families in Hungary. Martinovics, whose general views on aristocracy have already been noted,[5] entered the lists against the diet with his *Oratio ad Proceres et Nobiles Regni Hungariae*, in which he proclaimed the responsibility of the clergy and aristocracy for Hungary's backwardness.[6]

The legal and historical arguments which were used so liberally by the protagonists of feudal reaction, were refuted with unrivalled learning by József Hajnóczy who had been deprived of office on account of his non-aristocratic descent. Hajnóczy was concerned to demonstrate above all the almost

---

[1] A. Springer, *Geschichte Österreichs seit dem Wiener Frieden* (1863: Leipzig), i. 26–29.

[2] S. Tassier, 'Les Démocrates belges de 1789', in *Académie Royale de Belgique*, Classes des Lettres et des Sciences Morales et Politiques, Mémoires, xxviii/2 (1930: Brussels), pp. 213 ff.

[3] Ibid., p. 224.

[4] The draft is printed in full in L. A. Hoffmann, *Ninive*, appendix.

[5] *Supra*, pp. 13–14.

[6] Now published in full in K. Benda, *A magyar jakobinusok iratai*, I (1957: Budapest), No. 7, pp. 117–49.

complete lack of historical foundation for the Catholic clergy's political pretensions.[1]

In Vienna, opponents of feudal reaction decided to launch a periodical publication which was to demonstrate 'how very one-sidedly . . . His Majesty's call for the submission of the griev-ances and desires of the Estates . . . has been interpreted and perhaps even deliberately misrepresented, and what degree of audacity their claims and presumptions have reached'.[2]

The publication was entitled *Das Politische Sieb* and was edited under Sonnenfels's general direction by Steinsberg and Franz Xaver Huber. The former had been a contributor to the *Wöchentliche Wahrheiten*, the latter had just published a critical history of Joseph II's reign. In the pages of their paper, all excessive feudal claims and their protagonists were 'put through the sieve' of a highly unfavourable publicity which, it was hoped, would help to cool the heat of feudal enthusiasm generated in the diets.[3]

It was unfortunate for the privileged orders that the grievances and demands drawn up by the diets and the bishops could not be submitted directly to Leopold. They reached the Emperor only after they had been subjected to critical scrutiny and comment by Josephinian civil servants who allowed no legal and historical arguments put forward by the Estates to go unchallenged, and who proved them-selves a match in this respect for anyone the Estates could produce.[4]

After the debates in the Commission, the deputies of the diets were inclined to put the entire blame for their com-parative failure on the officials. The President of the Styrian Estates, Count Ferdinand Attems, therefore decided to appeal to Leopold for direct access to the throne:

The Ministries have ever been hostile to the Estates. Accustomed only to give orders, and never to accept advice or suggestions of

[1] Cf. his 'De Religione' in Benda, I, No. 16a, 260–7. For a discussion of the Hungarian political literature of 1790–1, cf. I. Kont, *Étude sur l'influence de la littérature française en Hongrie* (1902: Paris), pp. 181–205.

[2] Projekt Sonnenfels' zu einem periodischen Journal, s.d. (1791), *Kaiser Franz Akten*, F. 150, No. 10.

[3] Huber, *Charakteristik*, pp. 125 ff.

[4] Cf., e.g., Riegger's memorandum, Kerner, pp. 114–15.

any kind, . . . they have always looked upon the Estates as something to be kept down. . . . They have deliberately drawn out the conferences until Your Majesty's departure to Italy. [To this end] they have fomented divisions in the Estates . . . deliberately misconstrued their statements, and contradicted the most obvious facts. . . . In a word, they have treated the Estates not as representatives of a province, but as recalcitrants. . . .[1]

The experiences of the Styrian deputies were shared by those of the other provinces.[2] Even the Hungarians who had unceremoniously expelled the Josephinian bureaucracy from their country, had to observe with dismay how its scattered remnants reorganized themselves—some in the secret information service directed by Franz Gotthardi, the former police director of Pest,[3] others in the newly-created Illyrian Court Chancellery under Count Balassa. Both organizations acted as an effective brake on the activities of the Hungarian Estates, though their methods of work had of necessity to be rather underhand and indirect.

(iii) *Opposition to the policy of intervention in France*

There was little enthusiasm in Austria for a war of intervention against France.

For one thing, Austria was only just recovering from the hardships of the Turkish War, and was hailing Leopold II as a peacemaker.

But there were political reasons, too. Right from its inception the Revolution in France had enjoyed the sympathy of the common people in Austria.[4] The opponents of feudal restoration in Austria were aware of the affinity between their own political and social objectives and those of the French National Assembly: 'I liked certain aspects of the French Constitution of 1789 . . . because in my opinion our own is much the same, and it is based almost entirely on the principles which have been taught in our Universities . . .

---

[1] Majestätsgesuch Attems', s.d. (1791), *Kaiser Franz Akten*, F. 8, No. 16.
[2] Majestätsgesuch Hennigers, s.d., *Kaiser Franz Akten*, F. 10a, Konv. 2, fols. 6–13.
[3] Some of the records of Gotthardi's unofficial organization are to be found in *Vertr. Akten*, FF. 57 and 60.
[4] Noailles to Montmorin, 12 Aug. 1789, *Arch. du Min. des Aff. Étr., Correspondance Politique*, Autriche, vol. 356, fol. 282.

for some considerable time.' This was one of the replies of the Abbé Strattmann, van Swieten's friend and Custodian of the Imperial Library, when the police investigated his alleged Jacobinism in 1795.[1]

Speaking for the Styrian middle-class circles in which he moved, George Franz Dirnböck told the police at about the same time:

in short, we agreed with the first French Constitution, because we considered it to be conducive to the welfare of France and found it to contain several provisions which the Emperor Joseph had introduced in Austria. I mean the dissolution of monasteries, the abolition of serfdom, the new tax-regulation, etc.[2]

The French nation had risen against conditions of poverty and tyranny. But the subjects of the Habsburg monarchy had no need to follow this example, since a benevolent monarchical government had decided to amend such conditions of its own accord. That was the argument of the Austrian friends of the French Revolution.[3]

People holding such views on French affairs, would not look upon the French *émigré* nobles as victims of a political tyranny; but rather as kindred spirits of those who were striving for a full feudal restoration in Austria.

The prospect of a war of intervention against France as it emerged after the unsuccessful flight of Louis to Varennes, therefore aroused the keenest anxiety and controversy in Austria. The British Chargé d'Affaires in Vienna observed that 'the best informed people entertain great doubts of the Expediency of such a step'.[4] The less well-informed people evidently entertained very similar doubts. The move of the French king was being universally condemned. Coffee and winehouses became the scenes of 'National Assemblies' in which everyone, but above all students and young authors, spoke out for civil liberty, the rights of man, and the French Revolution.[5]

[1] Verhörsprotokoll Strattmanns, *Vertr. Akten*, F. 12, fol. 163.
[2] Verhörsprotokoll Dirnböcks, *Vertr. Akten*, F. 29, fol. 225.
[3] Verhörsprotokoll Strattmanns, *Vertr. Akten*, F. 12, fol. 160; cf. also J. v. Sonnenfels, *Handbuch der inneren Staatsverwaltung* (1796: Vienna), Introduction.
[4] Straton to Grenville, 9 July 1791, *Public Record Office*, FO. 7/24.
[5] Hoffmann's reports, 14 and 23 July 1791, *Vertr. Akten*, F. 58, fols. 187, 192.

After the publication of the Declaration of Pillnitz, the public criticism of the government seemed to assume unprecedented proportions. The spoken word was reinforced by leaflets and posters protesting against any kind of intervention in French affairs. Even the semi-official *Wiener Zeitung* became more outspoken.[1] The German publication *Kreuzzug wider die Franken*, also a protest against intervention, soon found its way into the Habsburg dominions, and, despite prohibitions, enjoyed a very wide circulation.[2]

(iv) *The political programme of the Fourth Estate*

Both the claims of the privileged Estates and the reports of the new constitution in France helped to stimulate political ideas among the Fourth Estate in the Habsburg dominions. The latter did not confine itself to combating the claims of the privileged, but countered them with claims of its own.

If the privileged orders demanded the restoration of lost feudal rights, the Fourth Estate was beginning to envisage the breaking up of feudal property and its transfer to the 'industrious' classes on the French model.[3] If the privileged orders demanded far-reaching powers for the diets, the Fourth Estate was beginning to demand adequate representation in these diets in no uncertain terms.

Joseph v. Sonnenfels, who already in the previous reign had pleaded for the limitation of absolutism by certain incontrovertible 'principles of government',[4] now suggested that the practical application of these 'principles' in the various provinces should be subject to consultation with truly representative diets: '. . . if the diets are to fulfil their fundamental purpose adequately, all classes of the nation must be entitled to send representatives to it.'

Sonnenfels envisaged the organization of the Habsburg provinces in four estates—Clergy, Nobility, 'Industrial

---

[1] Ah. Handbillet an Sauer, 3 Sept. 1791, and Au. Note Sauers, 8 Sept. 1791, *Archiv für N. Öst., Präsidialakten*, 1791/62. Sauer mentions a leaflet 'in welchem jeder abgemahnet wurde, sich in die französischen Angelegenheiten zu mengen'.

[2] Kressel to Kaunitz, 15 Oct. 1791, *Staatskanzlei, Noten v.d. Hofkanzlei*, F. 41; Leopold to the Palatin, s.d. (Jan. 1792), *Sammelbände*, F. 97, Konv. 1 c.

[3] Cf. Martinovics' memorandum, Oct. 1791, Benda, I, No. 31e, pp. 466–7.

[4] Cf. *supra*, p. 22–23.

Estate', and Peasantry. The Industrial Estate would include manufacturers, merchants, and owners of houses, the Estate of the Peasants all those peasants who owned land and paid a certain amount of tax in respect of it. Each estate would elect an equal number of representatives and voting would be by order.[1]

Andreas Riedel, a friend and unofficial adviser of Leopold II,[2] proposed about the same time a single 'People's Council' (*Volksrat*) for all the scattered Habsburg dominions, to be elected by universal suffrage.[3] Riedel freely acknowledged the source of his political inspiration, and suggested the following passage for the proclamation of the new constitution:

> Our beloved and faithful people need not be afraid of facing the difficulties involved in the administration of the State, because (1) thanks to the fortunate example of our neighbours, the path it has to follow is no longer doubtful, and there is no need to grope in the dark, (2) it can make use of the positive achievements of the French nation and improve on the latter's shortcomings.[4]

Riedel and Sonnenfels were not isolated in their plea for constitutional reform. Even in government circles the number of those advocating the admission of the Fourth Estate to the diets was considerable,[5] and in some of the Habsburg dominions the rank and file of the Fourth Estate took the field of political action in a campaign to secure its own representation.

In Belgium, the leader of the democratic party, Vonck, published a book demanding representation for the non-privileged.[6] In the course of 1790 and 1791, popular support for the Vonckists steadily increased. In February 1791 a popular rising in Brussels succeeded in dispersing the

[1] Votum Sonnenfels' über die Bittschrift des Landmanns in Steyermark, *Kaiser Franz Akten*, F. 10a, Konv. 1.

[2] Cf. *Vertr. Akten*, F. 62, No. 19.

[3] Riedel's project is printed in full in Valjavec, *Politische Strömungen*, app. ii *a*, *b*, *c*, pp. 454–90.

[4] Ibid., p. 460.

[5] For the views of the Chancellor Kressel and Councillors Grohmann, Edling, and Saurau, cf. *Kaiser Franz Akten*, F. 10a, Konv. 1; for the views of Councillor Keeß cf. Bidermann, pp. 40–41.

[6] Tassier, pp. 234 ff.

assembled Estates of Brabant who had refused to countenance any proposals for reform.[1] A petition organized by the Vonckists demanding reform of the Estates, attracted some 20,000 signatures.[2] When this drew only an evasive reply from the government, the democrats organized the society of the *Amis du Bien Public* which could boast branches in all provinces. Their discussions resulted in the publication of the *Observations sur la constitution primitive et originaire des trois États de Brabant*, a powerful echo of the ideas first propounded by Vonck in his isolation.[3]

In Hungary, the magnates' early attempt to exclude non-nobles from all offices, touched off an agitation among the towns for better representation in the diet. Deputations from the towns presented petitions to this effect both to the diet and to Leopold II, and a number of peasant communities followed suit.[4]

As far as the rest of the monarchy was concerned, the agitation of the Fourth Estate seems to have been strongest in those provinces where the claims of the privileged orders were particularly ambitious and obstinately upheld. In the Tyrol, of course, the right of the peasants to representation in the diet had never been abrogated, and they sent their deputies to the diets and delegations of 1790–1 in the usual way. There is no evidence so far of any agitation among the burghers and peasants of Lower and Upper Austria (whose Estates were comparatively moderate in their claims), or among those of Moravia, Silesia, Galicia, and Carinthia. However, the demand was strongly voiced, in one form or another, by the Fourth Estate in Styria, Carniola, and Bohemia.

The burghers of Styria, indeed, demonstrated an astonishingly high level of political maturity in their organization of the campaign.

Ever since the Counter-Reformation, the representation of the royal boroughs and towns of Styria had been confined

---

[1] H. v. Zeissberg, 'Zwei Jahre belgischer Geschichte', pt. i, in *Sitzungsber. d. Akad. d. Wissenschaften zu Wien*, cxxiii (1890), 38–39.

[2] Ibid., p. 50. [3] Ibid., p. 51.

[4] Reports of L. A. Hoffmann, 13 June and 21 Nov. 1791, *Vertr. Akten*, F. 58, fols. 145–6, 312–13; *Protokolle u. Indices der Kabinettskanzlei*, F. 58, Verzeichnis der Sr. M. nachgeschickten Stücke, No. 31.

to one single individual, the *Städtemarschall*. In the summer of 1790, when the full diet had assembled, the then *Städtemarschall*, Dr. Winterl, shocked that august gathering of lords and dignitaries by announcing that the estate of which he was the representative had required him to put before them a petition for a more equitable representation both in the main body and in the standing committee of the diet.[1]

This petition was the result of a campaign which had been carried on in all the Styrian boroughs and towns under the leadership of Franz Haas, a Graz innkeeper.[2] It was endorsed by duly accredited plenipotentiaries of the burghers from each of the five Styrian circles. Nevertheless, in the eyes of the privileged orders, the petition was merely a piece of outrageous presumption, and the diet unceremoniously ruled it out of order.[3]

The burghers' plenipotentiaries then decided to put a similar petition before Leopold, and sent three out of their midst to the Court for that purpose: Franz Haas; the chief magistrate of Leoben, Anton Raspor; and the Mayor of Knittelfeld, Joseph Wenninger.[4] In Vienna they got in touch with their friend and ally, the radical ex-Professor of Canon Law at Graz University, Dr. Franz Xaver Neupauer, who was at that time carrying on a legal practice in Vienna.[5] They were much encouraged by their reception in the capital. Their petition was considered by the Commission on Grievances and granted in the Court Resolution of 17 May 1791.[6]

The burghers' agitation and their success did not go unnoticed in the Styrian countryside, which was still seething with discontent at the reimposition of labour services and tithes. As the whole question of lord-tenant relationships was going to be discussed in the diet, the peasants were keenly interested in the question of the reform of the diet's composition.

A large number of peasants called on Franz Haas in Graz to discuss with him the possibility of securing peasant representation in the diet. Haas readily agreed to help organize

---

[1] Bidermann, p. 33.
[2] Schriftliche Aussage Dirnböcks, 3 Apr. 1795, *Vertr. Akten*, F. 29, fol. 23.
[3] Bidermann, p. 33. [4] Ibid.
[5] Verhörsprotokoll Wenningers, *Vertr. Akten*, F. 14, fols. 130–2.
[6] Bidermann, p. 37.

a campaign to this end,[1] presumably with the support of his fellow burghers who realized that their own representatives in the diet would be in great need of reinforcements against the preponderance of the three upper orders.[2]

As soon as the government's decision in favour of the burghers' claim was published, the peasants' campaign got into full swing. Appeals drawn up by Haas, calling on the peasants to follow the example of the burghers, were sent from village to village in each of the five Styrian circles. These appeals were accompanied by nomination forms which someone in each village took from house to house for signatures to endorse the nomination of plenipotentiaries, who would then be entitled to present a petition on behalf of the entire peasantry of Styria. A small sum of money to cover the expenses involved was collected from all who signed.[3]

By the end of July 1791, the election of plenipotentiaries was duly completed in each district, and the work of drawing up the petition was immediately taken up, so that it could be presented at the opening of the first session of the Styrian diet to be attended by ten burgher representatives, on 9 August 1791.[4]

These were the reasons (*Beweggründe*) which the peasants put forward for their petition in which they asked for the right to send three representatives from each of the five Styrian circles:[5]

1. The Estates are the representatives of the people. The peasants of Styria, numbering some 600,000 men, constitute the largest section of the people of Styria of whom there are 800,000 all told. Moreover, the peasants own more property than any other class. Therefore it is only just that the peasants should have their representatives in the diet like the other classes.

2. In every well-ordered state, all classes enjoy equal

---

[1] Protokoll der Untersuchungskommission über Haas, 29 July 1791, *Kaiser Franz Akten*, F. 8, No. 35.

[2] Votum Haas', 1 June 1792, quoted by Bidermann, p. 52.

[3] Aicherau to Stürkh, 19 July 1791 with enclosures, *Kaiser Franz Akten*, F. 8, No. 25.

[4] Majestätsgesuch der steirischen Bauern, 25 Nov. 1791, and Bittschrift an die Stände, 9 Aug. 1791, *Kaiser Franz Akten*, F. 10a, Konv. 1.

[5] Majestätsgesuch, Beilage B, ibid.

rights. Since all the other classes are enjoying the right to send their representatives to the diet, this right cannot be denied to the peasants, particularly in view of the latter's character and usefulness.

3. There is no reason why the peasants should *not* be granted the right to send their representatives to the diet like other classes.

4. He who contributes most to the obligations imposed by the country, should have the right to participate in the discussions concerning the affairs of the country. It is the peasant who bears the largest share of the country's burdens, and gives even his sons, of whose help he is in need, to the defence of his country.

5. The Estates assemble in the diet in order to advise His Majesty on questions concerning the welfare of the country as a whole, and consequently also the welfare of the peasant. But the peasant is himself the best judge of his own welfare.

6. In the diet as at present composed, there is no one to raise his voice on behalf of the peasants, if the latter's rights should suffer any infringement.

7. The right to send representatives to the diet would encourage the peasant to seek more enlightenment, which would of necessity benefit the country as a whole.

8. It would help the peasants to appreciate the necessity of the state taxes and make them more willing to pay these.

Despite all this elaborate reasoning, the diet simply refused to consider the petition, without even condescending to state the reasons for this in writing.[1]

The peasants now continued to follow the example set by the burghers a year earlier, and left for Vienna in November to lay their petition before the Emperor. In Vienna, Dr. Neupauer provided them with the necessary documents, instructed them in the rules of procedure to which they had to conform as legal petitioners, and did his best to organize support for their cause in government circles. At the same time he wrote to his friends, in Graz, who were very busy on behalf of the peasants there, urging them to see that

[1] Majestätsgesuch.

there should be no illegal incidents which might prejudice the peasants' case in the capital.[1]

While the petition was under consideration, its supporters were greatly encouraged by Leopold's appointment of a man of well-known liberal inclinations, Count Welsperg, as governor of Styria.[2] They now became a little less restrained in the public utterance of their opinions and aspirations. Their confidence increased still more, when they heard that Leopold had forbidden Count Attems, the representative of the Styrian lords, to come forward with any more requests to rescind the Court Resolution of 17 May 1791, and had ordered him to return to Graz forthwith (14 January 1792).[3]

The Countess Attems wrote to her husband:

> You will recognise Styria no more. The people here are not the same any more. . . . If the Emperor only knew all that is being said here, he would be quite as concerned at it as I am. Already the Jacobin Club [i.e. the burgher deputies and their friends and supporters] is deliberating how it can bring its influence to bear on Welsperg. . . .[4]

And elsewhere she reported:

> Lots of people here are busy . . . popularising the French Constitution. . . . There is a big traffic in books . . . with the result that there is now a general desire for the French Constitution and also the confidence that it will be attained. . . .[5]

while another Styrian aristocrat recorded with anxiety:

> The common people here speak quite loudly now—and their voice is the voice of Paris— . . . *intellegat qui potest*.[6]

For the agitation of the burghers and peasants in the neighbouring province of Carniola, there is only just enough evidence to show that it took place.[7] The peasants elected the lawyer Dr. Joseph Luckmann as their plenipotentiary who

[1] Verhörsprotokoll Neupauers, Fortsetzung, 6 Feb. 1796, *Vertr. Akten*, F. 12, fol. 312; Neupauer to Haas (copy), 23 July 1791, *Kaiser Franz Akten*, F. 8, No. 30.
[2] Wolff to Beer, 13 Jan. 1792, *Kaiser Franz Akten*, F. 10a, Konv. 1.
[3] F. Ilwof, *Die Grafen Attems* (1897: Graz), p. 195.
[4] Letter 8 Jan. 1792, *Kaiser Franz Akten*, F. 10a, Konv. 1.
[5] Letter 23 Dec. 1791, ibid.
[6] Dietmas Dietrichstein to Attems (copy), 8 Jan. 1792, ibid.
[7] Aufzeichnungen eines Kabinettsbeamten über die Stimmung der krainer Bevölkerung, s.d. (? late summer 1790), *Kaiser Franz Akten*, F. 10.

drew up the requisite petition on their behalf. To this he was able to append three tightly packed foolscap pages of signatures. The arguments put forward in the petition were very similar to those in the Styrian petition.[1]

In Bohemia, too, the burghers gave public expression to their desire to be represented more fully in the diet, where the lords paid but scant attention to the aspirations of the non-privileged.[2] But although the provincial government reported in favour of their claim,[3] the Bohemian burghers apparently had much less political initiative than those of Styria (who had to contend with a hostile provincial government). At any rate, there is no evidence of any organized campaign for Fourth Estate representation in the diet on their part.

One result of this, of course, was that the Bohemian peasants, whose desire for their own representation in the diet was none the weaker on that account, were left to their own devices. There was no Bohemian Haas and no Dr. Neupauer to instruct them in the tortuous legal paths towards their aim, and to see that they kept to it. It was even reported that two radical and unscrupulous freemasons were inciting them to take the law into their own hands.[4] Whatever the foundation of this report may have been, the fact was that representatives of the peasants appeared at the doors of the diet just as the final discussions on the commutation of labour services were due to commence (9 January 1792). They appeared, without any documents to show that they were duly elected plenipotentiaries, without any duly stamped petitions, in fact, without anything. And so they just had to go back.[5] But they have revealed to the historian how deeply rooted the idea of reforming the diets had become by the end of Leopold's reign.

3. *The Enlightened Despotism of Leopold II*

What was Leopold II's attitude to the democratic opposition described in the last section? Two views have been put

---

[1] Majestätsgesuch der krainer Bauern, June 1791, ibid., No. 3.
[2] Kerner, p. 111; Springer, p. 33.   [3] Kerner, p. 145.
[4] Rottenhan to Leopold II, 18 Jan. 1792, *Kaiser Franz Akten*, F. 10a, Konv. 2.
[5] Kerner, pp. 303-4.

forward. One is that his attitude was consistently one of sympathetic understanding,[1] the other, that it was one of equally consistent hostile suspicion.[2] Neither can provide a satisfactory explanation of Leopold's policies.

In July 1791 Count Mercy, the Austrian Minister Plenipotentiary in the Netherlands, asked Prince Kaunitz for definite instructions as to the policy he was to pursue in relation to the Belgian democrats. The Chancellor replied:

It is . . . up to Your Excellency, in each case as it arises, to pursue such a policy as may seem best calculated to bring about the restoration of the authority of the Sovereign and the return of public order, both of which are absolutely necessary if the King is to enjoy once more all the sources of the royal income.[3]

Kaunitz thus clearly indicated that the attainment of Leopold's principal aim ('wieder in den Genuß aller Quellen des königlichen Einkommens zu gelangen'), would require, not a consistent, but a flexible policy towards the democratic opposition.

It seems that Mercy was in any case quite well aware of the Emperor's way of thinking, as some months earlier he had reported to Kaunitz that he was optimistic about the early re-establishment of public order—'if, after the present crisis, the Estates become aware of the danger they are incurring (i.e. from the democratic opposition), and the democrats begin to realise that the fulfilment of their political aspirations depends entirely on the goodwill of the government'.[4]

In this formulation, it seems, lies the real clue to an explanation of Leopold's policies, not only in the Netherlands, but in all his dominions. We may summarize them as follows:

1. To welcome and encourage the expression of Fourth Estate opposition to the claims of the privileged orders as a weapon in the struggle to resist the latter.

2. To ensure the loyalty of the Fourth Estate to the monarchy by vigorously suppressing any signs of political independence, while encouraging it to look to

---

[1] e.g. Bidermann, p. 34.
[2] e.g. E. Mályusz, *Sándor Lipót főherceg-nádor iratai* (Budapest: 1926), Introduction, pp. 88, 142.   [3] Quoted by Zeissberg, p. 59.
[4] Ibid., p. 43.

him for the redress of grievances and the fulfilment of some at least of its political aspirations.

(i) *Encouragement and utilization of Fourth Estate opposition to the privileged orders*

The repeal of the Josephinian Patent on the land tax and labour services had made serious inroads into the sources of the royal income by reducing the tax obligations of the noble landowners and the 'taxability' of the peasants. Leopold had endeavoured to salvage as much as possible of the latter by stipulating in the patents of repeal that the return to the old system should be effected without imposing any additional burdens on the peasants.[1]

As soon as the peasants rose to secure retention of the Josephinian law, Leopold exploited this fact in his endeavour to restore the work of his predecessor.

Following his report on the peasant unrest in his province, the governor of Inner Austria was instructed to announce the appointment of royal commissioners to investigate the peasants' grievances, and to transmit the following order to the Estates:

> Since the complaints of the peasants in Inner Austria about their feudal obligations are so numerous and in some respects probably not altogether unjustified (it cannot, for instance . . . escape notice that in Carniola the peasant owes four days week-work in addition to all the other obligations customary in Inner Austria), and since the relations between lords and peasants are now strained to breaking point, so that it may soon be impossible to exact feudal obligations on the present scale . . . it is time for fundamental remedies . . . which in the present circumstances can only consist in a substantial reduction of feudal burdens. . . .[2]

A few days later the Estates were ordered to discuss specific proposals put forward by Count Cajetan Auersperg for the total abolition or commutation of labour services.[3]

Despite indignant protests from the Estates, who put the

---

[1] Kropatschek, *Sammlung*, i. 94.

[2] Ah. Handbillet an Kollowrat, 8 July 1790, and Hofdekret für Innerösterreich (draft), 9 July 1790, *Hofkanzlei*, IV M 3, Kart. 1342, 67 ex Julio 1790.

[3] Stürkh to Styrian Estates, 17 July 1790, *Steierm. Landesarchiv, Archiv der Stände*, Schuber 605, 17285 ex 1790.

blame for the unrest on subversive propaganda rather than excessive burdens, Leopold did not change his position.[1]

Towards the end of 1790, he transmitted the numerous petitions and complaints which he had received from peasants during his journey through Inner Austria to the Court Chancellery with the reminder that he was determined to secure alleviation for the peasants, and that he would act without the Estates' consent if the latter failed to submit proposals of their own.[2]

No such proposals had reached Leopold by the summer of 1791, when he was once more travelling through Inner Austria. He therefore ordered a number of officials to draw up proposals on various aspects of the problem,[3] and he encouraged the peasants in their campaign to secure representation in the diet.[4] The Estates, however, spent all their time trying to secure the withdrawal or modification of an earlier decision to grant real representation in the diet to the cities. On 25 January 1792 the Estates received a final ultimatum to submit proposals within a fortnight.[5]

The Styrian Estates had complained at one point that they were being singled out by Leopold for exceptionally 'harsh' treatment. It is possible to see, however, that the Emperor proceeded in exactly the same way in his negotiations with the Estates of other provinces. Those of Bohemia had been told in November 1791 that commutation of labour services would be enforced by decree, if a plan was not submitted by the next session of the diet.[6] They were, moreover, prevailed upon to accept the Josephinian land-survey as the basis of taxation, as well as the principle of equality of assessment as between peasants' and lords' land.[7] A plan for compulsory

[1] Majestätsgesuch der steirischen Stände, 13 July 1790, ibid. der kärntner u. krainer Stände, 19 and 28 July 1790; Au. Vorträge Kollowrats and Ah. Resolutionen hierüber, 24 July and 5 Aug. 1790, Hofkanzlei, IV M 3, Kart. 1342, 22 ex Aug. 1790.

[2] Hofdekret, 16 Dec. 1790, Steierm. Landesarchiv, Gubernialakten, F. 90, 31748 ex 1790.   [3] Kaiser Franz Akten, F. 8, Nos. 29, 40.

[4] Verhörsprotokoll Neupauers, Fortsetzung, 6 Feb. 1796, Vertr. Akten, F. 12, fol. 312.

[5] Welsperg to Styrian Estates, 25 Jan. 1792, Steierm. Landesarchiv, Archiv der Stände, Schuber 606.   [6] Kerner, p. 301.

[7] Rottenhan to Hatzfeld, 2 June 1792, Kaiser Franz Akten, F. 82/R. For further material on this point which seems to have eluded Kerner (p. 268), cf. Kaiser Franz Akten, F. 157, Konv. 2, No. 1.

commutation worked out by Councillor of State Friedrich v. Eger was also ready for enforcement in Lower Austria by the end of Leopold's reign.[1]

In Hungary, Leopold was at first very much on the defensive. The gentry were in an extravagant mood in the early months of 1790, and the government anxiously looked for signs of political action by the Fourth Estate which might exert a sobering effect on the hot-headed nobility. There were, of course, publications in 1790 stating the case of the Fourth Estate against the privileged.[2] But Leopold evidently wished to turn a stream into a torrent.

One potential author was soon at hand. Professor Leopold Alois Hoffmann had left Pest and come to Vienna, like Gotthardi, the former police director of Pest, for whom he had worked. He had offered to write against the Hungarian magnates in 1789, but Joseph II had turned down his manuscript because of certain references to the French Revolution.[3] The manuscript was now brought up to date, and published under the title *Babel* by special permission of Leopold, without the sanction of the official Board of Censorship or the knowledge of his chief ministers.[4] *Babel* was soon followed by a further attack, *Ninive*, which dealt specifically with the first draft of the new coronation oath which the diet wished to impose on Leopold II.[5] The aim of frightening the magnates away from their rebellion is evident on every page of these books:

The Hungarian burgher reads newspapers as well as the noble; he knows as well as his fellows in France that he is not the slave of the aristocracy. . . . He even asks quite loudly, why he should not . . . send his deputies . . . to the diet, as the burghers in France send theirs to the National Assembly.[6]

Leopold seems to have been satisfied with the effect produced by these publications, as he continued the experiment. The Hungarian expert in the Council of State, Izdenczy,

[1] V. Bibl, 'Das Robotprovisorium für Nieder-Österreich', in *Jahrbuch für Landeskunde Nieder-Österreichs*, Neue Folge, vii (1908), 240.

[2] Cf. *supra*, pp. 71–2.   [3] *Supra*, pp. 11–12.

[4] Kaunitz to Swieten, 24 Aug. 1790, *Staatskanzlei, Große Korrespondenz*, F. 405, Konv. B, fol. 145.

[5] *Babel; Ninive* (1790: Gedruckt im römischen Reiche); both anonymous.

[6] *Babel*, p. 90.

was instructed to write some books of this kind.[1] Hoffmann
procured another manuscript from an acquaintance.[2] János
Laczkovics, a former rebel, who had had to resign his commission, was restored to favour for his translation into Hungarian of Martinovics's *Oratio ad Proceres et Nobiles Regni
Hungariae*, in which he omitted the sections on monarchy
but developed those on aristocracy.[3] Martinovics himself
wrote another book in Latin, the *Oratio pro Leopoldo Secundo
Rege*, a well-reasoned statement of the case against the existing Hungarian constitution.[4]

In every case the book received the approval of Leopold,
was not submitted to the ordinary censorship, and was given
the widest possible circulation by Leopold's agents and their
assistants. In some cases there is evidence of financial re-
muneration for the author as well.[5]

Leopold was anxious that every group or class whose
interests conflicted with those of the dominant Magyar
nobility should come forward with their own claims and
aspirations, so as to confirm the reality of the threats implied
in the books he sponsored. The submerged nationalities had
a role to play in this connexion as well as the non-privileged
classes. Leopold encouraged the Greek Orthodox of Southern
Hungary to plead for the rights of the 'Illyrian' nation and
the Greek Church. Their petitions were favourably received
at Court,[6] and served as a pretext for the creation in February
1791 of a separate Illyrian Court Chancellery under a leading Hungarian Josephinian, Count Balassa.[7]

About the same time, Hoffmann was instructed to use his
influence among the citizens of Pest and Preßburg to induce
them to petition the Emperor for real representation in the diet.[8]
In this he succeeded and the petitions were duly published.[9]

[1] Izdenczy's memorandum, 11 Jan. 1793, *Kaiser Franz Akten*, F. 154, Konv. 1,
No. 7.
[2] Report of Hoffmann, 30 May 1791, *Vertr. Akten*, F. 58, fols. 139–44.
[3] Benda, I, No. 76, 150–70.
[4] Gotthardi to Francis II, 4 Mar. 1792, *Vertr. Akten*, F. 57, fol. 389.
[5] E.g. Laczkovics received 100 ducats for his translation (Benda, I, 634); for
anti-aristocratic pamphlets commissioned by the government, cf. also Gragger, pp.
77–82   [6] Adler, *Ungarn*, pp. 20–21.
[7] F. Walter, *Die österreichische Zentralverwaltung*, ii/4, p. 152.
[8] Report of Georg Mahl, 19 Apr. 1792, *Vertr. Akten*, F. 57, fol. 614.
[9] Report of Hoffmann, 4 Dec. 1791, *Vertr. Akten*, F. 58, fol. 317.

Martinovics, who had been introduced to Leopold by Gotthardi,[1] received similar instructions, though he was to work in a wider field:

> I and His Majesty agreed . . . secretly to induce the burghers and peasants in the whole of Hungary to send petitions to His Majesty before the next diet for recognition as Estates of the realm. . . . In the same way we intended to collect petitions from the poor parish priests and the poor county officials for better remuneration. . . .[2]

Martinovics's testimony deserves credence, for two individuals whose appointment in Hungary he suggested in this connexion, were in fact appointed in accordance with his propositions.[3]

We are told that Leopold was very well satisfied with the results of his policy.[4] It undoubtedly helped to curb the excesses of the Hungarian aristocratic opposition and to rescue some of the work of enlightened despotism in the kingdom.

By October 1790, all the most extravagant demands had been abandoned and moderate men assumed the leadership in the diet, which declared itself satisfied with the coronation oath of Charles VI, and accepted the Emperor's son, Alexander Leopold, as Palatin. In the course of 1791, the diet was prevailed upon to incorporate into Hungarian law the Theresian decree on limitation of labour services, the abolition of serfdom, and the principle of freedom of worship for Protestants.[5]

(ii) *Ensuring the loyalty of the Fourth Estate*

When one considers the means employed by Leopold II in his struggle against the privileged orders, one is almost tempted to comment that he played with revolution. This was not, however, the case. Like every other Habsburg,

---

[1] Gotthardi to Leopold, 18 Sept. and 20 Oct. 1791, *Vertr. Akten*, F. 60, fols. 21–23, 49–50.

[2] Martinovics to Francis II, 15 Mar. 1792, Benda, I, No. 44a, p. 644.

[3] Martinovics to Leopold, s.d. (? Feb. 1792) Ibid., pp. 640–3; undated Italian Cabinet Note, *Vertr. Aiken*, F. 60, fol. 137; Ah. Handbillet an Chotek, 15 Feb. 1792, *Handbilletenprotokoll*, 1792/198.

[4] Report of Georg Mahl, 19 Apr. 1792, *Vertr. Akten*, F. 57, fol. 614.

[5] Springer, i. 44–46.

Leopold demanded from the Fourth Estate above all obedience to the laws and to the government. Graciously though he might receive and encourage Fourth Estate petitioners craving his protection against the ambitions of the privileged, he was prepared to go to almost any lengths to silence Fourth Estate critics of his own considered policies. The widespread and bitter public criticism of the Declaration of Pillnitz provoked a savage outburst on the part of the Emperor:

I must ask you once again, he wrote to the governor of Lower Austria, to exercise the utmost vigilance, and I desire that you should do everything possible in close co-operation with the military and the police (if necessary by the promise of an attractive reward to informers) to discover and arrest one of those responsible for the dangerous and malicious leaflets which have been distributed, in order to set a warning example through his appropriate punishment to others like him, and thus . . . to nip this mischief in the bud.[1]

These were sharp words and they were repeated when similar situations recurred. But mere repression never became the main factor in Leopold's policy in relation to the Fourth Estate. He realized more clearly than his predecessor had ever done, that he must win and retain the confidence of the Fourth Estate if he was to hold his own against the privileged orders. Despite the political developments in the Fourth Estate, and despite the French Revolution, he believed that this was possible.

The Fourth Estate must be detached from the ranks of the opposition into which the policies of Joseph II had driven it. It must be persuaded to make its peace with the monarchy. All Leopold's secret agents claimed to be busily engaged in this task, and all claimed great successes.[2] To counteract French revolutionary influence among the freemasons and *Illuminati*, new 'loyal' masonic lodges were founded in accordance with the Emperor's secret instruc-

[1] Ah. Handbillet an Sauer, 3 Sept. 1791, *Archiv für N. Öst., Präsidialakten*, 1791/62.
[2] A typical example is Gabelhofer's claim: 'Zugleich war ich so glücklich den Bürgerstand, welchen man heimlich in das Komplott zu ziehen trachtete ganz für S.M. zu gewinnen', in Gabelhofer to Pergen, 29 Aug. 1793, *Pergen Akten*, viii/11, H8. Martinovics, Gotthardi, Hoffmann, and others frequently made similar claims.

tions.[1] New periodicals were launched with government assistance to influence public opinion in favour of the monarchy.[2]

On their own, none of these devices would have been very effective. The Fourth Estate in Leopoldine Austria cherished certain political demands. Unless he offered some concessions to these demands, Leopold could not hope to win the goodwill, far less the co-operation of the Fourth Estate. Even the secret agents were recruited on the basis of great political expectations rather than of personal reward. With a striking lack of humility, Martinovics wrote to the Emperor:

> I take my stand by the side of Your Majesty not . . . in order to enjoy undeserved favours from the throne at the expense of many deserving citizens, but . . . out of conviction. The Americans and the French have made good laws as a result of much bloody violence. Your Majesty makes good laws, which all enlightened men admire . . . without any revolution. This circumstance has prompted me to offer Your Majesty my services for the investigation of secret conspiracies. . . .[3]

Would Leopold be able to satisfy the Fourth Estate without endangering the absolute monarchy? His attempt is worth consideration.

The conclusion of the Turkish War, itself ardently desired by the Fourth Estate, made it possible to end a number of unpopular policies, as well as to secure at least a slight reduction in the high cost of living.[4]

Officially sponsored publicity on Leopold's government in Tuscany helped to wipe out the impression that Joseph's successor favoured the aristocracy, and aroused hopeful anticipations of a return to the reforming tradition on the grand scale.[5]

In one respect, however, the Fourth Estate desired to see a radical departure from Josephinian policy. The excessive

[1] Gabelhofer to Gotthardi, 20 Mar. 1792, *Vertr. Akten*, F. 57, fol. 576.
[2] Hoffmann to Francis II, 5 Mar. 1792, ibid., fol. 416.
[3] Majestätsgesuch Martinovics', 30 Jan. 1792, Benda, I, No. 36, p. 575.
[4] Immediatsbericht Welspergs, 29 Feb. 1792, *Kaiser Franz Akten*, F. 85/W.
[5] Report from Moravia sent in by Watteroth, s.d. (? Jan. 1792), *Vertr. Akten*, F. 64, fol. 249; Martinovics to Gotthardi, 22 Dec. 1791, Benda, I, No. 31 n, pp. 496-7, 499.

severities of the Josephinian penal code and the late Emperor's arbitrary violations of legality were deeply resented by public opinion and were utterly out of keeping with the prevailing trends of eighteenth-century thought. Leopold did much to bring government policy into line with public opinion.

He abolished the most cruel punishments which Joseph had devised and some of which had been inflicted in public, making the streets of Vienna—like those of Virgil's Tartarus—resound with the groans of the suffering and the clanging of chains.[1] In accordance with the philosophy of the Enlightenment, Leopold preferred 'to lead criminals back to their duty by a more lenient treatment, rather than to harden them against all decent inclinations by excessively severe penalties'.[2]

Joseph's violations of legality were brought to his successor's notice by petitions from the most notable victims, the bookseller Wucherer and Josepha Willias.[3] At first they merely requested a remission of their respective sentences.[4] But encouraged by their success—Wucherer was eventually allowed to return permanently and Willias was released[5]— they petitioned for compensation on the grounds of maltreatment by the police and wrongful conviction.[6] Leopold referred both petitions to the Supreme Judiciary.

The Minister of Police, Count Pergen, was alarmed by this decision, because it showed that the principle of his ministry's complete autonomy had been abondoned. In future the police would have to give account of its actions to the supreme judicial authority. Pergen warned the Emperor against the dangerous consequences which would inevitably

---

[1] The comparison was made by J. B. v. Alxinger, *Ueber Leopold den Zweyten* (1792: Berlin), pp. 14–15.

[2] Hegrad, p. 170.

[3] Cf. *supra*, pp. 40–44.

[4] Majestätsgesuche Wucherers, 12 July and 28 Oct. 1790 and 15 Jan. 1791, *Pergen Akten*, ix/5, H15, H18, H23: Willias's petition is not extant.

[5] Wucherer: Au. Note Pergens and Ah. Resolution, 27 Jan. 1791, ibid., H24: Dekret, 30 Jan. 1791, ibid., H25. Willias: Au. Note Pergens and Ah. Resolution, 13 May 1790, ibid. vii/4, H5.

[6] Wucherer's petition is not extant, but is referred to in detail in Au. Note Pergens, 24 Feb. 1791, *Pergen Akten*, ix/B5, H26; Majestätsgesuche Willias', 21 Aug. 1790 and 4 Jan. 1791, ibid. vii/4, H8, H13.

follow if he underestimated the importance of the police:
'... the police, without which order and security cannot be
maintained in this country any more than elsewhere, would
necessarily lose its prestige ... if the public noticed a certain
indifference (*Geringschätzigkeit*) on the part of Your Majesty.'[1]

The Supreme Judiciary submitted its findings concerning
Josepha Willias's petition on 10 January 1791, and recommended a commission of inquiry consisting of councillors of
the Lower Austrian government. After submitting the
matter to the Council of State, Leopold accepted the recommendation and instructed Pergen accordingly.[2]

The commission reported on 8 February. It found (i) that
the petitioner had been unable to substantiate her charges
of maltreatment, and (ii) that she was entitled only to 200
florins damages for losses incurred as a result of her arrest
by the police, assuming that she had been arrested not by
mistake, but through her own suspicious behaviour.[3]

In his covering note with which he submitted the commission's report to the Emperor, Pergen insisted that any
financial compensation must be awarded as a matter of grace
and not of right. He also supported the request of his subordinate officials for a vindication of their honour which had
been publicly impugned as a result of the publicity aroused
by the investigation.[4]

Very different were the comments of the Supreme Judiciary. Its sense of legality and fairness was evidently out-
raged by the facts which the investigation had brought to
light. In accordance with its recommendations, Leopold sent
a memorable instruction to Pergen which has not received
the attention from Austrian historians which it deserves.[5]
In the light of the treatment to which Willias had been subjected during her arrest by the police, Pergen was instructed
'to give a serious warning to his police officials that prisoners,

[1] Au. Note Pergens, 24 Feb. 1791, *Pergen Akten*, ix/B5, H26.
[2] *Staatsratsprotokoll*, 119 ex 1791.
[3] Referat der Regierungskommission, signed Wöber, Saurau, Hackher, *Pergen Akten*, vii/4, H17.
[4] Au. Note Pergens, 15 Feb. 1791, ibid., H18.
[5] I am unable to trace the Au. Vortrag of the Supreme Judiciary, dated 21 Feb. 1791, and base my conclusion on the wording of the Ah. Resolution in *Staatsratsprotokoll*, 686 ex 1791.

especially those remanded in custody, are to be treated with all possible respect and kindness . . .'. There follows a severe censure of certain specific abuses, such as the attempts which had been made to influence the prisoner's depositions, and the negligence of the prison doctor who was to be reprimanded for failing to attend to the prisoner promptly every time he had been requested. Instead of the 200 florins damages recommended by the commission, Leopold awarded 400.

Finally, Leopold decided (possibly on the basis of a separate recommendation by the President of the Supreme Judiciary, Count Seilern)[1] to issue a new general instruction designed to prevent as far as possible violations of legality by the police in future:

Since the unfortunate are also entitled to my full protection, I hereby order the Supreme Judiciary to see to it that every three months a Justice of the Court of Appeal and a Councillor of the [Lower Austrian] Government are sent to the *Polizeihaus* in order to inspect the treatment of prisoners. . . . Immediate steps are to be taken to ensure that no one is detained for more than three days without the notification of the authority concerned and the commencement of the investigation in which a Justice (*Justizmann*) is always to participate.

This section of the instruction was published as a decree for Lower Austria on 28 February 1791.[2] It was the first published instruction regulating the procedure of the police on the lines demanded by Sonnenfels and the adherents of the Enlightenment. They had good reason to be satisfied with a sovereign who had introduced to his country something of the principle of *Habeas Corpus*.

The Minister of Police saw less reason for satisfaction. His Note of 3 March, in which he expressed his objection to the Emperor's instruction on nine separate counts, was returned almost immediately with what was under the circumstances an insultingly brief and formal acknowledge-

[1] Wording of the Ah. Resolution, '. . . und habe hiernach so wie nach dem schlüslichen Antrag des Grafen v. Seilern . . . die Weißung gegeben . . .'.

[2] Kropatschek, *Sammlung*, iii. 232–3, N. 503. Wucherer was awarded no compensation, presumably because Joseph II had been personally responsible for his wrongful conviction (*Staatsratsprotokoll*, 903 ex 1791).

ment—*dienet zur Nachricht*.[1] Pergen was now desperate and took the probably unprecedented step of submitting his Note a second time, together with a statement from the reprimanded police doctor, because the instruction implied 'that Your Majesty accepts the charges proferred by the notorious Willias as true and as real abuses which have crept into the administration of the police under my direction'. He ended on a note of warning against those who had inspired the recent decisions: '[I beg Your Majesty] not to listen to those who through lack of knowledge disparage these institutions so important for mankind [i.e. the Ministry of Police], and who under the pretence of improving them, cause their destruction.'

In his reply, Leopold completely ignored the Note which had been sent to him a second time; he merely announced that there would be a separate investigation into the medical treatment of prisoners so that no injustice would be inflicted on the prison doctor.[2]

At this point Pergen tendered his resignation.

I am the more reluctant to divest myself of my burdensome office, he wrote, since I appreciate very clearly its importance and the dangerous consequences for Your Majesty and the state, which would follow if the administration of the police were not to be continued on the lines which have been laid down. Moreover, I am fully aware of all the underhand attempts that are being made under various pretexts to undermine this beneficial institution and to belittle it in the eyes of Your Majesty, if only because its very soundness arouses envy, and because His Late Majesty . . . allowed no other branch of the government to exercise any control over it. However, in view of my age and my long years of service, I am no longer able to bear insults (*Kränkungen*) without completely ruining my health.[3]

Friedrich Walter has described Pergen's resignation as coming 'rather unaccountably'.[4] However, in the light of the date[5] and the wording of his letter of resignation, there can no longer be much doubt as to its cause. Joseph II's Minister

---

[1] *Pergen Akten*, vii/4, H19.
[2] Au. Note Pergens, 5 Mar. 1791, and Ah. Resolution, ibid., H21.
[3] Quoted by Walter, 'Die Organisierung d. staatl. Polizei', p. 52.
[4] Walter, p. 52.
[5] It is dated 3 Mar., but Pergen's Note of 5 Mar. indicates that it was not sent to the Emperor until after that date.

of Police resigned in March 1791, because Joseph's successor put the hitherto autonomous Ministry of Police under the authority of the law.

Leopold did not appoint a successor to Pergen. The police administration of Vienna was entrusted to the governor of Lower Austria, Count Sauer. The other provincial governors were henceforth to refer to the Court Chancellery in matters of police as in all other matters. In only two respects was the Josephinian system allowed to survive: the provincial governors were allowed to correspond with Sauer to maintain the *gemeinschäftliche Verbindung der Polizey*, and Sauer was allowed direct communication with the Emperor.[1]

While Leopold thus reduced the Josephinian secret police to a skeleton, he was planning even more far-reaching changes in the administration of the 'public' police. Pergen's passion for the organization of secret police activities seems to have led to the almost total neglect of those 'public' tasks of the police which alone were legitimate according to the political theorists of the Fourth Estate—the maintenance of good order and the prevention of crime.[2] Leopold's intention in reorganizing the police in 1791 was to remedy this neglect and not, as has recently again been suggested,[3] to forge a better weapon against the danger of 'Jacobinism'. Clear proof of this is the fact that Leopold entrusted the working out of the plan for reorganization to Joseph v. Sonnenfels, the foremost antagonist in Austria of a political secret police.

Leopold regarded the matter as one of great urgency, and repeatedly brushed aside Count Sauer's assertion that the necessary practical preparations could not be completed within the year.[4] During the Emperor's absence in Italy, the Crown Prince had to see that there should be no delays.[5]

Sonnenfels worked out a scheme for the complete transformation of the Vienna police organization designed to fit it for its proper task of promoting public security and welfare in a city which had rapidly grown in size and population.

[1] Walter, pp. 52–53.
[2] A shocking state of affairs is revealed by Au. Note Sauers, 9 Nov. 1791, *Archiv für N. Öst., Präsidialakten*, 1791/2.
[3] W. C. Langsam, *Francis the Good* (1951: New York), p. 98.
[4] Au. Noten Sauers, 9 May and 5 June 1791, and Ah. Resolutionen, *Archiv für N. Öst., Präsidialakten*, 1791/2.   [5] Wolfsgruber, *Franz*, ii. 177.

This was to be achieved in the main as follows:

i. The city was to be divided into twelve police districts—four in the centre and eight in the suburbs—each of which was to have its own police organization under a 'District Director of Police'.

ii. A physician, a surgeon, and a midwife were to be appointed in each district to act as public health officers, and to give free treatment to the poor. The District Directors of Police were to see that the poor received prescribed medicines free of charge, and that those who could not be adequately nursed at home were taken to the general or maternity hospital.

iii. In order to speed up litigation, the District Directors were to be empowered to settle minor disputes not involving rights or property, and to act as arbiters if requested to do so by both parties to a dispute.[1]

Leopold approved Sonnenfels's proposals with certain modifications, and instructed him to draft the Patent by which the new system was to be proclaimed and inaugurated. Sonnenfels set about this task in the light of his own political principles, which required that the duties and powers of each public authority should be incorporated in public law to prevent arbitrary actions.[2] His draft is thus virtually a copy of the official instruction for the District Directors. Sonnenfels anticipated that after the escapades of the Josephinian police, the Austrian public would suspect that the District Directors had received further secret instructions in addition to the published ones. His draft, therefore, opens with a categorical assurance to the contrary: '. . . all those dubious methods, through which a number of police organisations have been diverted from their true task of protecting the welfare of the citizens, and debased into the frightful tool of an odious system of spying and oppression . . . have been banned from this organisation.'[3]

Though in retirement, Count Pergen seems to have been busily intriguing against Sonnenfels and his colleagues. His

---

[1] Plan v.d. Verfassung d. Polizei, *Archiv für N. Öst., Präsidialakten,* 1791/2.
[2] Cf. *supra,* pp. 22–23.
[3] Entwurf der Nachricht, s.d. (July–Aug. 1791), *Archiv für N. Öst., Präsidialakten,* 1791/2.

former subordinates of the Ministry of Police, who had been transferred to the Lower Austrian government, frequently came to see him at his Vienna residence, tried to win over Count Sauer to their views, and stirred up prejudice against the new system.[1] With Sauer they certainly achieved considerable success. In matters of police, the President of the Lower Austrian government allowed himself to fall under the influence of Pergen's former secretaries, Schilling and Mährenthal.

The wording of Sauer's Note which accompanied Sonnenfels's draft Patent is clearly that of Schilling who drafted it. Sauer merely struck out the most purple passages of his secretary's invective. True to the ideals of Pergen, the Note rejected as preposterous the idea that all the details of police administration from the highest to the lowest reaches should be made public. Sonnenfels had written a forty-nine page treatise instead of a proclamation. To inform the public of the details of government under present circumstances was to invite more public criticism and discussion of policy, of which there was more than enough already. Above all, Sauer and Schilling objected to the proposed assurance that there was no secret police in the new organization.

It is my innermost conviction that this assurance is not only entirely misplaced, but also extremely unwise and untrue; its author reveals a complete lack of political experience. Everyone who knows the first thing about *Staatspolizey*, knows that at a time like the present, and in so populous a city as Vienna where foreigners abound, an efficient police must set on foot many a secret supervision and investigation in order to track down subversive elements (*staatsgefährliche Personen*) and to nip in the bud their designs.[2]

Alongside Sonnenfels's draft Sauer submitted a shortened version of it in which the passages concerning the relations between the District Directors and the police department of the government, as well as the denunciation of the secret police, were omitted. This, too, he considered to contain far more than the public needed to know, and therefore added

[1] Report of Stieber, s.d. (Aug. 1791), *Kaiser Franz Akten*, F. 10b, fol. 639; report of Hoffmann, 23 July 1791, *Vertr. Akten*, F. 58, fols. 191–2.
[2] Au. Note Sauers, 12 Aug. 1791 (Schilling's draft and original), *Archiv für N. Öst., Präsidialakten*, 1791/2.

a third draft composed by himself (or more probably by Schilling), which was a model of Pergenite reticence. Of the three drafts submitted to him, Leopold chose the shortened version of Sonnenfels's, which was duly published as a Patent on 1 November 1791.[1]

The conflict between Sonnenfels and Schilling was not, of course, an argument as to fact. Sonnenfels must have known that Sauer had inherited some of Pergen's secret police functions. But he was evidently trying hard to persuade Leopold to lock up the skeleton of the Josephinian secret police in a cupboard, if not to bury it altogether. Schilling, on the other hand, was engaged in a joint attempt with his chief Sauer to restore the skeleton to some semblance of life. Sauer was flattered by the prospect of stepping into Pergen's shoes. His success in obtaining Schilling's appointment as his personal assistant in police matters seemed a favourable omen for the attainment of their joint ambition.[2] The publication of Sonnenfels's draft in full would have put an almost insurmountable obstacle in their way. Leopold's approval of the shortened version encouraged them to carry on with their scheme.

The next step was to try to restore the contact between the police organization in Vienna and those in the provinces, which had been severed after Pergen's resignation. Sauer submitted the case for this to Leopold in a Note of 3 October 1791:

The more I become familiar with police administration, the more grows my conviction that the police organisation in the capital will not be able to function adequately until it is enabled to observe from the centre, as it were, the state of public opinion throughout the Monarchy. It would therefore be advisable to instruct the provincial Directors of Police . . . to send in regular reports to the Director of Police in Vienna. Such an arrangement would be the more fitting in that a number of the provincial Directors of Police have not yet discontinued their correspondence with Hofrat v. Beer, and I have been taking the humble liberty of putting these reports before Your Majesty.

Sauer concluded with the plea that he should also be consulted before appointments were made to the provincial

[1] Kropatschek, *Sammlung*, iv. 471–94, N. 890.
[2] Au. Note Sauers, s.d. (July 1791), *Archiv für N. Öst., Präsidialakten*, 1791/34.

police organizations, and included a draft of a cabinet order to Kollowrat which would have given effect to his recommendations.[1]

To Sauer's bitter disappointment, Leopold declined to take any action on this. The new 'Sonnenfelsian' police organization was inaugurated on 1 November 1791. Within a short time it brought about a marked improvement in public security and a reduction in crime.[2] The population made full use of the free 'health service' attached to the new organization: more than 16,000 patients received free treatment during its first year of operation.[3] Leopold instructed provincial governors to report if and how the new system could be applied to the provincial capitals,[4] and considered projects for the further improvement of the district police organizations.[5]

Amid all this preoccupation with the 'public' police, Sauer and Schilling were quite unable to make any headway with their scheme for the revival of the secret police. At the end of Leopold's reign, Sauer had still not received a reply to his Note of 3 October, and a similar Note of 22 January had also remained unanswered.[6] Leopold received all the information he wanted directly through his own rather peculiar secret agents. He saw no reason, therefore, why he should antagonize the mass of his subjects by reviving the Ministry of Police which had aroused so much loathing that it had been thought advisable to drop the word 'police' altogether from the nomenclature of the organization inaugurated on 1 November.[7]

The Patents of 28 February and 1 November 1791 restored the authority of the law over the police, at least in principle. Was Leopold II prepared to go farther in the direction of the *Rechtsstaat* ideal so dear to public opinion? When he arrived from Tuscany, his reputation as a prince

[1] Au. Note Sauers, 3 Oct. 1791 (Schilling's draft), *Archiv für N. Öst., Präsidialakten,* 1791/2.
[2] Au. Note Sauers, 22 Jan. 1792, *Archiv für N. Öst., Präsidialakten,* 1791/2.
[3] H. Oberhummer, *Die wiener Polizei* (1938: Vienna), i. 60.
[4] Hofkanzlei Circulare, 19 Nov. 1791, *Ob. Öst. Landesarchiv, Präsidialakten,* F. 7, 25/74.
[5] Oberhummer, i. 61–62, 70.
[6] *Archiv für N. Öst., Präsidialakten,* 1791/2.
[7] Report of Hoffmann, 23 July 1791, *Vertr. Akten,* F. 58, fols. 191–2.

who respected the law certainly gave rise to some hopeful expectations in this respect. Sonnenfels thought the time had come to revive the project for the codification of public law which had made no headway whatever during the reign of Joseph II.

Under a monarch who has made the historic decision not to rule arbitrarily, but in accordance with and through the laws . . . the time seems to have come to revive with some hope of fair success the project for a political codification based on definite principles, and freely to express the wish that the foundation may thus be laid for a Constitution which alone can secure . . . the rights . . . of all classes, the general welfare, and the Throne.[1]

Though there was some delay, Leopold did finally justify Sonnenfels's expectations. On 12 February 1791 he ordered the Supreme Chancellor to set up a commission to prepare the codification of all political laws, and to appoint Sonnenfels as its reporter.[2]

Throughout the years of waiting, Sonnenfels had not changed his opinion that the first stage in the process of compilation was to establish general principles of government by reference to which the goodness or badness of particular laws could be judged. But by 1791 his ideas had developed further, and he advocated, as we have seen, that truly representative diets should be consulted about the application of the general principles in the different conditions of the various provinces.

Thus it came about that the Court Chancellery in its first report on the revived project put forward some interesting general propositions. The rights of man and the citizen, we read in this remarkable document, had lost none of their validity for having been made the pretext for reprehensible actions elsewhere. Leopold's proclaimed intention to consider the interests and welfare of all classes had convinced his subjects that the rights of man and the citizen were enshrined in his heart. The dignity and independence of the throne entitled the Emperor to lay down the principles in accordance with which the nation was to be governed. The rights of the nation and of the provinces to be consulted in

---

[1] Au. Promemoria Sonnenfels', 7. Apr. 1790, *Kaiser Franz Akten*, F. 149, No. 7.
[2] Adler, pp. 99–100.

matters affecting their welfare entitled them to express their opinion concerning the application of these principles.[1]

Warning voices were raised in the Council of State against the dangerous implications of some of these propositions, and against the political beliefs of Sonnenfels which conflicted with the power of the monarch and made it inadvisable to give him too much influence in the reform of legislation. The Emperor took note of the warnings, but resolved notwithstanding that the Estates were to be consulted about important changes in the laws (3 August 1791).[2]

We must try to establish, whether this decision was merely a further concession to the privileged orders, or a further contribution to the policy of reconciling monarchy and people in the age of the French Revolution by timely concessions; whether it was in fact the first instalment of genuine constitutional advance.

It will be well not to exaggerate the significance of Leopold's alleged constitutional principles. Their advertisement was intended to produce a specific political effect in the early months of 1790. We should look in vain for a consistent attempt at their implementation. Leopold's policy on constitutional reform in favour of the non-privileged was conditioned by what he believed to be the attitude of the latter towards the monarchy.

By the end of 1791, for instance, he had come to look upon the Belgian Vonckists as irreconcilable opponents of the monarchy.[3] A reform of the Estates would therefore strengthen the political forces hostile to the monarchy, and was not to be conceded in Belgium.

Quant aux projets de réformation quelconque des représentations des États chez vous je crois qu'il faut y aller doucement . . ., car ceci donnerait trop de credit et d'autorité aux Vonckistes et servirait dans le moment présent à fomenter des troubles, et je ne crois le moment présent à propos pour faire le moindre changement dans l'état actuel des choses.[4]

It is worth noting that Leopold's sister, who was governor

---

[1] Ibid., pp. 101–2.   [2] Ibid., pp. 103–4.
[3] Leopold to Marie Christine, 9 Oct. 1791, in A. Wolf, *Leopold II. und Marie Christine. Ihr Briefwechsel (1781–1792)* (1867: Vienna), p. 268.
[4] Leopold to Marie Christine, 31 Dec. 1791, in Wolf, p. 286.

of the Netherlands, was convinced that he was making a
mistake, and was driving the moderate Democrats into the
arms of the aristocratic and clerical opposition:

> ... je crois me persuader que quant aux Démocrates modérés, ils ne
> s'y laisseront entraîner que tout au plus dans le cas où il ne leur resterait
> d'espoir d'un changement de représentation que par le moyen d'une
> nouvelle révolution. ... Je ne puis m'empêcher ... de regarder ...
> comme des démarches très peu calculées et prudentes toutes celles qui
> aboutiraient à détruire absolument le reste d'espoir que pourraient
> avoir les soi-disants amis du bien public, de voir réaliser un pour [read:
> peu] les modifications salutaires, qu'on leur avait laissé entrevoir. ...[1]

The last few words are, of course, an allusion to the fact that
in Belgium, as in other provinces, the Democrats had earlier
been positively encouraged to press their claim for better
representation in the organizations of the Estates.[2]

Marie Christine's letter is interesting, because it describes
not only her own ideas, but also the policy which Leopold
did in fact pursue in some of his other provinces, where the
Fourth Estate seemed less deeply influenced by French
ideas and more tolerant of royal power.

On the basis of the available evidence, it is now difficult
to determine the relative importance of spontaneous political
action and semi-official prompting in bringing about the
petitions and campaigns of the Fourth Estate for better
representation in the diets. Their result, however, is not in
question: a stronger and more widespread desire for better
representation and the confident expectation that Leopold
would grant it.[3]

Leopold's policy was to grant it, if this seemed necessary
in order to retain the goodwill of the Fourth Estate, and if
the latter showed no alarming propensity of taking the law
into their own hands. He did so the more willingly in that
his action implied the sovereign's right to regulate unilater-
ally the constitution of the Estates. Unfortunately he died
when he had as yet taken only a few steps in this direction,
and we are left to surmise how much further he had intended
to go.

[1] Marie Christine to Leopold, 13 Jan. 1792, in Schlitter, pp. 231-2.
[2] Kaunitz to Mercy, 6 Feb. 1791, quoted by Zeissberg, I, p. 36.
[3] Cf. report of Georg Mahl, 19 Apr. 1792, Vertr. Akten, F. 57, fol. 614.

In January 1791, Leopold recognized Anton Raspor, mayor of Leoben, as accredited representative of the Estate of the cities and towns of Styria, and admitted him as such to the Commission on Grievances.[1] A Court Resolution of 17 May 1791, granted the Styrian cities and towns ten representatives in addition to the *Städtemarschall* in the diet and one in the standing committe of the Estates.[2] A decree of 7 January 1792 ordered all four Estates and the Styrian government to submit proposals on how best to attain the complete integration of the Fourth Estate in the organization of the Estates as a whole.[3]

The petition of the Styrian peasants for representation in the diet was sent to the Court Chancellery on 4 December 1791, with the unusual instruction that the Councillors were to submit separate recommendations on it. A bare majority recommended that the petition be granted in one form or another. At least one councillor was under the definite impression that Leopold in any case intended to grant it, and that the only question to be discussed was the manner of execution.[4] No decision, however, was announced before Leopold's death.

Martinovics asserts repeatedly that his confidential assignment in Hungary was to prepare the ground for a reform of the Hungarian constitution which was to be effected at the next session of the diet. He certainly submitted proposals for such a reform at the Emperor's request. The book which he was commissioned to publish and which appeared early in 1792, was manifestly designed to rally support for an impending reform of the constitution in favour of the nonprivileged.[5] Two men whom he wanted to see appointed in counties where opposition to such a reform was expected to be strong, were in fact appointed in these counties on 15 February 1792—'in conseguenza delle proposizioni di Martinovics'—as a cabinet official noted.[6]

---

[1] Bidermann, p. 34.   [2] Ibid., p. 32.
[3] Ibid., p. 50.
[4] Ah. Handbillet an Kollowrat, 4 Dec. 1791, and Vota der Hofräte, 12–14 Dec. 1791, *Kaiser Franz Akten*, F. 10a, Konv. 1.
[5] *Oratio pro Leopoldo Secundo*, pp. 90–99.
[6] Note of a cabinet official, s.d. (after 15 Feb. 1792), *Vertr. Akten*, F. 60, fol. 137; *Handbillettenprotokoll*, 1792/198.

There is further evidence that Leopold was also preparing to effect a reform of the Estates in Bohemia during the last months of his reign. There is a report from the British ambassador in Vienna, written on 15 October 1791, when Leopold was in Bohemia for the coronation:

His Imperial Majesty is supposed to have adopted the Idea that the dangerous contagion of French Reform can hardly be averted or at least that the fatal progress of that levelling spirit cannot be so effectually circumscribed as by new modelling the Constitution of several of the countries which belong to his dominions by voluntary concessions on the part of the Sovereign. . . . [It] seems to be the Emperor's Wish to begin by granting Bohemia . . . a determinate Constitution and regular meetings of Citizens and Peasants. . . . Such a project is believed to occupy His Imperial Majesty's most serious thoughts.[1]

Unfortunately the ambassador did not fulfil his promise to send further information on this matter with the next safe conveyance.

We know, however, that a *Hofdekret* of 4 November 1791, gave notice to the Bohemian Estates of Leopold's intention to amend their constitution in favour of the non-privileged: His Majesty would soon make known to them how he desired their newly granted right to be consulted about important changes in the laws to be brought into harmony with the rights of the other classes.[2] This clearly establishes the connexion between the promised consultation on important changes in the laws and the reform of the Estates. The admission of the Fourth Estate to the diets was not to be an empty gesture.

In February 1792 the deputies of the Bohemian Estates were in Vienna to discuss the decision that the Josephinian land-survey was again to become the basis of taxation in Bohemia. On 12 February 1792 Sonnenfels submitted to Leopold—*Ihrem Befehle gemäß*—the draft of a *Hofdekret* through which the royal decision to admit representatives of all classes to the diet was to be announced to these deputies.[3] The result of Leopold's death on 1 March 1792 was that the

---

[1] *Public Record Office*, FO. 7/28, No. 109; cf. the report of the Prussian ambassador quoted by V. Bibl, *Der Zerfall Österreichs* (1922: Vienna), i. 41–42.
[2] Quoted by Sonnenfels, *Kaiser Franz Akten*, F. 10a, Konv. 2, fol. 2.
[3] Ibid., fols. 2–3.

Bohemian deputies heard no more either of the Josephinian land-survey, or of the rights of the non-privileged classes.

Some general evidence for the assertion that Leopold intended to embark on far-reaching reforms in favour of the Fourth Estate may, finally, be found in his later administrative measures. Professor Watteroth was instructed to organize civil servants of Josephinian outlook in a secret association which was to help them to detect, report, and overcome aristocratic obstruction in the bureaucracy.[1] As from 1 January 1792, Leopold established regular direct contact between himself and the provincial governors, who were instructed to make known to him those civil servants who were particularly assiduous in carrying out their duties.[2] At the same time, he appointed two quite junior civil servants to a kind of control commission with powers to inspect all the great departments of state, and to report on the manner in which his orders were being carried out.[3] One may hazard the conclusion that the Emperor was thereby strengthening his own control over the bureaucracy with a view to facilitating impending controversial reforms.

Among all this uncertainty, we can be certain only that the non-privileged, and especially those in close contact with the Emperor, cherished the confident hope that fundamental reforms would be effected, and that Austria would enjoy the benefits of revolution without having to suffer from the violence which normally accompanied such an event. That is to say, Leopold II's policies were producing the desired effect.

[1] Immediatseingabe Watteroths, s.d. (? Oct.–Nov. 1791), *Vertr. Akten*, F. 64, No. 2, fols. 21–22; some subsequent folios consist of reports on civil servants by members of the association.

[2] Kropatschek, *Sammlung*, iv. 597, N. 955.

[3] Ah. Handbillet an Hatzfeld, 1 Dec. 1791, Walter, *Die österreichische Zentralverwaltung*, ii/4, 156.

III

THE END OF ENLIGHTENED
DESPOTISM

1. *Reversal of Leopold II's Policies*

LEOPOLD II had trusted no one but himself. None of his ministers had enjoyed his full confidence. At times he had deeply distrusted even his sons, the Crown Prince and the Palatin of Hungary. Part of the preparations for his projected reforms had been the promotion of small men to inspect and control the bureaucracy at all levels.

Francis II, succeeding unexpectedly at the age of twenty-four, lacked confidence in himself, distrusted himself. He was bound, therefore, to lean heavily on his advisers. He gave his former tutor, Count Francis Colloredo, the title of cabinet minister, clearly indicating to all who cared to understand that he would not make his own decisions. He respectfully deferred to the advice of his chief ministers, the Supreme Chancellor Kollowrat, the Hungarian Chancellor Pálffy, the Minister of State Hatzfeld, and to that of his brother, the Palatin of Hungary.

The final abandonment of enlightened despotism was the inevitable consequence of the new relationship between sovereign and ministers. Kollowrat, Pálffy, Hatzfeld, and Colloredo, had long ceased to believe in enlightened despotism, if indeed they had ever done so. The crisis in the Habsburg dominions and the French Revolution had convinced them that lasting stability could be secured only by the complete abandonment of all fundamental reform, and the restoration of the weakened influence of clergy and nobility.

Prince Kaunitz, who remained unshaken in his principles, might have been able to counteract to some extent the influence of the other ministers. But Kaunitz had ceased to maintain direct contact with his sovereigns ever since Joseph II's illness. And his go-betweens, Spielmann and Philipp Cobenzl, unscrupulously betrayed their chief, tempting Francis into the senseless adventure of a war which was the grave-digger of enlightened despotism in Austria.

(i) *The abandonment of the projected reforms*

The Estates of Bohemia had already sent deputies to the Court to hear and discuss Leopold's demands concerning taxation and labour services. After the Emperor's death, many weeks elapsed without the announcement of any decisions.[1] Meanwhile the Bohemian diet proclaimed that the lords could never agree to a general commutation of labour services.[2] In the final decree on the land tax, the demand for a return to the Josephinian land-survey was dropped.[3]

By April 1792 Councillor Eger's plan for compulsory commutation of labour services in Lower Austria was completed. Francis II, who as Crown Prince had interviewed so many Lower Austrian peasant petitioners, was inclined to give his approval. He was dissuaded from doing so by Counts Kollowrat and Hatzfeld, who urged the dangers inherent in so far-reaching a reform at a time of general revolutionary unrest. Commutation was to be left to voluntary agreements between individual lords and their tenants.[4] Labour services did not disappear from the Habsburg dominions until 1848.

The lords soon realized that a new wind was blowing from Vienna, and took the opportunity to raise their demands on the peasants. They reverted to the threats uttered after the repeal of Joseph II's February Patent, and were confident that the government was on their side.[5]

Leopold II's plans for constitutional reforms in favour of the Fourth Estate dropped like hot bricks from the hands of his successor. The devious and underhand means by which Leopold had decided to further these plans, were quite alien to the simple and straightforward outlook of Francis II. He dismantled the new controls and kept at arm's length all his father's confidential collaborators.[6] Many of the latter's

[1] Rottenhan to Hatzfeld, 2 June 1792 (copy), *Kaiser Franz Akten*, F. 82/H.
[2] Springer, i. 32.   [3] Kerner, p. 268.
[4] Bibl, 'Das Robotprovisorium für N.Ö', pp. 240–1, 273; Kerner, p. 302.
[5] Au. Note Sauers, 22 Mar. 1792, *Archiv für N. Öst., Präsidialakten*, 1792/6.
[6] Walter, *Die österreichische Zentralverwaltung*, ii/5, No. 10, pp. 35–36; Gotthardi to Colloredo, 16 Mar. 1792, *Vertr. Akten*, F. 57, fol. 483.

reports and projects were consigned to the flames. Francis did not want to know anything about 'certain things his father may have done, or about the people he may have used'.[1]

The books written and distributed according to Leopold's secret instructions were now confiscated and destroyed by the authorities who had been deliberately circumvented in their publication.[2] The pensions granted to their authors were cancelled. The honours and posts promised by Leopold to his collaborators did not materialize.[3] Their political dreams and personal ambitions were thus simultaneously shattered.

In August 1792 the Styrian burgher deputies were instructed to exclude from their list of further demands any mention of peasants' representation in the diet.[4] All attempts to keep the campaign alive had soon to be abandoned, and the Styrian burgher deputies were condemned to remain a rather ineffective minority in the body of the diet. The confident hopes of January 1792 were gone, and there was no more cause for aristocratic alarm.

(ii) *Censorship*

Censorship regulations had been steadily tightened up since 1789. The new regulations of 1792, however, amount to something more than just a continuation of this policy. After the accession of Francis II, the government's fear of the printed word dictated policy to the exclusion of every other consideration.

On 11 March the *Strassburger Kourier* was banned on the recommendation of Count Sauer, the governor of Lower Austria and *quasi* Minister of Police.[5]

A Cabinet Order issued two weeks later, required the suppression of all kinds of political speculation and discus-

[1] Wolfsgruber, *Franz*, ii. 225, cf. also Martinovics to Laczkovics, 10 Dec. 1792, Benda, I, No.66, p. 866.
[2] Kollowrat to Sauer, 15 May 1792, *Archiv für N. Öst., Präsidialakten*, 1792/80.
[3] Gotthardi to Colloredo, 7 Apr. 1792, *Vertr. Akten*, F. 57. fol. 545.
[4] Hofdekret, 11 Aug. 1792, *Steierm. Landesarchiv, Gubernialakten*, F. 91, 13205 ex 1792.
[5] Au. Note Sauers, 10 Mar. 1792, *Hofkanzlei*, IV M 2, Kart. 1333.

sion in newspapers. Censors were to pass only simple reports of ascertained facts.[1]

On 28 June, again on Sauer's recommendation, Francis ordered the banning of the Jena *Allgemeine Literatur Zeitung*, one of Germany's leading cultural publications, on the grounds that its principles might easily become detrimental to public order.[2]

Sonnenfels prevailed on the Court Chancellery to plead for a reprieve of this publication on account of its learned contents, but in vain; Francis insisted on the ban.[3]

After the events of August 1792 in France, the government was more than ever anxious to prevent the dissemination of 'unsuitable' news through the cheap, popular papers. A reminder to this effect was sent to Kollowrat on 24 September.[4] Francis seems to have been extremely sensitive on this point, and finally ordered that the censorship of the popular Viennese papers should be taken over by the former secretary at the Ministry of Police, Friedrich Schilling.[5] The era of Sedlnitzky was dawning.

(iii) *War*

Despite the hopes of the French *émigrés* and the fears of their opponents, the Declaration of Pillnitz had not been followed by a Leopoldine crusade against revolutionary France. After Louis XVI's formal acceptance of the new constitution, Leopold acknowledged that there were no longer any grounds for active intervention. He therefore proposed that the European Powers should confine themselves to a passive 'Concert of Observation', and keep themselves in a state of readiness for joint action in case the situation in France deteriorated.[6] The blustering diplomacy inspired by the Gironde orators tempted Kaunitz early in

---

[1] E. V. Zenker, *Geschichte der wiener Journalistik von den Anfängen bis zum Jahre 1848* (1892: Vienna), p. 89.

[2] Ah. Handbillet an Kollowrat, 28 June 1792, *Handbilletenprotokoll*, 1792/295.

[3] C. Glossy, 'Schreyvogels Project einer Wochenschrift', in *Jahrbuch der Grillparzergesellschaft*, viii (1898), 307; *Staatsratsprotokoll*, 3625 and 4381 ex 1792.

[4] *Handbillettenprotokoll*, 1792/437.

[5] Ah. Handbillet an Sauer, 26 Nov. 1792, *Archiv für N. Öst., Präsidialakten*, 1792/168.

[6] Schlitter, pp. lxxxv–lxxxvi.

1792 to assume a more threatening tone towards France.[1] But though a defensive alliance with Prussia was concluded on 7 February, Leopold and Kaunitz consistently rejected all pleas for active intervention in France without prior commitments by all major European Powers.[2]

Francis II allowed himself to be tempted into abandoning this cautious policy. Spielmann, acting behind his chief's back, and the Prussian emissaries Bischoffwerder and Schulenburg, succeeded in making Francis regard a war against France as a most attractive proposition. They did this by linking the idea of intervention on behalf of the French royal family with that of territorial compensation. Prussia was to participate in a new partition of Poland, the way for which was being prepared by the destruction of the new Polish constitution with Russian arms. Austria was to be allowed to exchange the Netherlands for Bavaria and to get some unspecified additional compensation.

Having accepted the advice of Spielmann, Francis had no choice but to accept also the resignation of Kaunitz. Spielmann had hoped to win Kaunitz for his scheme by reviving the Bavarian exchange project, to which the Chancellor had been greatly attached in earlier years. Under the circumstances, however, Kaunitz had the gravest doubts both as to the political morality and the expediency of the new policy, which he considered unworthy of a great self-respecting power.[3]

Thus, within only a few months of the general pacification of Jassy, Austria was once more locked in war against a major power, with only one weak and unreliable ally at her side. The new war was to have the most far-reaching implications for the further development of Habsburg internal policies. While Leopold II had striven to secure the loyalty of the Fourth Estate in order to resume the work of enlightened despotism, his son now strove to secure the support of the privileged Estates for the prosecution of the war.

[1] Schlitter, pp. xcv–xcvi.
[2] Ibid., pp. ci–cii; Kaunitz to Leopold, 25 Feb. 1792, in A. Beer, *Joseph II., Leopold II. und Kaunitz. Ihr Briefwechsel* (1873: Vienna), p. 427.
[3] Au. Vortrag Kaunitz', 25 June 1792; A. v. Vivenot, *Quellen zur Geschichte der deutschen Kaiserpolitik Österreichs* (1873 ff.: Vienna), ii. 114–15, No. 481.

(iv) *Securing the support of the privileged Estates*

Above all, the government needed subsidies from the Estates of Brabant and Hungary, and spiritual support from the clergy. For these it was prepared to pay a high political price. The goodwill of the Estates of Brabant was the most immediately necessary. To secure it, Francis abandoned one by one the positions which Leopold and the Archduchess Marie Christine had long and tenaciously defended against the Estates.[1]

To the Hungarian Estates, who voted a subsidy of four million florins, he sacrificed the Illyrian Court Chancellery[2] and the recently won rights of the Protestants.[3]

Clerical opinion was reconciled by a gradual relaxation of the Josephinian restrictions on various forms of public devotion,[4] the dissolution of the Commission for Ecclesiastical Affairs and the compulsory retirement of its President, Baron Kressel, in November 1792. Thereafter, even such regulations as had not been officially relaxed could not be enforced as strictly as they had formerly been.

The dissolution of the Ecclesiastical Commission was accompanied by a general reorganization of the central administration which gave Francis the opportunity of carrying out a purge of the most ardent Josephinians from the ranks of his bureaucracy. The true import of this large-scale compulsory retirement of officials may best be gauged from the almost untranslatable words which Francis himself used when he informed his brother, the Palatin of Hungary, of what he had done: 'Die Veränderung bei den Dikasterien . . . ist mit gutem Erfolg geschehen, und habe ich so viel möglich alle räudigen Schaafe ausgeputzet.'[5]

By the end of 1792, it had become clear that the beginning of Francis II's reign had spelt the end of the era of

---

[1] Zeissberg, 'Zwei Jahre belgischer Geschichte', pt. ii, in *Sitzungsberichte d. Akad. d. Wissensch., Wien*, cxxiv (1891), 21 ff.

[2] Ah. Handbillet an Balassa, 29 June 1792, *Handbillettenprotokoll*, 1792/297.

[3] Palatin to Francis, 6 Nov. 1792, Mályusz, No. 81, pp. 560–1.

[4] C. Wolfsgruber, *Kirchengeschichte Österreich-Ungarns* (1909: Vienna), p. 56.

[5] Francis to the Palatin, 6 Dec. 1792, Mályusz, p. 575. Sonnenfels was not removed from the new *Directorium*, but was instructed to confine his activities exclusively to questions of style.

enlightened reform, and it looked very much as though an era of war and reaction was coming to take its place.

About this time Alxinger wrote to his friend Wieland:

> Our Emperor is well-intentioned. But our ministers are implacably hostile to the Enlightenment; they have failed to keep pace with the times. They would fain rule in the fashion of a century ago, denounce everyone who is critical of the old ways as a Jacobin, and are determined to have it their own way whatever the cost. Freedom of the press and literature have incurred their fierce hatred, and anyone who has ever expressed himself in favour of these, has not the slightest chance of promotion now. Censorship is stricter than ever, and there are no traces left of the great spirit which animated Joseph. . . .[1]

Having so recently hoped for so much, a large number of people found it very difficult to reconcile themselves to so sudden a darkening of the future outlook.

2. *Opposition to the 'New Course'*

The sudden reversal of policies by the government of Francis II was bound to have a profound effect on public opinion. There were, of course, those who turned like straws in the wind, and abandoned enlightened principles as soon as they realized that they were no longer favoured in government circles. Lorenz Leopold Haschka, once the bard of limited monarchy,[2] now tried to stir up enthusiasm for the war against France.[3] On the whole, however, the reigns of Joseph II and Leopold II had brought about too great a development of political consciousness to make possible a mere passive or fatalistic acceptance of the new policies.

(i) *The demand for further reform*

The revolutionary events in France were exploited by the conservative opponents of enlightened reform in the Habsburg dominions. These violent upheavals, it was argued, were the natural consequence of undermining the power and privileges of clergy and nobility; the Enlightenment was the

---

[1] G. Wilhelm, 'Briefe Alxingers', in *Sitzungsberichte d. Akad. Wissensch., Wien.* cxl (1899), 71.

[2] *Supra*, p. 24.

[3] Cf. the poems published in the early numbers of the *Magazin für Kunst und Literatur*.

catspaw of revolution. In time, the September Massacres and the execution of the French king were adduced as confirmation, both horrifying and definitive.[1]

Against this theory, which was rapidly becoming the official philosophy of the government, the adherents of the Enlightenment stated the case for further enlightened reform. Not Enlightenment but the lack of it was responsible for the bloodshed in France. So far from leading to revolution, enlightened reform was the best possible insurance against it. Leopold II had taken this view.

In a courageous book published early in 1793, Sonnenfels protested against the new censorship policy, and tried to present the problem of disaffection as Leopold had seen it:

> Could [monarchs] ever forget ... that they ... have the Enlightenment to thank for the deference of their subjects and the general obedience given to them? ... When Omar consigns the books to the flames to heat the baths of Alexandria, his subjects are left in no doubt that he means to rule them by ... the sword alone. ... Could monarchs hesitate for a single moment in their choice between subjection exacted by fear alone ... and the respectful obedience which flows from the heart and is endorsed by the reason?[2]

The ideas here expressed were the guiding principles of a new periodical, the *Österreichische Monatsschrift*, the first issue of which appeared in January 1793. The editor was Alxinger, the well-known poet who had been critical already of Joseph II's despotic methods. Originally conceived as a counterblast to the obscurantist effusions of Leopold Alois Hoffmann,[3] the *Monatsschrift* became Austria's first opposition journal—opposing a government which had embraced a good deal of Hoffmannist philosophy.

There was certainly some evidence to show that the abandonment of enlightened reform increased rather than diminished the danger of unrest.

[1] To argue this case was the chief purpose of the officially sponsored *Magazin für Kunst und Literatur* edited by the Abbé Hofstätter, which ran from 1793 to 1796.

[2] *Betrachtungen eines österreichischen Staatsbürgers an seinen Freund* (1793: Vienna), pp. 87–89.

[3] Alxinger to Wieland, in Wilhelm, p. 72. Hoffmann had allowed himself to drift into the anti-Enlightenment party by personal resentment against Gottfried van Swieten and Sonnenfels.

The decision to leave commutation of labour services to 'voluntary' agreements between lords and tenants, encouraged the former to raise their demands, and therefore aroused bitter resentment among the latter. We have evidence of agitation and unrest among the peasants particularly from those areas where the incidence of feudal burdens had been traditionally very heavy, Bohemia and Inner Austria. A secret police agent, specially sent to Bohemia at the end of 1792 to investigate the unrest in that province, found among the peasants there a universal hatred of their lords and a determination to rid themselves of their excessive burdens by force.[1] Outright refusal to render feudal dues became frequent once again, and military force was on occasion necessary to enforce obligations.[2] So clear and single-minded was the demand of the Bohemian peasants for the re-enactment of the Patent of February 1789, that the typical epithet for the rebel in this province was not 'Jacobin' but 'Josephinian'.[3]

In the provinces of Inner Austria the situation was equally tense. There, too, a secret police agent was sent at the end of 1792 to report on the discontent. His reports have, unfortunately, been largely lost,[4] but we know from other sources that the peasants in Styria kept up a continuous agitation against labour services and rents in kind, and that Josephinian civil servants like Mitscha, Pucher, and Dirnböck (all of whom were later involved in the Jacobin trials) did their utmost to prevent the lords from increasing their exactions.[5] In Carinthia, the peasants' demand for general commutation was so strong that the governor fully expected that they would enforce it by their own strength if the garrisons stationed in his province were to be transferred to the front.[6]

The relaxation of the Josephinian restrictions on various

---

[1] Report of Ratoliska, s.d. (Jan. 1793), *Pergen Akten*, x/A2, H15.
[2] e.g. Lazansky to Pergen, 16 May 1793, *Polizeihofstelle*, 1793/347.
[3] Cf. the conclusion of a revolutionary leaflet found in Feb. 1793: 'Aus dem (bisher) geheimen Nationalkonvent des josephinischen freyen Böhmen in Prag', *Polizeihofstelle*, 1793/138.
[4] The surviving ones are in *Pergen Akten*, x/B3.
[5] Verhörsprotokoll Dirnböcks, *Vertr. Akten*, F. 29, fols. 12, 36–37.
[6] O'Donnel to Kollowrat (copy), 18 Jan. 1793, *Polizeihofstelle*, 1793/197.

kinds of public devotion was probably welcomed by the Austrian peasants who adhered staunchly to traditional cere-monials which were the outward expression of their spiritual and social life. But it aroused strong antagonism among the considerable section of the capital's population who found the austere 'enlightened' Catholicism enforced by Joseph II more in keeping with contemporary ways of thought, or who had even embraced some form of agnosticism.

Cardinal Migazzi was sufficiently encouraged by the new trend in government policy to attempt again the removal of an unorthodox Josephinian preacher who taught that practical morality was more important than observance of ceremonies. The reaction of the affected congregations was, however, quite as vigorous as it had been in 1786, the last time the Cardinal had attempted to suspend a preacher for unorthodoxy.[1] Once more, Leopold Felberer, now a master cobbler, organized a petition for reinstatement which was signed by some four hundred members of the congregation. An official inquiry into the affair took place, conducted by Councillor Lorenz, head of the ecclesiastical department of the Lower Austrian government. Lorenz firmly rejected the Cardinal's anti-Josephinian contention that he owed no explanation to the government for his action, and refused to regard the petition as invalidated by the assertion that it was 'Jacobin-inspired'.[2] The councillor's spirited advocacy of the petitioners' case and the vigorous reaction of the congregation eventually secured the reinstatement of the preacher.[3]

The government's new policy of conceding greater in-fluence to the clergy again, was also resented by the Pro-testant minority. They saw in it the end of their hopes of full equality which had been aroused by the 1781 Patent of Toleration. As a result, disaffection was spreading among them, and they looked with envy at the situation in France, where all discrimination against their co-religionists had disappeared.[4]

[1] *Supra*, pp. 7–8.
[2] Auszug aus dem Verhörsprotokoll Felberers, *Erzbisch. Ordinariatsarchiv, Regesten*, No. 773; *Archiv für N. Öst., Präsidialakten*, 1793/42; ibid. *Geistliche Akten*, 1793/C20, 982.   [3] Wolfsgruber, *Migazzi*, pp. 823–4.
[4] Au. Vortrag Saurdus, 17 July 1793, *Pergen Akten*, x/B1, H42.

(ii) *Opposition to the war*

The war of intervention against France was unpopular from the start. It remained unpopular despite the September Massacres, the execution of the King, and the looting in Belgium.

In the countryside, the popular opposition to the war expressed itself in the traditional reluctance of the peasant to sacrifice his life or that of his son in a struggle which he did not feel to be his own concern:

> Was kümmern mich die Großen,
> Die Narren die.
> Schon Ströme Blutes flossen
> Dahin für sie.
> Wer Händel hat, mach selbe aus.
> Ich bleib bei meinem Geld zu Haus.[1]

Since this represented the general attitude of the peasants to the war, recruiting officers frequently had great difficulties in carrying out their task.[2]

There was also a more intellectual aspect of the opposition to the war. The Austrian newspaper reader had acquired a limited but genuine knowledge of the French Revolution. Hence many of them did not share the fatal error made by the government in calculating that the defeat of revolutionary France would be a matter of months. They knew that Francis would not be able to defray the expenses of the war out of his privy purse (as he had promised) for very long, and that he had embarked on a hopeless enterprise. Lieutenant Hebenstreit of the Vienna garrison, the one Austrian Jacobin to ascend the scaffold in 1795, said: '. . . I have always predicted an unfortunate issue to this war, as I shall never be able to convince myself that armies can be effective against a whole people.'[3]

Towards the end of 1792, when the French armies were rapidly advancing into Germany and Belgium, public opinion expressed itself much more openly on the question of the

---

[1] Quoted in Haselberger's Chronicle, in *Mitteilungen d. Gesellsch. für salzburger Landeskunde*, lxix (1929), 118.
[2] Lazansky to Pergen, 23 Feb. 1793, *Polizeihofstelle*, 1793/184.
[3] Verhörsprotokoll Hebenstreits, *Vertr. Akten*, F. 2, fol. 886.

war.[1] Numerous leaflets called for an end to the fighting. It is interesting to note that Leopold II's former confidential collaborators were among the authors and distributors of these products. They were applying the methods chosen by Leopold for his struggle against the privileged orders to their struggle against the new Emperor. Just as Leopold had been trying to frighten the nobility by stimulating symptoms of peasant revolution, so Riedel, Gotthardi, Martinovics, and others now tried to frighten Francis by writing and distributing leaflets and appeals, and submitting reports designed to create the impression of a revolutionary situation.[2] They hoped by these means to frighten Francis into ending the war and returning to a policy of enlightened reform. Francis decided instead to re-establish the Josephinian secret police in order to suppress the opposition.

3. The Re-establishment of the Autonomous Ministry of Police

(i) Rebuilding the organizational foundations

Count Sauer, who had been trying unsuccessfully to rebuild a nucleus Ministry of Police under Leopold II, had sensed very soon that the conditions for the attainment of his ambition were much more favourable under the new sovereign. As early as June 1792 he had on his own account taken the first steps in the desired direction by detaching the registration department (*Anzeigewesen*) from the rest of the police administration and putting it under the direct control of himself and Hofrat Beer, Pergen's former deputy, whose functions had practically disappeared since the minister's resignation.

Märenthal, one of the two secretaries of the former Ministry of Police, was detailed exclusively to assist Beer in the new special police department. As the other secretary of the former Ministry of Police, Schilling, was already acting as Sauer's assistant in police matters, the nucleus of Pergen's former secret police department had thus been effectively re-established.

---

[1] Rottenhan to Colloredo, 11 Nov. 1792, *Sammelbände*, F. 348.

[2] For Gotthardi and Martinovics, cf. their 'reports' in Benda, I, No. 59, pp. 797-814, No. 63, pp. 849–60, and Gotthardi's confession, *Vertr. Akten*, F. 4, fol. 224; Riedel's 'Call to the German Nation' is published in full in Valjavec, *Die politischen Strömungen*, appendix iv, pp. 505–15.

Seeking official sanction for the changes he had introduced, Sauer argued that the Leopoldine police constitution had led to a paralysis in precisely that part of the police administration which was of especial importance 'in the present circumstances'.

The system of police-registration has been neglected, [and] there is inadequate police-supervision of foreigners. . . . [Yet] there can be no doubt about the presence of several French emissaries here, who conceal their activities in such a way that only prolonged and close observation can lead to their discovery. But this, in turn, requires an efficient system of police-registration, the active co-operation of all police officers, and the consistent direction of a man thoroughly experienced in all matters of police. Moreover, the French Revolution has its defenders not only among the foreigners, but here and there also among Austrian subjects, who speak in its favour . . . more or less openly. It is indeed essential to know these people and their character, in order . . . to correct or punish them, and to forestall any disorders which might result from their talk. This too requires prolonged and close observation, which, without penetrating into the circle of intimate relationships, must keep watch over all actions and people likely to become dangerous to the state, over all public places such as coffee-houses and inns, and above all over all secret organisations and societies.

Francis sanctioned Sauer's dispositions, and went on to observe that 'altogether the administration of the police is not properly organised'. He demanded that a plan for its improvement be submitted to him after his return from the coronations.[1]

Thus only half a year after the establishment of the Leopoldine police, the whole question of police administration was in the melting-pot once more. Sonnenfels, the author of the Leopoldine reform, must have been bitterly disappointed to see his work so soon endangered, and did his utmost to parry the offensive of the secret police protagonists. A request by the governor of Galicia for a financial grant for secret police purposes gave him a welcome opportunity to launch a fierce counter-attack in which he condemned even the meagre remnants of the autonomous

---

[1] Au. Note Sauers and Ah. Resolution, 10 June 1792, *Archiv für N. Öst.*, *Präsidialakten*, 1791/2; the resolution is in Schloißnigg's handwriting.

secret police which had remained in Sauer's hands.[1] A defence against Sonnenfels's attack was submitted by Schilling, the real source of all ideas on matters of police put forward by Sauer. The stakes were now set high, and Schilling called for nothing less than the complete dissolution of the Leopoldine police organization, and a return to the autonomous Ministry of Police as it existed in the later years of Joseph II's reign:

No one acquainted with the internal situation of the State will fail to realise the utility and necessity of a well-organised police, especially in the highly critical period in which we are living.

Similarly, no one can fail to realise that the police organisation introduced here in Vienna by the Emperor Leopold simply does not meet the requirements for the sake of which the State organises a police.

If the police was to meet these requirements, two things were necessary according to Schilling's submission: centralization of the police organization throughout the monarchy, and exclusion from its duties of all activities not relevant to these requirements. Schilling calculated that whereas the Leopoldine police was costing about 150,000 florins a year, a police organized on the lines he was putting forward need cost only 10,000 florins a year.[2] It was clear that few of the real social requirements that were met by the Leopoldine police would be catered for by the police as envisaged by Schilling and the 'police-party'. But the prospective reduction of costs must have seemed very tempting to Francis who had just promised that he would not impose any new taxes to finance the war against France.

The submission of the dispute to the Council of State gave Prince Kaunitz an opportunity of putting on record his own opposition to the idea of an autonomous secret police such as Schilling was canvassing once more:

As far as the principles of a secret police and its more important activities are concerned, it is my opinion that the former must be fully

---

[1] A. H. Benna, 'Organisierung u. Personalstand der Polizeihofstelle (1793–1848)', in *Mitteilungen d. Öst. Staatsarchivs*, vi (1953), 214.

[2] Äußerung Schillings, Aug. 1792, *Polizeihofstelle*, 1814/15. My attention was drawn to this document by the work of Dr. Benna.

known to the Court Chancellery and to the Council of State, and that the latter must be sufficiently under the control of the Court Chancellery to prevent the secret police from exceeding the bounds of its proper jurisdiction and . . . from becoming a hated and pernicious instrument of espionage and arbitrary arrests.[1]

Though the allocation of the secret police fund to the governor of Galicia was for the moment refused,[2] neither the bitterness of Sonnenfels's polemic nor the prestige of Kaunitz succeeded in modifying the growing desire of the new government for the old centralized and autonomous Ministry of Police. Both of Francis II's most influential advisers, Colloredo and Schloißnigg, pushed the Emperor in this direction.[3] The secret police, wrote Colloredo, 'must be completely independent of all Ministries, must submit its information . . . solely to Your Majesty, and receive its orders from Your Majesty alone . . .'.[4]

These were of course exactly the views of Joseph II's Minister of Police, Count Pergen. Colloredo was aware of this; for, instead of submitting his own detailed views on the organization of the secret police, he drew the Emperor's attention to the 'Secret Instruction' drawn up by Pergen in 1786.[5]

Already on 5 September 1792 an official communication from the Emperor was sent off to Pergen:

As I wish to set the secret police onto a proper footing, and as this department to my knowledge best fulfilled its purpose under your direction, you will inform me as soon as possible of the plan according to which it carried out its tasks, and submit to me your suggestion as to how this institution, so necessary and conducive to the welfare of the State, could be re-established.[6]

Pergen, evidently biding his time, declared himself unable

[1] *Kaunitz Voten*, 4293 ex 1792.
[2] The wording of the notification makes it clear that Sonnenfels carried the day: 'da es zu geheimen Ausspähungen ohnfehlbar keiner besonderen Geldverwendungen bedärfen würde . . .', indirect rendering in Au. Note Pergens, 4 Feb. 1793, *Pergen Akten*, xviii/C1, H22.
[3] Au. Vorträge Colloredos, 8 and 28 Oct. 1792, *Staatskanzlei, Informationsbureau, Polizeiberichte*, F. 4, Konv. 1, fols. 32–33 and 30–31, 22; Vortrag Schloißniggs, s.d. (? summer 1792), ibid., fols. 20–21, 86.   [4] Au. Vortrag, 8 Oct. 1792.
[5] Au. Vortrag, 29 Oct. 1792; a copy of the 1786 Instruction is attached.
[6] *Handbillettenprotokoll*, 1792/394.

to offer any detailed suggestions, since Leopold had kept
him ignorant both of the reasons for the overthrow of the
Josephinian police and of the principles underlying the new
system. He did not, however, miss this opportunity of adding his own condemnation of the Leopoldine police to those
which had already been heard:

> [I do not know why Emperor Leopold] has introduced a new police
> system which is, so far as I have heard, very complicated and extremely
> expensive, and occupies its officials with writing rather than with
> action. . . . But it is certain that an effective police can be established
> only if its actions are not impeded by a lot of scribbling or by com-
> missions of various kinds. . . .[1]

Count Sauer now hastened to pick up again the threads
of the secret police correspondence from the provinces,
which had for the most part ceased after Pergen's resignation in March 1791, and to prepare the ground for the full
re-establishment of the Ministry of Police in other direc-
tions.[2] By demonstrating his zeal in bringing about the
reorganization desired by Francis, Sauer was no doubt hoping
to draw attention to his own fitness for the post of Minister
of Police. Pergen, however, had adroitly declined to make
his experience available to any other minister, confident that
the young Emperor would hesitate to undertake the constitution of the Ministry of Police altogether without his
co-operation.

He had calculated correctly. Colloredo had already hinted
at the desirability of recalling Pergen, who appeared to have
all the qualities and all the experience which he thought a
Minister of Police should have.[3] Francis evidently agreed
and offered Pergen the resumption of his former office.
Pergen accepted, asking only for a deputy to carry on the
work of the ministry during the summer months when he
himself would have to rest in view of his failing health.
Francis readily agreed to this, leaving the choice of deputy
to Pergen himself.[4]

---

[1] Au. Note Pergens, 10 Sept. 1792, *Pergen Akten*, xix, H8.
[2] This is clear from the wording of the Ah. Handbillet an Sauer, 5 Nov. 1792,
Pergen Akten, xviii/A1, H7.
[3] Au. Vortrag, 8 Oct. 1792.
[4] Ah. Handbillet an Pergen, 30 Dec. 1792, *Handbillettenprotokoll*, 1792/619.

When all was ready for the final step—the actual date was
3 January 1793—Count Sauer received a curt order to hand
over the police administration 'both in Vienna and in the
hereditary dominions' to Pergen.[1] Simultaneously, the country was briefly informed that the Ministry of Police had
been re-established 'as it existed in the reign of … Joseph II',
i.e. as a branch of government whose methods, jurisdiction
and powers would be unknown both to the public and to the
other ministers.

Pergen's first concern was to disburden his organization
from the 'useless scribbling' imposed on it by Sonnenfels
and Leopold II. Already on 25 January the District Directors of Police received orders to discontinue their arbitration
in minor disputes.[2] Soon after, the civilian police guard set
up in December 1791 to improve public security and crime
detection, was disbanded.[3] No doubt, the free 'health service'
which had been attached to the police administration under
the Sonnenfelsian system would also have fallen victim to
Pergen's exclusive passion for the secret police, had he not
been forced to conclude that the sudden abolition of this
widely used and appreciated institution would cause serious
unrest in Vienna. Under the circumstances, Pergen had to
content himself with a number of 'cuts' to reduce the cost
of the service. These amounted to the introduction of a
means test on those who wanted to use the service, the issue
of regulations to keep down the cost of prescriptions, and
the limitation of the service as far as possible to treatment in
hospital.[4]

On 1 April Pergen informed Francis that he had chosen
as his deputy Count Francis Joseph Saurau. He was to be
in charge of the ministry from May to September every year.[5]

The machinery was now complete. Much would depend
on how it was going to be used, and what powers Counts
Pergen and Saurau would manage to arrogate to themselves.

[1] *Handbillettenprotokoll*, 1793/4.
[2] Oberhummer, i. 83–84.
[3] Ibid. i. 84.
[4] Au. Note Pergens, 29 Mar. 1793, and Dekret an Polizeioberdirektion, 7 Apr.
1793, *Polizeihofstelle*, 1793/375.
[5] *Polizeihofstelle*, 1793/1.

(ii) *Surveillance and suppression*

Even before the full re-establishment of the Ministry of
Police, the emphasis of police activity was shifting noticeably
from its 'public' to its 'secret' duties.

The outbreak of the war against France was followed
almost immediately by new measures for the supervision of
foreigners and especially of Frenchmen. A growing number
of official reports now alleged the infiltration of French
agents for various purposes.[1] Reminding governors of their
duty to keep all foreigners under the constant supervision
of the police, the Court Chancellery now further directed
them not to allow any foreigners to enter their provinces
until their passports had been inspected by the police.[2]

The large number of anti-revolutionary French *émigrés*
desiring to enter the Habsburg dominions especially after
the August Revolution, gave rise to the apprehension that
French agents would now endeavour to effect their entry in
the disguise of *émigrés*. To guard against this possibility the
Austrian government decreed in November 1792 that all
prospective immigrants would have to obtain a passport from
the Austrian Chancellery of State or from an Austrian resident minister.[3] The following January, when the Ministry
of Police had been re-established, it was further stipulated
that a police permit was required before actual residence
could be allowed.[4]

In practice the new regulation affected not only would-be
immigrants, but also foreigners already resident in Austria
before their publication. For many of these failed to satisfy
the stiff requirements of the new regulations concerning
qualifications for residence. They accordingly received the
consilium abeundi from the police and had to leave, usually at
very short notice.[5]

The particular displeasure and suspicion of the govern-

---

[1] e.g. *Archiv für N. Öst., Präsidialakten*, 1792/75, 91, 97.
[2] Circulare an sämtl. Länderchefs, 15 June 1792, *Hofkanzlei*, IV M 3, Kart. 1353.
[3] *Staatsratsprotokoll*, 5490 ex 1792.
[4] Circulare an sämtl. Länderchefs, 17 Feb. 1793, *Polizeihofstelle*, 1793/13.
[5] Pergen to Beer, 12 Feb. 1793, contains a list of the first batch of expellees,
Polizeihofstelle, 1793/118. Expulsions continued throughout the subsequent period:
e.g. ibid. 1793/238.

ment was incurred by those Frenchmen who habitually gathered together in social circles of various kinds. Both the numbers attending such circles and the frequency of their meetings increased sharply after the French victories in the autumn of 1792. A police agent who attended the largest of these gatherings and daily shadowed its members, reported that the Frenchmen did not hesitate now openly to display their leanings to the French revolutionary cause even in the coffee-houses and inns they frequented.

The high spirits of the French residents coincided with a spread of defeatism and a growing desire for an end to the war among Austrian subjects, which were equally the result of the French victories. Intent on continuing the war, the government was bound to react strongly to this situation. On 1 December 1792, Count Sauer put the results of the police investigations into the activities of the French residents before the Emperor, and asked for permission to round up the largest of their social gatherings in its entirety at the next meeting, in order, as he put it, 'to reduce the numbers of these undesirable gatherings and to set up an example to them'. Francis endorsed the proposal which was duly carried out. It was the first large-scale political round-up to be made by the Austrian police.[1] Its victims were detained in prison for more than a month without any definite charges being preferred against them. After the conclusion of the police investigations, in the course of which the prisoners' correspondence and papers were searched, about half of them were deported, though they had not been convicted of any definite offence.[2]

The cold wind of the new police régime was to be felt by Austrian subjects no less than by the French residents.

Already when Sauer had made the first preparations for the re-establishment of the secret police shortly after the out-break of the war against France, he had adduced as one of his reasons the necessity of constantly observing the trends of political opinion among Austrians. Towards the end of 1792, the state of public opinion in various provinces was described as so deplorable that a number of police agents

---

[1] Au. Note Sauers, 1 Dec. 1792, *Polizeihofstelle*, 1793/135.
[2] Ibid. 1793/135, 156, 229.

were sent on special missions for the specific purpose of measuring the political temperature.[1]

By the turn of the year, the Russo-Prussian deal on the Second Partition of Poland crowned the failure of the whole foreign policy design for the sake of which the war had been undertaken. The government of Francis II now replied to the ignominious defeat sustained in France and the perilous isolation imposed by the Second Partition by bringing a new level of organization into its system of internal police supervision and repression.

At a Conference of Ministers (*Ministerialkonferenz*) held to discuss the implications of the forthcoming Second Partition, the Earl Marshall, Prince Starhemberg, moved that the conference should go on to consider the problem of internal security. A country involved in external complications with a revolutionary power, he urged, must do its utmost to forestall the dissemination of revolutionary principles within its own frontiers. In this respect he held up England as an example to the conference, specifying her voluntary anti-Jacobin committees which were taking it upon themselves to secure the suppression of revolutionary and the circulation of anti-revolutionary literature.

As Austria had a different constitution from England, the government of the former, according to Starhemberg, must undertake what the 'private patriotism' of the latter had taken upon itself—i.e. to secure the suppression of revolutionary and the widest possible circulation of anti-revolutionary literature.[2]

Though doubts were expressed about these proposals by some members of the Council of State, Francis endorsed both. Early in February 1793 the following instructions, designed to reinforce the internal security of the Habsburg state in its period of external peril, were issued to all governors:

1. No secret conventicles to be tolerated whatever their pretext;
2. Careful vigilance to be exercised over all French emigrants and their correspondence; . . .
3. The existing censorship regulations prohibiting the printing,

[1] *Supra*, p. 114.
[2] Protokoll der Ministerialkonferenz, 3 Jan. 1793, Vivenot, ii. 458–9.

copying, or importation of all books favourable to the French
Revolution, or dealing with such . . . principles as are opposed
to the principles of the Habsburg States, to be strictly enforced;

4. Great care to be taken that the newspapers refrain from mentioning anything which might throw a favourable light on the
French Revolution; journalists and authors . . . should be induced by the promise of a suitable reward to publish books setting
forth the evil results of the French Revolution in a manner both
lively and comprehensible to ordinary people;

5. As private printing-presses offer the best method of bringing
dangerous publications into circulation in the teeth of the best
censorship regulations, the suppression of such presses to be a
priority task for the police . . .[1]

By the time these new instructions were issued, the
Ministry of Police had been re-established, and Pergen
made it his principal task to ensure their full execution.
Accordingly he insisted that all his subordinates give absolute priority to the duty of keeping close and continuous
watch on each and every trend of public opinion; no police
report was to be regarded as complete unless it contained
information on that point. Other tasks standing in the way
of this were to be left to the municipalities if necessary.[2] The
provincial governors were told not to regard anything connected with public opinion as too trivial to report to Vienna,
and to follow up all denunciations, however unfounded they
might appear at first sight.[3] They received large sums of
money for the payment of secret agents.[4]

Himself convinced that revolutionary upheavals were
generally the work of secret societies,[5] Pergen gave the
widest possible interpretation to the instruction concerning
the suppression of 'secret conventicles'. Directly and indirectly he subjected the surviving masonic lodges to such
strong pressure to discontinue their activities, that by the
end of 1793 all had ceased to meet.[6] All other places, such
as coffee-houses, where people came together to air their

[1] *Staatsratsprotokoll*, 5987 ex 1792.
[2] Dekret an die Polizeioberdirektion, 29 June 1793, *Polizeihofstelle*, 1793/463.
[3] Pergen to Lazansky (draft), 21 Feb. 1793, ibid. 1793/137.
[4] *Handbillettenprotokoll*, 1793/112; *Kabinettsprotokoll*, 1793/1519, 1625.
[5] Au. Note Pergens, 1 May 1797, *Pergen Akten*, x/A1, H8.
[6] Au. Note Pergens, 9 Dec. 1793, *Polizeihofstelle*, 1793/855.

political views or to read newspapers, were put under constant and obvious police supervision, so that free discussion became impossible outside the privacy of the home.[1] Finally, even gatherings in the private home felt the chilly wind of Pergen's unlimited suspicion.[2]

As under Joseph II, Pergen again asserted after his reappointment that questions of censorship came within his jurisdiction.[3] Acting on this assumption, both he and Saurau made numerous recommendations concerning the suppression of publications passed by the Censorship Department. In March 1793, for instance, Pergen submitted to Francis a secret police agent's report to the effect that Schubart's attempt to explain rationally the acts of violence carried out in France was giving offence to 'the better class of people', and secured the banning of his *Chronik*.[4] In January 1794 he drew the Emperor's attention to the fact that the new French calendar, which he considered 'detrimental to morality' (*sittenverderblich*), had been passed by the Censorship Department, and secured the reversal of this decision.[5] A little later, he sent Francis the January number of the *Österreichische Monatsschrift*, having marked a number of places in which earlier revolutions were not put into a sufficiently repelling light. As a result, the Emperor demanded much stricter censorship of this publication in future.[6]

Pergen and Saurau repeatedly complained of a situation in which action was frequently taken only when much harm had already been done. Too often the views of the Censorship Department did not coincide with those of the Ministry of Police, largely (they thought) because of the former's inadequate acquaintance with the trends of public opinion.[7] To remedy this situation, Pergen requested towards the end of 1793, that the Censorship Department should be instructed to hold regular consultations with his ministry before making their decisions.[8] The far-reaching readjustment of responsi-

[1] Ratoliska's report, 23 Mar. 1795, *Polizeihofstelle, ältere Polizei-Akten*, ii/2, H10.
[2] *Kabinettsprotokoll*, 1793/1942; 1794/78.
[3] Cf. *supra*, pp. 44–45.   [4] *Polizeihofstelle*, 1793/193.
[5] *Kabinettsprotokoll*, 1794/39.
[6] Ibid.
[7] Au. Vortrag Sauraus, 17 May 1793, *Polizeihofstelle*, 1793/322.
[8] Oberhummer, i. 87–89.

bilities envisaged by Pergen was not to be achieved all at once, but Francis approved of the general design to extend the power of the Ministry of Police. On 2 January 1794, a Court Resolution informed Pergen that he was to receive fortnightly lists of all permitted and prohibited publications from the Censorship Department, and that all cheap publications intended for mass circulation would in future have to be approved by his ministry before permission to print could be granted.[1] Pergen might well be confident that it would not be long before the Ministry of Police took over the Department of Censorship altogether.

(iii) Count Pergen and the rule of law

By resuscitating the autonomous Ministry of Police, Francis II had reopened the question of its relationship to the Supreme Judiciary and the law. Did the decisions of Leopold II which had caused Pergen's resignation in 1791 stand, or did Pergen's recall imply the retrospective vindication of police action in the Wucherer and Willias cases?[2]

The latter was evidently assumed by Count Sauer, when he was instructed to prepare the ground for the re-establishment of a centralized Ministry of Police. Reporting on the case of Polz who had confessed to having spoken favourably of the French Revolution, the would-be Minister of Police did not hesitate to recommend that the offender be put indefinitely under precautionary police arrest. Sauer's argument was of a simplicity which scarcely indicates that a vital principle was at stake: 'The necessity for the arrest ... has been imposed upon the State by [the offender] himself through his dissemination of principles which under the present circumstances are very dangerous for the State, and to which he still adheres.'[3]

Francis II's simple endorsement of Sauer's recommendation[4] probably led Pergen to expect that precautionary arrest of suspected subversives who could not be convicted at law,

[1] Dekret an die Polizeioberdirektion, 7 Jan. 1794, *Archiv für N. Öst., P.-Oberdirektions Akten*, 1794/38.
[2] *Supra*, pp. 91–5.
[3] Au. Note Sauers (draft), 31 Oct. 1792, *Archiv für N. Öst., Präsidialakten*, 1792/156.
[4] *Kabinettsprotokoll*, 1792/1915.

was going to be one of the regular features of his ministry's activity, and he began with the practical preparations for the reception of a large number of detainees.[1]

Yet Pergen moved cautiously. He was evidently taken aback by the adverse comment and deep apprehension aroused by the reappearance of his ministry, which found expression even in the usually quite docile *Wiener Zeitung*.[2] In the case of Polz, which he inherited from Sauer, we find him—surely for the first time—trying to shift the responsibility for continued detention onto another minister, viz. the Vice-Chancellor of State, Philipp Cobenzl. As the latter emphatically declined the responsibility, Polz was released.[3] When the investigation of Stieber and Rühle, who had also been arrested by Sauer, was completed, Pergen refrained from any specific recommendations, leaving Francis to decree the indefinite detention of these two on his own account.[4] Apart from these, only one other person, Spaun, was at this stage 'sentenced' to indefinite detention because of his expressed pro-French opinions, but the records of his case have been so badly damaged by fire, that it is not possible to determine how the decision was arrived at.[5] All three were detained in the fortress of Kufstein.

The special instruction which Pergen issued at the beginning of April to all provincial governors, is still notably restrained on the question of suspected subversives:

. . . the police officials are to carry out a preliminary investigation, and if it seems that there might be a basis for criminal proceedings, a judge is to be appointed to continue the preliminary investigation jointly with the police officials. A joint report is then to be submitted to the Governor, as to whether the case can be transferred to the Criminal Court, or whether the joint investigation is to continue and the suspect is to remain in the hands of the police (*'und der Inquisit polizeymässig anzusehen sey'*).[6]

---

[1] Pergen to Wallis (draft), 14 Jan. 1793, *Polizeihofstelle*, 1793/28.
[2] Pergen to Colloredo, 12 Jan. 1793, *Sammelbände*, F. 143.
[3] Pergen to Cobenzl, 15 Jan. 1793, *Staatskanzlei, Noten v.d. Polizei*, F. 29; Cobenzl to Pergen, 18 Jan. 1793, and Au. Note Pergens, 21 Jan. 1793, *Polizeihofstelle*, 1793/43.   [4] Au. Note Pergens and Ah. Resolution, 16 Jan. 1793, ibid. 1793/34.
[5] Ibid. 1793/125. For Spaun's career, cf. L. Böck, 'Ein Linzer als Staatsgefangener in österreichischen Festungen', in *Linzer Tagespost, Bilderwoche*, 1930, No. 24.   [6] *Steierm. Landesarchiv, Miszellen*, Kart. 223.

The reason for Pergen's caution was probably that he anticipated that the critics of his ministry would keep a careful watch for any cases of unlawful or arbitrary actions carried out by himself or his subordinates. And in fact this seems to have been the case. On 16 June 1793 Francis informed Pergen that cases of arbitrary arrests which were not followed by any kind of investigation, had been reported to him from Galicia, and instructed him to remind all his subordinates of Leopold II's *habeas corpus* decree of February 1791.[1]

Nothing could have been more unwelcome to Pergen than this reminder of the Leopoldine decree. For despite his recent caution, the Minister of Police was still determined to secure the removal of all legalistic shackles on the activity of the police, which in his opinion impeded the maintenance of 'internal security'. The deterioration of Austria's external position after the comparative failure of the 1793 campaign, and the growing dissatisfaction of the people with the government's policies, seemed to him to have made the detention of the more articulate and talkative critics a matter of real urgency. But the establishment of a sound legal case against such critics had not become any the easier for that. Pergen therefore decided that the time had come to go over to the offensive and to secure once and for all the powers he wanted.

Towards the end of 1793, a case had arisen which was not unlike that of Willias. An alleged prostitute had been given the *consilium abeundi* by the police and had appealed to the Supreme Judiciary against the order, as she had not been legally convicted of an offence. Pergen took the opportunity to reject as decisively as he could the claim of the Judiciary to scrutinize the actions of his ministry. Against the principles of the Enlightenment, he pitted his own:

It is truly amazing how certain fashionable theorists and agitators take every opportunity to shift the demarcation line between Judiciary and Police. The Judiciary is competent only in cases involving a *ius quaesitum*; but in cases involving mere disciplinary measures, a public nuisance, or any kind of danger to the State, it has always been for the police to act, without consideration of person. . . .[2]

---

[1] *Polizeihofstelle*, 1793/452.
[2] Au. Note Pergens, 12 Dec. 1793, *Pergen Akten*, ix/B18, H6.

As far as cases 'involving any kind of danger to the State' were concerned, Pergen was, of course, exaggerating. He had still to obtain the power to act in the way he considered necessary, that is to say, the power to impose on his own authority precautionary detention for an indefinite period on persons whose freedom of movement he considered detrimental to 'internal security', but who could not be convicted of a definite offence against the law.

To get precisely this power, was the purpose of a Note submitted by Pergen on 2 December 1793, in which we find no traces of the restraint distinguishing his earlier utterances:

Your Majesty is well aware, how difficult it is to establish a watertight legal case against persons [engaging in seditious activities], and to secure their conviction in a court of law, however obvious their subversive principles and their efforts to disseminate them through insolent talk might be. . . . Yet such fanatics are none the less dangerous to the State in the present circumstances, and the police is always at a loss how to deal with people of this sort whose numbers are constantly growing.

I therefore beg Your Majesty to let me have some instructions as to the punishment the police should inflict in cases like this.

There is no difficulty with regard to foreigners not permanently residing here; if their ways of thought or their actions arouse suspicion, they can be given the *consilium abeundi*. But with regard to Your Majesty's subjects, . . . the appropriate method would be to discharge them after the first offence with the caution that if they persist in expressing their pernicious principles openly and thereby lead wellthinking and peaceable citizens astray, they will be punished with the loss of that liberty which they have abused to the detriment of the security of the State, and remain in detention for as long as the present circumstances last.[1]

Though Francis had not hesitated in the past to order precautionary detention in particular cases, he declined to give Pergen the requested *carte blanche*: 'It is not possible to lay down once and for all the procedure to be followed with this kind of offender, and it will have to depend more or less on the nature and seriousness of the offence.'[2]

---

[1] *Polizeihofstelle*, 1793/827.
[2] The date of the resolution (4 Dec. 1793) indicates that this was a cabinet decision, arrived at without consultation of the Council of State.

The decision is a tribute both to the Emperor's simple sense of justice, and to the vitality of the legal ideals of the Enlightenment which outlived the extinction of enlightened despotism in Austria. But it did not mark the end of Count Pergen's offensive against the rule of law.

IV

THE 'JACOBIN CONSPIRACY'

1. The Activities of the Austrian 'Jacobins'

IF one is to pass a fair judgement on the apprehensions of Count Pergen and the subsequent activities of his ministry, it is necessary to investigate the actual strength and character of the active internal opposition in the Habsburg dominions in the troubled months of 1793–4. The evidence is inadequate, but must serve as far as it goes.

Out of the frustrated political aspirations of the non-privileged had developed an active political opposition to the policies of Francis II's government. But the government, so far from yielding to this opposition continued and consolidated its policies, and revived the Ministry of Police for the purpose of dealing with the opposition. This left opponents of the government's policies with the alternative of either discontinuing their opposition and keeping their views to themselves, or of getting together unobtrusively with like-minded men to organize and co-ordinate their opposition with the aim of securing a change in policy while such a change was still feasible.

According to all the evidence available, the various activities which have gone into history as the Jacobin Conspiracy were little more than such an attempt to organize and co-ordinate the active opposition to the policies of Francis II's government.[1]

There already existed a strong tradition of regular gatherings of men of 'advanced' opinions in places where foreign newspapers and periodicals were available, a tradition which dated from the days of Joseph II. As the political vanguard of the non-privileged turned into the political opposition under Francis II, these gatherings graduated into 'demo-

---

[1] For what follows, cf. in general the voluminous depositions and confessions of the arrested 'Jacobins' in *Vertr. Akten*, FF. 1–32 and the documents published by K. Benda, *A maygar jakobinusok iratai*, II. Specific references would expand these notes to unmanageable proportions.

cratic' or 'Jacobin' assemblies in the official parlance of the time. For the increasing official disfavour in which they and their ideas were held by the government could only strengthen the democrats' desire to meet like-minded people, to discuss political developments with them, and to exchange ideas.

With the gradual disappearance of foreign newspapers and periodicals at the instance of Counts Sauer, Pergen, and Saurau, and even more with the imposition of an uncomfortable and obnoxious police supervision over all coffee-houses and inns, the scene of political discussions shifted from public to private places beyond the reach of the watchful eye of the police. And within the four walls of private establishments the general tone of the discussions became more radical, hopes more exalted, and projects more daring.

Such democratic gatherings existed probably in all provinces of the monarchy, but the evidence we have is necessarily of those whose activities eventually brought down upon themselves the full force of the police, i.e. those in Innsbruck, Upper Styria, Vienna, and Hungary.

The Innsbruck circle consisted entirely of university students who were brought together by an Italian enthusiast for the French Revolution. The latter, a servant of Sir Levett Hanson, instructed his young hearers in the history of the Revolution, as a result of which the latter decided to dedicate themselves to the cause of liberty and equality.[1]

The Styrian circles, of course, consisted in the main of the burghers' deputies to the diet and some of their electors, who had been compelled to give up their promising campaign for peasant representation in the diet, but who were still trying to achieve full equality with the upper orders in the organization of the Styrian Estates.[2]

In Vienna there was more than one group, though the different groups overlapped to a certain extent. The most important was that which gathered in the house of Baron Andreas Riedel, the confidant of Leopold II, who had tried

[1] The material concerning the Tyrolean Jacobins is to be found in *Polizeihofstelle*, 1795/496, because no regular criminal proceedings were taken against them.
[2] Bidermann, pp. 51–57; F. M. Mayer, *Steiermark im Franzosenzeitalter* (1888: Graz), pp. 9–12.

to induce his successor to desist from the war against France. Here Lieutenant Hebenstreit was a frequent and honoured attender, and expounded his view that human misery would continue so long as men said 'mine' and 'thine' and refused to have things in common.[1] In this circle high and low seemed to mix on equal terms.

A more purely intellectual group was that of Professor Wollstein, the Director of the Vienna School of Veterinary Surgery. This circle included the poet and magistrate Prandstätter, ex-Professor Neupauer, and the lawyer Dr. Jutz.

Lastly, there was the circle of the poet Blumauer and his landlord Johann Hackl,[2] which included such diverse personalities as Martinovics, the Abbé Strattmann, a friend of Gottfried van Swieten, and the police commissioner of Lemberg, Troll, who had carried out some secret assignments for Leopold under Gotthardi's direction.

The members of each of these groups were mostly acquainted also with those of the others. Apart from the houses of Riedel, Wollstein, and Hackl, the premises of a small number of 'democratic' shops in the centre of Vienna were used by them for short gatherings and discussions during the day.

The chief occupation of all these groups was political discussion, especially of developments in France, and the circulation of prohibited newspapers and books amongst themselves. Clauer's *Kreuzzug wider die Franken* was avidly read by Dirnböck and the Styrian burghers' deputies. Tom Paine's *Rights of Man* circulated in a French translation. Prohibited newspapers were smuggled in from Salzburg. News of French victories was always received with general acclamation, as it seemed to bring nearer prospects of peace.

The social life of the groups was fairly well developed, and there were numerous dinner parties, especially when there were guests from abroad or from other provinces to be entertained. When spirits were high, the *Marseillaise* and *Ça ira* would be sung.

[1] For Hebenstreit's socialism, cf. Verhörsprotokoll Hebenstreits, *Vertr. Akten*, F. 2, fol. 888–9, 950–4.

[2] Hackl belonged to the opposition for personal, not political reasons (*Vertr. Akten*, F. 12, fols. 153–4, 181).

The political activity of the democrats consisted above all in their sustained effort to spread their own ideas among their fellow citizens. This was done either by the direct method of introducing new members into the groups, or by disseminating leaflets, pamphlets, songs, and so forth, both of popular and more refined appeal. Riedel was the author of several satirical pamphlets. Prandstätter translated Batthyány's *Ad Amicam Aurem*,[1] and Gilovsky one of Robespierre's celebrated speeches. Both Martinovics and Riedel worked on a 'Catechism', setting out their ideas in that form of question and answer which Jesuit education had made so familiar. Georg Ruszitska, a member of the Riedel group, showed his prowess by composing an appeal to the peasants to resist the reimposition of labour services, which Jelline, a very ardent democrat, undertook to translate into Czech. Hebenstreit was the author of a long Latin poem entitled *Homo Hominibus*, in which the usual ideas of the Enlightenment were interspersed with utopian socialist notions of common ownership.

Hebenstreit, who was nothing if not versatile, was also the creator of the most successful of the 'Jacobin' propaganda efforts, the *Eipeldauerlied*. To words written by Captain Beck, who had died in 1793, he had supplied the melody which helped to carry the words far and wide.[2] The *Eipeldauerlied* strikes a new revolutionary note, since it assumes that Francis has given himself up completely to the aristocracy, and for the first time completely identifies Emperor and aristocracy:

> Schauts enker Kaiser Kind nur an,
> Mit'n Adel tut er's halten,
> Der Ludwig hat's halt a so than,
> D'rum haben s'n ja nit g'halten.

Some of these pamphlets were still unfinished at the time of the arrests. Most of them circulated only in handwritten copies. Riedel, however, insisted that Hebenstreit's *Homo Hominibus* ought to be printed, and the manuscript was finally taken to a printer in Steinamanger who was a relation of one of the members of Riedel's group. But it was

---

[1] This translation is to be found in *Vertr. Akten*, F. 7. Cf. *supra*, p. 71.
[2] The *Eipeldauerlied* is to be found in *Vertr. Akten*, F. 4.

already too late. Before the corrected proofs could be returned to the printers, Hebenstreit and his friends were under lock and key.

The chief limitation of the democratic propaganda in Vienna was its almost complete lack of contact with the peasants of the surrounding countryside. In this respect the Styrian democrats enjoyed an important advantage. From the days of the joint campaign of burghers and peasants for constitutional reform in Styria, there existed a close contact between the opposition in town and country. Hence democratic propaganda in Styria was also organized around the commutation of tithes. The peasants looked to the burghers' deputies to draw up their petitions for them. And Franz Haas and Joseph Wenninger were not the men to miss such an opportunity of disseminating their political ideas and attacking their opponents.

An important part of the democratic propaganda both in Styria and Vienna was propaganda for peace. Among the varied political opinions confessed to in the course of the subsequent trials, opposition to the war against France was common to all who were investigated. To strengthen the opposition against the war, good use could be made of any news of French military successes. The ostentatious clerical support that was given to the war was an easy target for democratic satire. The passage of French prisoners of war presented opportunities for most effective demonstrations of the desire for peace and friendship with the people of France. And the Styrian experience in the technique of political campaigning provided an excellent foundation for an organized peace campaign with circulars, petitions, and signatures, which was initiated by the burgher deputies of the Judenburg district.[1]

The problem of giving some sort of organization to the democratic groups and winning new members for them on a large scale, so that they might become instruments for effective action other than propaganda, was only just beginning to be tackled at the time of the arrests.

Baron Riedel introduced the idea of using a sign by which all those in agreement with the aims of the groups could

---

[1] Geständnis Dirnböcks, *Vertr. Akten*, F. 29, fols. 23–24.

recognize each other and thus form some idea as to the numerical strength of the democrats. Some of the more ardent younger members, among them the physician Dr. Menz, devised a formula for an oath to be taken, 'in the name of Nature, Reason and Freedom', and pledging unceasing struggle against despots and fanaticism. When early in July 1794 a deputation from Styrian burghers which included Dirnböck came to Vienna, they sought and found contact with some of the Vienna democrats. As a result long discussions on the French Constitution took place. A strong common attachment to political freedom kindled the desire for a closer union between them. To cement such a closer union the Styrian deputies joined their Viennese friends in a quasi-masonic ceremony on top of a hill in the Brühl near Vienna at which the above oath was taken.[1]

The news of this procedure seems to have been received with satisfaction in the democratic circles, but there is no evidence that it was repeated by anyone else.

In Hungary the democratic groups were more numerous than anywhere else in the Habsburg dominions. A very large group existed in the capital and met in the house of Ferenc Abaffy, a prominent aristocratic reformer in the Diet of 1790. Among the members of this group we find József Hajnóczy, author of several learned books refuting aristocratic and clerical pretensions,[2] the ardent young Ferenc Szentmarjay who translated Rousseau's *Contrat Social* into Hungarian, Professor Antal Kreil of the University of Pest, and many other intellectuals, lawyers and civil servants. Democratic groups, some large, some small, met regularly in the provincial centres of Kaschau, Großwardein, and Güns.

The propaganda activities of the Hungarian groups differed little from that of the Austrian ones. Martinovics, however, who abandoned all hope of frightening Francis II into a change of policy, assumed the leadership of the Hun-

---

[1] Concerning this oath-taking ceremony, cf. Verhörsprotokoll Menz', answers to questions 8–21, *Vertr. Akten*, F. 1. Menz alone admitted the serious character of the ceremony, all other participants stoutly maintained that it was a joke. Menz quoted the formula of the oath as follows: 'Im Namen der Natur, der Vernunft u. der Freyheit schwöre ich mich zu verbrüdern zur Tugend, schwöre Haß den Despoten u. der Hierarchie des dreygekrönten Ungeheuers, schwöre Gutes zu thun nach meinen Kräften, zu steuern dem Fanatismus u. den Mißbräuchen u. uns zu lieben als Brüder.'   [2] Cf. *supra*, pp. 71–72.

garian democrats in the spring of 1794. Claiming to be in contact with the Committee of Public Safety, and holding out the prospect of French aid, he persuaded them to set up a regular underground organization called *Gesellschaft der Freiheit und Gleichheit*. Its 'Catechism' envisaged a Hungarian republic freed from feudal dominion. To acquire the necessary strength for the initial rebellion, Martinovics founded a second secret society—the *Gesellschaft der Reformierten*—which had the specific purpose of attracting the nationalist gentry to the cause of rebellion, so that they might provide its spearhead as they had done in 1789 and 1790. Naturally, the gentry were kept ignorant of the anti-feudal *Gesellschaft der Freiheit und Gleichheit*, which was waiting in the wings to reap the harvest of the victorious rebellion by transforming it into a middle-class revolution. By the summer of 1794, Martinovics and his 'directors'—Hajnóczy, Laczkovics and Szentmarjay for the democrats and Count Jakab Sigray for the gentry—had recruited about 300 members to their respective secret societies.[1]

No one among the Austrian 'Jacobins' shared the Hungarians' clear political perspective. There was little awareness that the realization of their aims might require revolutionary action. Consequently the possibility and nature of such action remained the subject of purely theoretical speculation on which the most varied views were being expressed. Riedel himself seems to have regarded the 'dullness' of the Austrian peasantry as an obstacle which would prevent revolutionary action for a long time to come. The socialist Hebenstreit, on the other hand, could not believe that the French and Polish peasant was more 'enlightened' than the Austrian, and was convinced that the dire poverty of the artisans in the growing towns would ensure the success of a revolutionary appeal to them at any time.[2] Neither attempted to draw any practical conclusions from their theory.

It is clear that there was no regular contact with any democratic organizations abroad. But the Riedel circle had

[1] A short but thoughtful and scholarly account of the Hungarian conspiracy by Professor Benda is now available in German: 'Die Ungarischen Jakobiner', in *Maximilien Robespierre 1758-1794. Beiträge zu seinem 200. Geburtstag*, ed. W. Markov (1958: Berlin), pp. 447-68.

[2] Verhörsprotokoll Hebenstreits, *Vertr. Akten*, F. 2, fols. 971-2.

a secret which they very much wanted to impart to the French government. Hebenstreit had been stimulated by the agrarian revolts of 1790–2 to consider the problems facing an ill-equipped peasant army in defending itself against a well-equipped cavalry. As a result, he had designed a 'war-machine', based on the principle of the *chevaux de frise*, which he and his friends were convinced would be of great service to the French in their struggle against the Austrian forces and therefore help to bring the war to an end. One member of the Riedel circle, the Protestant pastor Karl Traugott Held, had a contact which finally enabled him to take the secret to the French capital.[1]

Held came from Saxony, and was acquainted with the Polish patriot Count Soltyk, who was in Vienna in the early months of 1794 trying to buy arms for Kosciusko.[2] Held imparted his secret to Soltyk on condition that the latter co-operated in making it available also to the French. Soltyk immediately sent a courier with the design of Hebenstreit's invention to Kosciusko, and gave Held 200 florins for the journey to Paris, as well as a letter addressed to Barsch, the Polish chargé d'affaires in Paris.

Held, accompanied by a young German, Denkmann, arrived in Basle on 28 April 1794, where the secretary of the French Embassy referred them to General Schérer. The latter thought that the design might be of great importance, and enabled them to proceed to Paris.[3] They arrived on 9 May, but were promptly arrested before they had a chance to acquaint the Committee of Public Safety with the purpose of their journey. However, they explained Hebenstreit's invention in writing and managed to convey the material to the committee. As a result of this and a persuasive petition, the committee decided to release them on 9 August.[4] Whether the committee tried to make any use of the invention it is not at the moment possible to say.

---

[1] For Held's mission to Paris, we are not exclusively dependent on the deposition of the arrested 'Jacobins', because we have also the detailed account which he gave in his petition to the Committee of Public Safety, 20 Thermidor, an II, *Archives Nationales, AF* ii. 57, pl. 415, fols. 28–29.

[2] Kollowrat to Pergen, 23 Apr. 1794, *Polizeihofstelle*, 1794/288.

[3] Bacher to Buchot, 16 Floreal an II, *Arch. du Min. d. Aff. Étr., Correspondance Politique*, Suisse, vol. 446, fol. 42.   [4] *Actes du Comité de Salut Public*, xv. 793.

2. *The Crisis of the Summer of 1794*

Clearly, the evidence concerning the various 'Jacobin' groups in the Habsburg dominions does not trace even the outlines of a powerful 'conspiracy' menacing the foundations of the monarchy. The question therefore arises, why the Ministry of Police should have come to the conclusion that they did represent an acute danger, and should have so strongly insisted on ruthless counter-measures. To find a convincing answer to this question it is necessary to turn from the activities of the 'Jacobin' groups to the general political situation in which these activities were carried on.

The failure of the campaign of 1793 had shattered whatever hopes of a short war had survived the earlier disasters. The preparation of the 1794 campaign involved new financial burdens (though the name of 'war-tax' was avoided) and a new drain of the badly needed manpower from the land to re-form depleted regiments.[1] The continued requirements of army provisions helped to push up prices from the already high level prevailing since the Turkish War and jeopardized supplies for the capital.[2] The attempt to suppress exports to Revolutionary France and, after April 1794, also to Revolutionary Poland inflicted considerable dislocation on Austrian commerce and industries.[3] Everywhere an acute lack of money and men made itself felt. To crown all, the 1794 harvest in Hungary, the monarchy's principal granary, was threatened by a severe drought.[4]

Inevitably, the brunt of all the hardships was borne by the non-privileged, who were still waiting for the concessions which had seemed at hand at the close of Leopold II's reign, but which had been shelved in that of his son.

Under these circumstances, the police reports on the general state of public opinion were bound to give rise to serious misgivings at the Ministry of Police.

Relations between landlords and peasants continued to be

---

[1] Vortrag der Ministerialconferenz, 16 Dec. 1793, *Nachlaß Kollowrat*, F. 14, No. 1257; Patentaufsatz (copy), 10 Jan. 1794, *Staatskanzlei, Noten v.d. Hofkanzlei*, F. 46.

[2] Au. Note Wallis', 10 Aug. 1794, *Kriegsarchiv, Hofkriegsrat*, 1794/44/563.

[3] Straton to Grenville, 17 May 1794, *Public Record Office*, FO. 7/37, No. 9.

[4] Palatin to Francis, 13 Aug. 1794, Mályusz, No. 134, p. 700.

strained to breaking-point. The danger of peasant risings in
support of their demands was ever present.[1] Despite the war,
partly perhaps because of it, the example of the French
peasants who had shaken off the feudal yoke still inspired
many of Austria's peasants, whose notions of the revolutionary achievement may have been a little exaggerated.[2]

The war had never enjoyed popular support, but by 1794
war-weariness had assumed very pronounced forms of expression. Peasant resistance to recruitment became more
obstinate. Drafted against his will, the peasant carried his
resentment and his opposition to the war with him into the
army, and even into the front line. He was confirmed in his
attitude by the letters he received from home, which reflected the growing disgust with the war on the part of those
he had left behind, told of the manifold hardships and burdens due to the prolongation of the war, and concluded with
the fervent desire for the return of the army, 'which would
put an end to all the hardships'. This desire was fully shared
by the soldiers themselves, who received every order to retreat with undisguised joy, because it seemed to bring nearer
the prospects of peace.[3]

For the French 'enemy' the Austrian soldier tended to
feel sympathy rather than hostility. Both shared a common
hatred for the landed nobility. The longer the Austrian
soldier remained on French soil, the more did he assimilate
the language and outlook of the men he was supposed to
fight, the ideas of '89. The growing number of desertions
was but one expression of this mutual understanding. 'I am
dissatisfied with the . . . troops under Wurmser', Francis
wrote to his brother the Palatin early in 1794, 'there is a
great deal of political discussion even among the officers,
desertion is frequent, and they continually hold friendly
conversations with the enemy's advanced guards.'[4]

The problem of growing sympathy for the French soldiers
on the part of those who came into close contact with them
was not confined to the front line. It emerged in all the

[1] E.g. Circulare des Kreishauptmanns Mitscha an alle Zehendobrigkeiten, 27
Dec. 1794, *Polizeihofstelle*, 1795/636; Mayer, pp. 21–23.

[2] Stampach to Pergen, 1 Oct. 1794, *Polizeihofstelle*, 1794/928.

[3] Anon. to General Rollin, 13 Aug. 1794, *Kaiser Franz Akten*, F. 78d.

[4] Francis to the Palatin, 2 Jan. 1794, *Sammelbände*, F. 98, Konv. 6.

Habsburg provinces through which French prisoners of war had been transported, and even more in those where they finally settled. Everywhere the population showed a keen desire to come into contact with the prisoners, and it was not long before the relations established were so friendly that an alarmed Ministry of Police urged decisive intervention.[1] The uniform buttons, inscribed with 'Liberté, Egalité', which the prisoners had distributed, had to be surrendered to the authorities. But the new attitudes which had sprung from the contact with the prisoners could not thereby be uprooted.[2]

With regard to this general internal situation, Count Pergen officially declared that the active co-operation of the military with the police was essential to the maintenance of internal tranquillity.[3]

Thus, at the height of the crisis in the war against France, the need to retain large garrisons in the Habsburg provinces had become a major military consideration.[4]

Such, then, was the mood of the Austrian people when they heard of the disastrous defeats inflicted on their army in France and the Netherlands in June and July 1794. The great sacrifices which had been imposed upon them had resulted in the loss of the Netherlands to France. All the normal resources of the monarchy were exhausted; it was impossible to see where the means to finance a new campaign would come from.[5]

The disasters on the battlefield need not have weakened the internal position of the government. They had strengthened the general desire of the people for peace, the conclusion of which was now openly advocated even in the highest places.[6] There had long been a tendency to regard the Austrian Netherlands as a source of weakness rather than

[1] Welsperg to Pergen, 29 Apr. 1794, *Polizeihofstelle*, 1794/304; Au. Note Wallis', 23 Feb. 1794, *Kriegsarchiv, Hofkriegsrat*, 1794/9/583, fols. 8–15; cf. also *Polizeihofstelle*, 1793/788a, 896.
[2] Barco to Wallis, 7 Aug. 1794, Benda, II, No. 3.
[3] Pergen to Wallis (draft), 25 Dec. 1793, *Polizeihofstelle*, 1793/899.
[4] Au. Note Wallis', 23 Feb. 1794, *Kriegsarchiv, Hofkriegsrat*, 1794/9/583.
[5] Au. Note Kollowrats, 21 July 1794, *Nachlaß Kollowrat*, F. 15, No. 1317.
[6] Graf Karl Zinzendorf, *Selbstbiographie* (1879: Vienna), p. 234; Au. Note des Palatin, 1 Aug. 1794, Mályusz, No. 132, p. 697; Straton to Grenville, 23 July 1794, *Public Record Office*, FO. 7/37.

strength to the monarchy.[1] Moreover, since most people in
Austria considered that Prussia had not fulfilled her obligations under the Austro-Prussian alliance,[2] few would have
regarded an Austrian withdrawal from the war as dishonour-
able. On the contrary, it would have been widely regarded
as a long-overdue precaution against Prussian and Russian
aggrandizement.

Francis II, however, decided to ignore the advice of his
Minister of State, Count Zinzendorf, who advocated peace,
and to adopt that of his Minister of Foreign Affairs, Baron
Thugut. There could be no question of peace, the Emperor
declared; more money and troops were to be raised in the
monarchy until such time as a subsidy might be secured
from Great Britain.[3] Francis further antagonized public opinion by sending his army into Poland (19 July 1794). This
action ranged Austria firmly on the side of Russia and Prussia against Kosciusko as a full partner in the now inevitable
Third Partition of that unfortunate country.[4]

Apparently unaware of the difficulties in the way of a
rigorous prosecution of the war, Francis had accepted
Thugut's suggestion to summon the Hungarian diet for the
purpose of obtaining money and recruits. The government
at Ofen, however, had not shared Thugut's easy confidence;
the Lord Chief Justice, Count Zichy, had hastened to Vienna
to warn the Emperor of the consequences of the step he was
proposing to take. Under the circumstances, the assembly
of the diet would almost certainly mark the beginning of a
new revolutionary upheaval in Hungary.[5] Reports from
Hungary at this time indicated an almost universal unwill-
ingness to pay for the continuation of the war.[6] From the
Military Commander in Ofen, the War Council received

[1] Cf. the Memorandum of Philip Ritter v. Stahl, 14 Aug. 1794, *Kaiser Franz Akten*, F. 78d.

[2] Straton to Grenville, 9 and 19 July 1794, *Public Record Office*, FO. 7/37, Nos. 21 and 24.

[3] Ah. Resolution proclaimed in the Conference of Ministers 13 Aug. 1794, Mályusz, p. 698.

[4] For evidence of widespread sympathy for the Polish revolutionaries, cf. Gragger, pp. 86, 153.

[5] César to Frederick William II, 25 June 1794, *Staatskanzlei, Interiora, Interzepte*, F. 2 (1794), fols. 42–43.

[6] Voten Izdenczys, 21 and 28 July 1794, Mályusz, p. 692.

urgent requests for immediate and considerable reinforcements.[1]

The government's determination to continue the war
despite the military disasters in the summer of 1794 had
brought the internal crisis in the Habsburg monarchy to a
head. It is in the light of this crisis that we must consider the
policy of the Ministry of Police with regard to the Austrian
'Jacobins'.

3. The Arrests

The police had been aware of the identity and movements
of some of the 'Jacobins' since the summer of 1793,[2] and
later that year Count Pergen had asked Francis for the
power to arrest these people against whom he was unable to
establish a legal case.[3]

Soon an opportunity to proceed with some arrests and
convictions under the 'political code', which comprised the
less serious so-called police-offences, presented itself. For in
January 1794 an informer denounced to the police the vigorous religious discussions taking place among the cobblers,
tailors, and apprentices in the suburbs of Vienna.[4] These
men were still attending the sermons of their favourite
Josephinian preachers—Anton Kick, the vicar of Penzing,
and the Benedictines Wenzel and Liechtensteiner who
looked after the suburban parish of Schottenfeld. By now
many of them aired fully-fledged atheist views.[5] The police
were not obliged to present a legal case against these men,
because they could be dealt with under the 'political code'
and convicted of blasphemy. This was done, and a large
number—the 'seducers'—were sentenced to the pillory and
one year's imprisonment, while the 'misled' were dismissed
with a severe caution.[6]

---

[1] Barco to Wallis, 7 Aug. 1794, *Kriegsarchiv, Hofkriegsrat,* 1794/44/563, fol. 32.
[2] Au. Vortrag Sauraus, 17 July 1793, *Pergen Akten,* x/B1, H42.
[3] *Supra,* pp. 130–1.
[4] Vortrag der polizeilichen Untersuchungskommission, 24 Mar. 1749, *Polizeihofstelle,* 1794/197.
[5] For the general tendency of these preachers' sermons and the evolution of
their listeners' views, cf. *supra,* pp. 16–19.
[6] *Polizeihofstelle,* 1794/197, 262, 308, 309.

Though the investigations had revealed that the accused had rejoiced in news of French victories and had been airing 'Jacobin' as well as atheist views, Pergen and Saurau must have known that the suppression of the *Schusterkomplott* had not affected the roots of Austrian 'Jacobinism'.

However, after the initial successes marking the early stages of the 1794 campaign the internal situation improved a little, and the anxiety of the Ministry of Police subsided accordingly. Saurau struck a note of confidence when he wrote at the beginning of June to Colloredo, who was accompanying the Emperor on a visit to the front: 'Des gens malintentionnés, dont on ne manque nulle part, ne cessent pas de troubler l'alégresse que nous causent les bonnes nouvelles, et de semer partout l'alarme et le découragement. Heureusement leur nombre n'est pas fort grand et on les survaille autant que possible.'[1] While Austrian arms were winning successes at the front Saurau was confident that he could keep the critics at home under control.

But soon success gave way to failure; the French advanced victoriously into Belgium. Saurau's comparative confidence gave way to concern. In a Note to the Emperor of 18 June he again drew attention to the fact that 'ill-disposed people' welcomed unfavourable news and spread it as fast as they could. This time, however, he does not add the confident assertion that their number was small and the vigilance of the police adequate to keep them in check. Instead he pointedly returns to a familiar complaint: 'Unfortunately it is not possible to establish legal proof of their malicious intentions. . . .'[2]

It was at about this time that the Austrian authorities found out that Held and Denkmann had gone to Paris, and that their journey from the French frontier had been financed by the French government. According to their source of information the purpose of the trip was to inform the Committee of Public Safety of the existence of a powerful revolutionary society in Vienna and to obtain financial support for it.[3]

[1] Saurau to Colloredo, 1 June 1794, *Sammelbände*, F. 162.
[2] *Staatskanzlei, Informationsbureau, Polizeiberichte*, F. 4, Konv. 1, fol. 249.
[3] Tassara to Thugut, 29 May 1794, *Staatenabteilungen, Schweiz, Berichte*, F. 193.

Meanwhile, Cardinal Migazzi and the Court Chancellery had been studying the confessions of the atheist cobblers, which showed clearly enough that it was the arguments of the 'Josephinian' preachers which had started them off on the spiritual road to atheism. Migazzi therefore suspended the Benedictines and proceeded to put the Vicar of Penzing into monastic confinement on 20 June.[1] Among the inhabitants of the capital this unlawful action provoked an outburst of indignation and criticism which brought Pergen out of his summer retirement to report personally on the situation.[2]

The incident helped to convince Pergen that the internal crisis had become sufficiently acute and the 'Jacobins' sufficiently influential to bring insurrection well within the bounds of practical possibility.[3] Rebellion was rife in the neighbouring countries, among the Poles and the Grisons. Jacobin 'conspiracies' were being brought to light in other capitals, in Turin, in Naples, in London.

In Vienna, therefore, the Minister of Police roused himself to another desperate effort to wrest from a reluctant Emperor the power to carry out precautionary arrests on a large scale:

The Lord preserve humanity and Your Majesty's subjects from the despotism of ministers and officials and from *lettres de cachet*. But between these and the due processes of the law there is a middle way, and this must be followed if public order and our whole system of government is not to be exposed to immediate danger. In this critical period, when dangerous ideas have gone to so many people's heads, cases arise for which no precedents can be found in the judicial records. Precisely in these cases it is always impossible to furnish sound legal proofs which would satisfy the professors, partly because witnesses . . . are reluctant to testify in public, and partly because the government itself must insist that certain sources of information which are known to Your Majesty, remain an official secret.

Pergen considered that the British government, which

---

[1] *Erzbischöfl. Ordinariatsarchiv, Regesten*, No. 789.
[2] Au. Noten Pergens, 23 and 24 June 1794, *Kabinettsprotokoll*, 1794/783, 802.
[3] Cf. Geheime Anzeige Degens, 8 July 1794, *Vertr. Akten*, F. 8 (Riedel), fols. 39–44.

had just suspended *Habeas Corpus*, had thereby provided him with a most effective argument:

> At all times, even under the mildest governments, cases involving the security of the State and of public order have been exempted from the rules of judicial formality, and even England, so jealous of its Constitution, has recently departed from constitutional procedure and has taken measures appropriate to the requirements of the present situation.
>
> If [the criminals] are to be brought into the dock only when their crimes can be legally proven, then it is only too likely that the catastrophe will be upon us when the case opens, and that our provinces will be in a state of revolt. It is the first duty of a properly constituted police not to allow crimes to mature. The police must therefore be endowed with the powers necessary to fulfil this great duty. . . .[1]

Francis again refused to make a definite decision on this question, and sent Pergen's Note (which contained a number of far-reaching proposals on other matters)[2] to the Council of State. Pergen knew that this step precluded an early decision on his request and made a favourable decision at a later date at least unlikely.

As soon as the failure of Pergen's bid for wider powers of arrest had become clear, Saurau resorted to an alternative method of securing the arrest of the leading 'Jacobins', for which, we must presume, he had secured Pergen's approval.

Since May 1794 Saurau had been receiving the bulk of his information on the Viennese 'Jacobins' from the book-seller Joseph Vinzenz Degen, a former business partner of Alois Blumauer, who had long frequented some of the democratic gatherings.[3] On 27 June, i.e. four days after the submission of Pergen's last Note, Saurau revealed to Francis the identity of his informer and the nature of his information. The purpose of Saurau's Note, written in his own hand, was to secure endorsement for the informer's request that he be never called upon to testify in public against those whom he was denouncing, lest his business suffer as a result. He did not hesitate to recommend that this request be granted, be-cause his spy's information would be such as to render his

---

[1] Au. Note Pergens, 23 June 1794, *Polizeihofstelle*, 1794/1004.
[2] These proposals are discussed in the last chapter.
[3] *Vertr. Akten*, F. 8 (Riedel), fols. 27–44.

own testimony quite superfluous. Saurau's words reflect an
assured confidence as to the possibility of soon procuring
legally adequate evidence, a confidence which strangely contrasts with the doubts on this point expressed by Pergen only
four days earlier: 'Your Majesty may be assured that the
police will do all in its power to track down all dangerous
plots and to collect such evidence as will prove their existence beyond a shadow of doubt, and thus provide the
grounds for the arrest of the ringleaders.'[1]   Unfortunately
the economical wording of Francis's endorsement gives us
little indication of the extent to which he was aware of the
intentions of his Deputy Minister of Police.[2]

The records reveal very clearly the grounds for Saurau's
confidence. He had, in fact, lighted upon the perfect solution
to the difficulties created for the police by the champions of
the rule of law and the legal rights of citizens. But we must
let Saurau's agent speak for himself. On 20 July Degen sent
in the following account of his day's work:

As a result of my arrangement with Jellenay[3] that we should intro-
duce to one another our respective acquaintances, he brought a certain
Willek[4] and Franzl to my flat to-day. At first this revolutionary trio
seemed to consider my flat a little too elegant for a genuine *sans-culotte*,
but after I had made some sarcastic remarks about those who live in
even better quarters, they were prepared to do justice to my principles.

When I had succeeded in getting them into a mood . . . favourable
to my designs, I put before them my plan which will, I trust, meet
with Your Excellency's approval, since I flatter myself that it is calculated to achieve the twin aims of gaining the confidence of these
people and enabling Your Excellency to get a view of the plot . . . in
all its ramifications. As I had from the beginning displayed a timid
attitude towards these people in order to ward off any possible suspicion, I began the presentation of my project in a similar spirit.

'The unexpected victories of the French (I said), the strong revolutionary inclination among the younger generation, the intensification
of police supervision which is putting many of us into an ever more
hazardous situation . . .—all this makes it necessary for those who have

---

[1] *Pergen Akten*, x/B1, H48.

[2] *Kabinettsprotokoll*, 1794/814: 'Ich genehmige Ihr Einrathen u. erwarte über den
Erfolg dieser Anstalten die weiteren Anzeigen.'

[3] Should read: Jelline; cf. *supra*, p. 136.

[4] Should read: Billek; a member of Riedel's circle.

come together on the basis of their common outlook, to enter into a closer union. In such a union we should become aware of our numerical strength, . . . while the resulting concentration of forces would create new opportunities of action. Since, however, the now necessary circumspection precludes gatherings on a large scale, it will be necessary to meet in groups of five. Each suburb would have its own group. The same would apply to the provinces, except that the numbers and the distances involved will necessitate further sub-division. This means that they would also have to have a representative committee in the Capital, which would be qualified on account of its affiliations to fulfil the functions of a central committee. The suburban committees would set up their own central committee, and the whole organisation would then be placed under the direction of a supreme central committee. . . .'

As a suitable member of this supreme committee I proposed Riedel, who would certainly be able to suggest some other prominent persons qualified to assume leadership. . . . Jellenay agreed to report our discussion to Riedel and Hebenstreit.[1]

Degen's provocation immediately produced the desired result. Already the next day he was able to write to Saurau triumphantly:

My plan has done the trick. Hebenstreit has asked me to meet him in the Brigittenau to-day. Your Excellency will not fail to appreciate how strongly this confirms my assertion that nothing is easier than to stir up trouble in the provinces and even in the Capital with a little money and some *esprit d'intrigue*.[2]

Thus, on the evening of 21 July 1794, Hebenstreit came together with Degen in the *Augarten* to discuss revolutionary tactics. Jelline was there (the second witness required by the Law), but Hebenstreit did most of the talking. The following day, Degen wrote a full report of the discussion for Saurau:

Jellenay has talked to Jutz[3] about my plan for setting up committees. The latter has rejected it as premature and too dangerous. He maintains that for the present only propaganda work was practicable; the rest would follow of itself as a result of the increasing internal tension and the victories of the French.

Hebenstreit's opinion . . . is altogether different. He maintained that public opinion was prepared already, because every journeyman and

---

[1] *Vertr. Akten*, F. 8 (Riedel), fols. 45–47.   [2] Ibid., fol. 48.

[3] A member of Wollstein's circle; cf. *supra*, p. 135.

labourer was conscious of the fact that throughout the monarchy those who work have nothing, while those who do nothing live in plenty. What was needed was not enlightened but rather energetic people. . . . It was necessary to go to work without very elaborate preparations. A central committee directed by prominent people was not much use. . . . Organisation and propaganda in the provinces was dangerous and useless for the time being. First there must take place a *coup d'éclat* in the Capital, then the provinces would follow suit automatically. Only in Prague it should be arranged that the rising breaks at the same time as in the Capital. . . .

He knew most of the existing democratic groups, but did not think that any of them were capable of organising the *fait d'éclat* on which everything depended; they could only be of use afterwards. . . . He was trying to organise a more appropriate association consisting of students who would have to go to the more popular inns, try to make contact with the journeymen and labourers, draw them into useful discussions . . ., and ask them what they were prepared to do in case of a rebellion. . . . The most that associations consisting of our sort of people could hope to do was to collect money to enable such drinking apostles to devote themselves to their business of seduction.

As to the organisation (of such a *coup d'éclat*), he had the following plan. Altogether only some three and a half thousand energetic (*handveste*) people were needed. These would have to assemble under fourteen reliable leaders—he himself would be inclined to chose military persons—at a number of distant places where sharpened iron bars, pikes, clubs and forks had been buried for this purpose. From there they would have to advance on the city at an appointed time during the night, overwhelm the sentries, confine and besiege the fuseliers of the garrison in their barracks (he hoped for active co-operation on the part of the cavalry and especially the artillery), seize the treasury, kill more than three hundred aristocrats with their retinue, lay hold of the person of His Majesty the Emperor, compel him to sign a few dozen *cartes blanches*, and then —— him too. The next day proclamations would have to be issued to the people, a provisional government set up, and deputies from the provinces summoned in the Emperor's name to a people's assembly. . . . One of these proclamations would have to effect the total abolition of feudal dues from peasants to landlords or to the former sovereign. . . . In justice to Jellenay I am bound to mention that he expressed to me his horror at Hebenstreit's murderous plan. He much prefers my plan for associations. I got him to sound Baron Riedel on it and am expecting his report. . . . Your Excellency will see . . . how easy it is to lead these people on to any length you may wish, and that it will not be too difficult to secure legal proofs, should it be deemed advisable to make criminals. . . . In case Hebenstreit should become involved in something more than a purely political investigation and moral considerations should enter into it, I must for truth's sake further add that he had consumed a whole mug of beer before our conversation.[1]

Degen evidently considered that the criminals were as yet not quite 'made', and that the process of manufacture was to continue. Saurau, however, had decided that in view of the state of public opinion, the arrest of the 'Jacobins' brooked no further delay.[2] He therefore preferred to take it that his *agent provocateur* had put an adequate *rationem capturae* into his hands—beer or no beer. On 24 July Hebenstreit and his closest associates were arrested.[3] Saurau would see to it that adequate convictions followed. Meantime it was a relief to think that the popular agitation for peace had lost its spearhead.

[1] *Vertr. Akten*, F. 8 (Riedel), fols. 49–54.
[2] Cf. Fraknói's summary of the Au. Note Sauraus, 21 July 1794, *Széchényi Kvt.* (*Budapest*), *Ms. Fol. Germ.* 1071. The original Note is lost.
[3] *Kabinettsprotokoll*, 1794/968.

V

THE JACOBIN TRIALS

1. *The Preliminary Investigation—Further Arrests*

IN accordance with Count Saurau's advice, Francis appointed a special commission immediately after the arrests to conduct the preliminary investigation. This commission (the *Untersuchungshofkommission*) was to consist of representatives of the Judiciary and the Ministry of Police, and was to meet under the presidency of Saurau himself. As persons of military status and later also numerous Hungarians were among the arrested, a representative of the War Council and two councillors from the Hungarian Court Chancellery were added to the commission.[1]

The existence of the Hungarian 'conspiracy' was revealed to the police only as a result of this investigation. Martinovics had been arrested as a frequenter of the compromised Viennese groups,[2] but mistakenly concluded from his arrest that all had been discovered. Consequently he soon confessed and gave the police their first information of his secret societies.[3] This led to the arrest of all his collaborators in Hungary, as well as to that of his former partner Gotthardi whom he had let into his secret.

By comparison, the investigation of the Austrian prisoners yielded little that was entirely new to the police. The investigators, guided by Schilling, discovered all those who had been in any way concerned in Held's journey to Paris; they eventually induced Riedel to confess to the authorship of the 'Call to the German Nation';[4] and they found that among the accused there were, in fact, the authors of a considerable

[1] Au. Note Sauraus, 24 July 1794, *Kabinettsprotokoll*, 1794/968; Ah. Handbillet an Wallis, 25 July 1794, *Kriegsarchiv, Hofkriegsrat*, 1794/44/407; Ah. Handbillet an Clary, 25 July 1794, *Handbillettenprotokoll*, 1794/399; Ah. Handbillet an Pálffy, 21 Aug. 1794, ibid. 1794/428.

[2] Cf. the extract of the Au. Note Sauraus, 21 July 1794, which appears as document No. 1 in Benda's publication, II, p. 25.

[3] Francis II to Palatin, 14 Aug. 1794, Mályusz, p. 704.

[4] *Supra*, p. 117; Franz Xaver Pauer had been wrongfully convicted of its authorship: cf. *Vertr. Akten*, F. 3.

proportion of the seditious leaflets, poems, and songs whose wide circulation had been the source of so much anxiety for the police in recent years.[1] As in the case of Martinovics, the evidence given incriminated a considerable number of people of whose complicity the police had been unaware, and thus led to a number of further arrests in the course of August and September 1794.

Count Pergen and his deputy were particularly anxious to discover the identity of the participants in the Brühl oath-taking ceremony, which Degen had been unable to ascertain.[2] For there was reason to believe that this might make possible the arrest of some of the Styrian democrats for which Pergen was now pressing very insistently, in view of the discontent which was still openly expressed in their province. Their capacity for doing harm was, in Pergen's view, very considerable 'because their official positions and their popularity make them very influential and they can easily exploit this influence to disseminate their pernicious principles among the people'.[3]

The governor of Styria, Count Welsperg, had hitherto consistently declined to proceed with arrests on the grounds that the data supplied by the various informers were too vague and would have to be supplemented before any action could be taken.[4]

At length, the desired opportunity came. There were a number of people whom the commission suspected of having participated in the oath-taking ceremony; among them was a young landscape-painter called Laurenz Schönberger. Saurau thought it might be possible, as he put it, 'to exploit Schönberger's youth and lack of experience with a view to inducing him to make a full confession by the promise of immunity'.[5]

Whatever the nature of the methods indicated in this

[1] It seems that the reports of Saurau's investigating commission for the year 1794 were destroyed in the fire of 1927. I have therefore had to infer from the depositions and confessions in *Vertr. Akten*, FF. 1–32, what was new to the police and what was already known.
[2] *Vertr. Akten*, F. 8 (Riedel), fol. 53.
[3] Pergen to Welsperg, 6 Jan. 1795 (draft), *Polizeihofstelle, Ältere Polizei-Akten,* ii/2, H3.   [4] Welsperg to Pergen, 14 Jan. 1795, ibid. H5.
[5] Sitzungsprotokoll der Untersuchungshofkommission (? 23) Mar. 1795, ibid. H11.

laconic description, they had the desired effect: Schönberger confessed and named all the participants. Those who lived in Vienna were immediately arrested, while a police commissary was sent off to Styria to effect the arrest of the two Styrian burgher deputies who had joined in the ceremony, Dirnböck and Wipplinger. Dirnböck, the former champion of the Styrian peasants, lost his head and turned King's evidence, incriminating three of his friends, who were promptly arrested.[1] Among the latter was Wenninger, Mayor of Knittelfeld and burghers' deputy in the diet, one of the leaders of the movement which had won for the Styrian burghers the right to representation.

In the course of its work, Saurau's commission got together an indictment against nearly all of those who had been arrested. Minor details apart, the following offences made up the bulk of the indictments:

1. Offences committed as a result of Degen's provocation—i.e. the preliminary planning of a revolt (Hebenstreit, Jelline, Billek, Franzl).
2. The dispatch of a model of Hebenstreit's war-machine to France (Hebenstreit, Riedel, Prandstätter, Jutz).
3. The illegal oath-taking ceremony in the Brühl (Menz, Müller, Schedel, Dirnböck, Wipplinger).
4. The sign of mutual recognition to be used by the democrats (Riedel, Hebenstreit).
5. The dissemination of seditious books, leaflets, pamphlets, songs, &c. (Gilovsky, Riedel, Hebenstreit, Prandstätter, Müller, Jelline, Ruszitska, Troll, Gotthardi, Hackl, Dirnböck, Wenninger).
6. Aiding and abetting[2] (Hackl, Gotthardi, Troll, Prandstätter, Wenninger, Stegmüller, and, to some extent, nearly all the accused).[3]

2. The Trials

By the beginning of October 1794 the preliminary in-

[1] Ibid. H 18; Sitzungsprotokoll, 8 Apr. 1795, ibid. H38.
[2] This category includes *Mitwissenschaft*, i.e. mere knowledge of illegal activities if it was not followed by denunciation.
[3] In the absence of the commission's reports of 1794, I have again had to infer from the depositions and confessions; the indictment against those arrested after Jan. 1795 is contained in the Au. Vortrag Sauraus, 24 June 1794, *Polizeihofstelle, Ältere Polizei-Akten*, ii/2, H58.

vestigations of those arrested between July and September were nearing completion. The next step was to decide what was to be done with the accused in the light of the findings of Count Saurau's commission. It seems that no one entertained much doubt as to what was to be done with the Hungarian prisoners. The Emperor, the Palatin, and Count Saurau all feared that any attempt to deprive the regular Hungarian courts of their jurisdiction in this case would revive the flames of the nationalist fire of 1789–90, the embers of which were still glowing. Agreement was therefore quickly reached on the transfer of the Hungarian prisoners to the King's Court at Ofen after the completion of the preliminary investigations.[1] The transfer was effected towards the end of November, and the regular trials commenced a few weeks later.[2] Measures were taken to ensure that the documents passed through as few hands as possible.

The procedure to be followed with regard to the trial of the Austrian prisoners was not so quickly settled.[3] In staging the anti-Jacobin *coup*, Saurau's chief purpose was to impress public opinion, to intimidate the 'insolent critics'. Moreover, like Pergen, he objected to the idea of other government departments scrutinizing police records, particularly, one may surmise, records of the kind which provided the basis of the more serious indictments in this case. To let this case go through the inevitably slow processes of the law would serve neither the cause of intimidation nor that of secrecy, not to mention the risk of acquittals which such a procedure would entail. Therefore, having submitted the findings of his commission to the Emperor, Saurau went on to conclude that the exceptional importance of the case, and in particular the need for the utmost expedition and secrecy, made trial by the ordinary criminal courts inappropriate. Instead there should be set up a special *ad hoc* tribunal, a *judicium delega-*

[1] Palatin to Francis II, 3 Sept. 1794, Mályusz, No. 144; Au. Note Sauraus, 17 Sept. 1794, *Kabinettsprotokoll*, 1794/1999.　　　　[2] Benda, II, Nos. 24 ff.

[3] Huber's account of the trials (*Beiträge . . .*, pp. 224 ff.) is inaccurate. Most modern accounts, e.g. Bibl, *Der Zerfall Österreichs*, i. 79–83; W. C. Langsam, 'The Emperor Francis and the Austrian Jacobins', in *American Hist. Rev.* l (1945); L. Stern, 'Zum Prozess gegen die österreichische "Jakobinerverschwörung"', in *Maximilien Robespierre*, ed Markov, are based on Huber and other vague contemporary reminiscences, which have been inadequately checked against the sources.

tum cum derogatione omnium instantiarum, whose nucleus was to be the accusing *Untersuchungshofkommission*, and which was to be presided over by Count Clary, the President of the Supreme Judiciary.[1]

Significantly, it appears that Saurau did not propose that those whose profession put them under military law should be withdrawn from the jurisdiction of the military courts. This fact would seem to indicate that one purpose of his recommendation was to make possible the imposition of the death penalty which had been abolished for civilians (except under martial law) by the Josephinian Code of 1784.

Whatever may have been Saurau's intentions, the astounding fact is that Francis sanctioned his recommendation immediately and without prior consultation of the Council of State. Considering the gravity of the point at issue, this was a most extraordinary procedure and provides an impressive illustration of the enhanced influence of the Ministry of Police since the *Untersuchungshofkommission* had embarked on its labours. Saurau's Note is dated 1 October. On 2 October a Cabinet Order was sent to Clary with instructions to organize the special tribunal.[2]

The Habsburg monarchy was about to take a long stride towards the establishment of the police state. The implications of the introduction of trial by an all-powerful special tribunal were even more far-reaching than those of investing the Ministry of Police with the power of precautionary arrest. The Council of State had been effectively circumvented. As there is every reason to believe that Count Clary would have complied most readily with the Emperor's orders in this case,[3] the historian is bound to ask himself whether, but for an accident, October 1794 would have marked for Austria the final breach with the enlightened traditions of the *Rechtsstaat*.

The accident referred to was the absence of Count Clary

---

[1] Au. Note Sauraus, 1 Oct. 1794, *Kabinettsprotokoll*, 1794/1953. The Note itself is lost and we have only the brief summary in the register indicating Saurau's proposition. I have assumed that the wording of the subsequent Cabinet Order to Clary (*Vertr. Akten*, F. 33, fol. 27) is based on Saurau's formulations.

[2] *Vertr. Akten*, F. 33, fol. 27.

[3] Cf. his Au. Vortrag, 1 June 1795, *Vertr. Akten*, F. 152, fol. 239, in which he refers to the Order of 2 Oct. 1794 with warm approval.

who was away for a few days on his Bohemian estates when the Emperor's order for the establishment of the special tribunal arrived at the Supreme Judiciary. In Clary's absence, the order was opened by the Deputy President, Karl Anton Freiherr v. Martini, the veteran leader of the Austrian School of Natural Law.[1]

The order which Martini had just received represented a complete denial of all that he had taught and stood for throughout his life.[2] Only a few months before, he had submitted the first instalment of his codification of Austrian law.[3] And now he was to co-operate in a totally inexcusable breach of the law by his sovereign, whose first duty it was, in Martini's view, to uphold its integrity.

Martini refused to resign himself to the bitter reflection that the legal ideals of the Enlightenment had been but a convenience to the sovereigns of Austria, taken up for a time, only to be discarded when yesterday's conveniences had become the inconveniences of today. Accordingly he asked Francis whether he might set out in writing his thoughts concerning certain 'difficulties' to which the procedure envisaged would give rise. Francis consented.[4]

Martini's exposition of the 'difficulties' he had in mind constitutes a document which deserves to be widely known, both as an example of its author's courage and ideals and as a milestone in the constitutional history of Austria.

He objected to the procedure recommended by Saurau on five main counts:

1. Three of the men appointed to serve on the special tribunal lacked the qualifications prescribed by the law for all members of criminal courts.

2. The accused would have good cause to complain about the recommended procedure because 'even the greatest criminals have the right to claim the protection of the law which is going to inflict punishment on them, and to demand trial according to the regular judicial procedure'. Though the sovereign, as supreme law-giver, had the right to order

[1] Au. Anfrage Martinis, 2 Oct. 1794, *Vertr. Akten*, F. 152, fol. 300.
[2] *Supra*, pp. 19–20.
[3] Adler, p. 107.
[4] This is indicated by the opening sentences of Martini's memorandum quoted below.

exceptional measures in cases of emergency, such a departure from the due process of law 'must be presumed to
promote the general welfare, and must not be indulged in
to such an extent that someone is simply deprived of the
rights to which he is entitled'. Exceptional procedures for
which there was no apparent and urgent necessity impaired
the prestige of the law and left a most unfavourable impression on public opinion, as was shown by several examples
still fresh in the public memory.[1]

3. In all previous cases of *derogatio omnium instantiarum*,
the aim had been to ensure a more complete fulfilment of
the law. In this case, it would amount to nothing less than
a *derogatio legum*, because not only would the accused be
deprived of their lawful right of appeal but the trial would
not be subject to review by a superior court which was
prescribed by the law, even in cases of less serious crimes.
'What children expect from their father, subjects expect
from their ruler—a wise, well-considered, mature verdict.
It is the wish of every well-thinking citizen that the accused
should be declared innocent rather than guilty.'

4. In other countries, conspirators and traitors had recently been tried, and everywhere, in Naples, Piedmont,
Sweden, and England, they had been tried in accordance
with the ordinary processes of the law. In all these countries
the danger of rebellion was greater than in Austria. Against
this danger the law in any case provided the procedure of
martial law. 'Just and wise laws, which must be based on . . .
long experience, but which must also be scrupulously observed, are the strongest and safest pillars of the Throne.'

5. Even if a trial might be speeded up by confining it to
the judgement of a single court, it did not follow that the
competent courts could simply be passed over: the shortest
way was not always the best. There might well be delay in
the end, if some, or even one, of the accused should object
to condemnation by a single court and appeal for the protection to which he was entitled by the law. If any of the documents were to reach the Council of State, the councillors
would certainly recommend the observance of the ordinary

---

[1] This is probably a reference to Joseph II's violations of legality which have
been described in Chapter I.

procedure. In any case, it was not impossible to speed up the normal processes of the law. This could be done in numerous ways, and the possibility of unforeseen delays at a later stage would be forestalled. As to the need for secrecy, the minimum number of judges required by the ordinary procedure was in any case fairly small, and the judges could be reminded of the oath of secrecy by which they were all bound.[1]

Despite the growing influence of Saurau and the Ministry of Police, Francis II had not become completely impervious to this kind of advice. He sent Martini's Note to the Council of State, which unanimously endorsed the demand for justice, and submitted drafts for the appropriate orders to be dispatched to Clary and Saurau.[2] The Palatin, who added his opinion to those of the Councillors of State when he was in Vienna, also cast his vote in support of Martini and the observance of the law, especially because he had recently insisted that the Hungarian prisoners be handed over to the ordinary criminal courts.[3]

It was perhaps the most serious weakness of the Emperor Francis II at this time that he allowed himself to be strongly influenced by badly chosen advisers. In this case, however, we must pay tribute to the courage with which he acted after Martini, the Palatin, and the Council of State had succeeded in convincing him that he had been badly advised. He was prepared to swallow his words and to reverse the order he had issued less than three weeks earlier. On 21 October 1794, Clary and Saurau received orders which rendered null and void the respective orders they had received on 2 October.

Dear Count Clary,
    In order to give my subjects no grounds for anxiety, and to enhance the reputation which Austrian justice already enjoys abroad, I have decided . . . that the individuals who have been investigated for High Treason by Count Saurau . . . should be handed over to the Vienna Criminal Court together with all the relevant documents, records, statements, etc. There they are to be tried as speedily as possible, but in

---

[1] Au. Vortrag Martinis, 15 Oct. 1794, *Vertr. Akten*, F. 152, fols. 290-8. cf. Appendix.

[2] Au. Note Vogels, 19 Oct. 1794, concerning 3564 ex 1794, *Kaiser Franz Akten*, F. 94.

[3] Votum des Palatin concerning 3564 ex 1794, *Kaiser Franz Akten*, F. 91.

accordance with all the formalities prescribed by the law. The sentence is to be submitted to the Court of Appeal in conformity with the usual procedure and from there to the Supreme Judiciary. The secrecy essential in cases of this sort will have to be observed throughout. You will know what steps to take to put this order into effect.[1]

As far as can be ascertained, Count Saurau did not venture any comment on the Emperor's sudden change of mind concerning his recommendation. The first veiled protest came from Clary, the President of the Supreme Judiciary since 1792, the man who above all others should have been concerned with the scrupulous maintenance of the rule of law. But Clary preferred the original order of 2 October, and tried to secure at least a partial reversion to it. As in cases of high treason the final decision rested in any case with the Supreme Judiciary, he argued, the question of appeals to a higher court did not arise: the lower courts were not really imposing a sentence, but merely giving an advisory opinion. From this Clary concluded that it would be quite 'lawful' as well as conducive to speed and secrecy if the Court of Appeal sat in joint session with the Supreme Court in cases involving high treason.[2]

Francis referred Clary's proposal to the Council of State. The council severely censured Clary for his 'unlawful' suggestion, and took this opportunity of reaffirming emphatically their stand for full legality.[3] Adopting the draft resolution put forward by the council, Francis ordered that the cases be heard by the three courts, in quite separate session, 'in order to secure Austrian justice from all possible criticism and reproach'. The only concession won by Clary was the admission of two non-voting observers from the Ministry of Police to the sessions of the Supreme Judiciary dealing with the Jacobins.[4] When the Vienna Criminal Court was

[1] An Clary: *Vertr. Akten*, F. 33, fol. 29; an Saurau: *Staatsratsprotokoll*, 3564 ex 1794. The wording of these orders must be Eger's or Zinzendorf's.

[2] Au. Note Clarys, 5 Nov. 1794, *Vertr. Akten*, F. 152, fols. 280–2.

[3] Au. Note Vogels, 13 Nov. 1794, concerning 3816 ex 1794. A short extract of Zinzendorf's *Votum* is quoted by Bibl in *Zerfall Österreichs*, i. 398, n. 106, but Bibl was confused as to the point under consideration.

[4] *Staatsratsprotokoll*, 3816 ex 1794. The admission of the two observers is the only justification I can discover for the practice of giving a special name (*Hofkommission in Hochverratsangelegenheiten*) to the sessions of the Supreme Judiciary dealing with this case.

instructed to commence the trial, it was ordered to omit the usual entries in its registers, and to keep the records strictly apart from the rest.[1]

Meanwhile, a North German legal expert, Dr. Paulsen, had completed a long and elaborately argued treatise purporting to prove that it would be 'lawful' to impose capital punishment even on civilians convicted of high treason in an Austrian court, despite the fact that the criminal law as it then stood excluded it. On 1 November he sent the treatise to Pergen 'on His Majesty's orders'.[2]

In all probability this treatise had originally been intended to clear the way for the imposition of death penalties by the special tribunal envisaged by Saurau. Since Francis had reversed his original decision, consulted the Council of State, and made up his mind to observe the law, the ground had more or less disappeared from under Paulsen's feet. Inevitably, the treatise was now submitted to the Council of State, which recommended its reference to a joint commission of the Supreme Judiciary and the Commission on Legislation.[3]

In this way the treatise finally came into the hands of Martini, who was the President of the Commission on Legislation. He roundly condemned it as a 'legal monstrosity', both impudent in its pre-judgement of a case which was still *sub judice* and dangerous in its substitution of emotional for legal considerations. Martini asked the commission to conclude that

such perversions of the law, which are aimed at instilling into it a severity it does not possess . . . deserve not only no consideration but rather punishment, especially at a time when the political mood of the nations enjoins the utmost care to keep a Sovereign, beloved of his people, free from the hateful reproach of . . . a severity exceeding the bounds of the law, a severity which is closely akin to despotism and which would altogether forfeit the affection of the people. . . .

Martini's exposure of Paulsen's preposterous legal fallacies was incontrovertible and was adopted by the joint commission as the basis of its own report. Only the demand for Paulsen's punishment was omitted. The cause of the

---

[1] *Vertr. Akten*, F. 152, fol. 264.   [2] Ibid., fols. 220–7.
[3] Au. Note Vogels, 13 Nov. 1794, concerning 3817 ex 1794. Only Eger voted for outright rejection.

treatise was irretrievably lost. Francis resolved that it was to be put *ad acta*.[1]

When we consider Martini's stand on the question of the special tribunal and the irregular imposition of capital punishment, we may well be tempted to conclude that some of those who were arrested as Jacobins in 1794 and 1795 owed their lives to the principles of natural law and to the courage with which Martini was prepared to champion these principles.

Neither, of course, could save the lives of those whose nationality put them within the jurisdiction of the Hungarian courts or whose profession within that of military law. For capital punishment had been reintroduced in Hungary in 1793; in military law it had never been abolished. The consideration of the consequent inequality of treatment as between the various groups of prisoners had been adduced by Paulsen in support of his argument. It induced the President of the War Council, Count Wallis, to embark on what was to be the last attempt to secure the imposition of death sentences on the civilian prisoners.

Lieutenant Hebenstreit had not been the worst offender, Wallis argued, yet he was to suffer the worst punishment. Death sentences could undoubtedly be imposed on some of the other Jacobins, since crimes so pernicious and universal as theirs were clearly not envisaged in the Criminal Law of 1784. New crimes demanded new punishments. Had not the Ancient Greeks punished patricide, though the crime was unknown to their code when first committed?[2]

Martini's words were too fresh in the Emperor's mind when Wallis's proposal reached him for the argument therein propounded to make much impression. It was sent back with the rejoinder which it undoubtedly deserved—a curt order to its author to mind his own business.[3]

---

[1] Au. Vortrag Clarys u. Martinis, 27 Nov. 1794, and Ah. Resolution, *Vertr. Akten*, F. 152, fols. 190–205. Bibl is, of course, quite wrong in his assertion that capital punishment was inflicted retrospectively on anyone.

[2] Au. Vortrag Wallis', 24 Dec. 1794 (draft), *Kriegsarchiv, Hofkriegsrat*, 1794/ 62/2240. Wallis was writing after the military court had passed sentence of death on Hebenstreit.

[3] Ah. Handbillet an Wallis, 2 Jan. 1795, *Handbillettenprotokoll*, 1795/5: '. . . nur aber finde ich zu erinnern, daß es mir zum Wohlgefallen gereicht, wenn sich jede

This much, then, was settled: the accused Jacobins were
to be tried and sentenced in accordance with the normal legal
procedure laid down in the criminal law as codified in 1784.
We must not conclude from this, however, that they were
accorded a trial which could be described as fair by present-
day standards. The confinement of the prisoners seems to
have been very harsh despite the Leopoldine regulation that
anyone not convicted of a crime was to be treated with
leniency. The prisoners themselves frequently referred to the
rigours of their confinement, and the justice of their complaints is borne out by their investigators' frequent references
to a state of 'deep depression and bitter remorse' among the
accused. One of the prisoners (Gotthardi) died soon after his
conviction, and another (Wenninger) went insane while still
under investigation.[1] Though special circumstances contributed to this tragic issue in both cases, neither throws a
very favourable light on the general conduct of the trials.

This was the more serious in view of the fact that the
accused had to defend themselves as best they could, and did
not enjoy the services of defence counsel. It was obviously
the tactics of the investigating commissioners to wear down
the moral resistance of the accused, though in theory it was
their duty to elicit equally and fairly the evidence for and
against them. The *Referat* submitted to the court had to
cover the case for the defence as well as that for the prosecution.

Only if we bear this in mind will we be able to appreciate
the significance of Count Clary's order that the two magistrates who had been appointed to the *Untersuchungshofkommission* and who had conducted most of the preliminary
investigation on its behalf, should be among the four magistrates who were to constitute the criminal court, and
should, as far as possible, conduct the criminal investigation.[2]
The result was that there was little to distinguish the pre-

Behörde nur mit in den in ihren Wirkungskreise einschlagenden Angelegenheiten
beschäftiget . . . .'

[1] Au. Note Sauraus, 13 July 1795, *Staatskanzlei, Informationsbureau, Polizeiber.,*
F. 4, Konv. 1, fol. 159; Au. Note Pergens, 5 Nov. 1796, *Polizeihofstelle, Ältere
Polizeiakten,* ii/2, H141.

[2] *Vertr. Akten,* F. 152, fol. 264. A corresponding order was issued to the Court of
Appeal: ibid. F. 19, fol. 5.

liminary investigation from the criminal investigation—the latter was but a continuation of the former;[1] the prosecution held the entire field.

However, this procedure, too, was challenged by someone reared in the legal traditions of the Enlightenment, someone occupying a less exalted position than that of Martini. He was, in fact, one of the accused—the lawyer Dr. Jakob Ignaz Jutz.

Fully versed in the intricacies of the law, Jutz knew his rights and, moreover, had the moral courage to claim those which he felt had been denied him. Above all, Jutz demanded different investigating commissioners so as not to be judged by his accusers.[2] In its comments on the petition, the Supreme Judiciary could not find much to say in defence of its President's action. While claiming that the extraordinary procedure had been 'necessary', it agreed that on the whole one should not depart from the rules 'more than was necessary'. It declared itself ready to appoint different investigating commissioners and to remove all police personnel, 'lest the impression be given that a political control was being exercised over these criminal proceedings'. Francis accepted this and ordered that the magistrates who had conducted the preliminary investigation should not be employed in the criminal proceedings.[3]

Jutz's courageous action did a great deal to make the subsequent criminal investigations fairer to the accused than they would otherwise have been. They began with a clean slate and did not, like the earlier ones, merely continue where the preliminary investigation had left off. Unfortunately Jutz's action came too late to affect the most important cases, which had reached or were about to reach the concluding stages by the time the Supreme Judiciary felt impelled to mend its ways.

---

[1] In all the earlier cases there is only one *Verhörsprotokoll*, which covers both the preliminary and the criminal investigation. The latter simply continued where the former had left off.

[2] Petition to the Criminal Court, 9 May 1795, *Vertr. Akten*, F. 9, fols. 245–6; memorandum to the Supreme Judiciary, 14 May 1795, ibid., fols. 249–52.

[3] Au. Vortrag Clarys, 1 Aug. 1795, and Ah. Resolution, *Vertr. Akten*, F. 9, fols. 347–8.

3. *The Convictions*

The indictments submitted by the *Untersuchungshofkommission* were upheld by the Vienna Criminal Court whose verdicts were, in the main, confirmed by the Court of Appeal and the Supreme Judiciary. The military tribunal, too, found the charges of the police proven. Most of the accused were found guilty of lese-majesty and high treason under the Criminal Code of 1784.

The military tribunal was the first to complete its work. It sentenced Gilovsky and Hebenstreit to death by hanging. As the former had committed suicide during the preliminary investigations, the prescribed execution was carried out on his corpse. Hebenstreit mounted the scaffold on 8 January 1795.[1] According to the Styrian democrats who had not yet been arrested at this time, his dying words were: '*Solventur vincula populi*'.[2] Captain Billek[3] was sentenced to 10 years *Festungsarrest mit Eisen*.[4] Professor Wollstein was let off with the five months imprisonment he had already undergone at the time of conviction. Among the reasons put forward for this unusually light sentence was the consideration that 'the State would be the greatest loser if he should be removed from his post, especially because so much has been spent on his training'.[5]

The Hungarian courts sentenced 18 of the accused to death and 16 to various terms of imprisonment. Seven of the death sentences were carried out: Martinovics and his four 'directors' were executed on 20 May 1795, and two lawyers a little later. The other death sentences were commuted by Francis II to imprisonment for an indefinite period.[6]

Before making a final decision on the sentences imposed on the Austrian civilian prisoners, Francis referred the cases to the Council of State. He ordered, however, that the records should not be deposited in the Council's archives,

[1] *Kriegsarchiv, Hofkriegsrat,* 1794/62/2339; *Kabinettsprotokoll,* 1795/23.
[2] *Vertr. Akten,* F. 29, fol. 278; according to another tradition they were 'Vincula sol ventur. Valete.'
[3] Brother of the Billek mentioned in Degen's report, *supra,* p. 149.
[4] *Kriegsarchiv, Hofkriegsrat,* 1794/62/2239, fols. 20–26.
[5] Ibid., fols. 39–40.
[6] Benda, 'Die ungarischen Jakobiner', p. 470. The date of Martinovics' execution is here wrongly given as 20 June.

but returned to the Cabinet, and that the case of Riedel and those closely connected with it should be witheld from Councillor Eger, who had himself been dangerously implicated by Riedel's evidence.[1]

Count Zinzendorf alone seems to have raised his voice in protest against the manner in which the police had 'made criminals'. He denounced Degen's provocation as 'an abuse of the secret police which should not be regarded with indifference', and dismissed Schilling's justfication of it as quite unconvicing. The 'unpleasant, declamatory style' and 'insulting expressions' employed by the Supreme Judiciary in its judgements were intolerable in a court whose duty it was to be 'as cold as a code'.[2] In the case of Riedel, Zinzendorf considered that the seriousness of the crimes had been grossly exaggerated, and recommended a reduction of the sentence.[3]

He pleaded in vain. Riedel was sentenced to 60 years *langwierig schweren Festungsarrest*, Gotthardi and Ruzsitska to 35 years, Jelline, Prandstätter, Leopold Billek, Hackl, Menz, Müller, and Dirnböck to 30 years, and Schedel to 20 years.[4] Lighter sentences of *zeitlich gelinden Arrest* were passed on Jutz, Troll, Franzl, and Wipplinger. Wenninger, who had lost his sanity during the trial, and five others were acquitted.

---

[1] Note Vogels, 9 July 1795, *Kaiser Franz Akten*, F. 95. Riedel had said in evidence that Eger had expressed approval of Hebenstreit's *Homo Hominibus (Vertr. Akten*, F. 8 (Riedel), fol. 301).

[2] *Vertr. Akten*, F. 33, fol. 152.

[3] Ibid., fols. 118–20.

[4] The fortress in their case was Munkács about which the Ministry of Police made the following official declaration: 'Die für Staatsverbrecher bestimmte Festung Munkács wäre vermöge ihrer phisischen (sic!) Lage von der Art, daß die dahin Verurtheilten ihrem Lebensende bald entgegensehen.' (*Vertr. Akten*, F. 24, fol. 429.)

THE CONSEQUENCES OF THE TRIALS

1. Enhanced Prestige and Influence of the Ministry of Police

DESPITE Saurau's failure to secure trial by special tribunal for the Austrian 'Jacobins', the episode as a whole resulted in a marked increase in the prestige and influence of his department. There is no doubt that the evidence elicited by the investigating commissioners made Francis II feel that he owed a great debt of gratitude to Pergen, Saurau, and their subordinates. He sanctioned without hesitation whatever Pergen recommended as suitable rewards.

Degen, whose provocation had made the trials possible, was granted handsome financial compensation for 'loss of business' suffered as a result of public suspicion concerning his activities. Eventually he was appointed an official publisher to the Imperial Court, and to this day a street in Vienna is named after him.[1]

Ratoliska and Bannwarth, who had carried out most of the shadowing and the arrests, were promoted to the status of *Regierungssekretär*. Schilling, who had drafted the questions of the preliminary investigation and elicited most of the important confessions, became *wirklicher Hofrat* with a rise in salary of 1,000 florins a year.[2]

Saurau himself was appointed governor of Lower Austria while retaining his position in the Ministry of Police. Count Sauer, whom he replaced, was not offered another appointment, and had to go into retirement. Saurau's services in the Ministry of Police were specifically mentioned among the reasons for his promotion.[3] The wheel had indeed come full circle. Leopold II had subordinated the police to the civil government; now the latter became a department of the Ministry of Police.

[1] *Pergen Akten*, viii/12, H1-7.
[2] *Handbillettenprotokoll*, 1795/25; ibid. 1794/548; *Pergen Akten*, xix, H11.
[3] Hofdekret an Saurau, 23 Aug. 1795, *Steierm. Landesarchiv, Ständ. Archiv, Nachlaß Saurau*, 60/666.

2. *Genesis of the Vormärz*

The opponents of enlightened despotism among the Emperor's advisers had long been proclaiming the close connexion between reforms and revolution, and had pointed to France as the classic illustration of their case. The trial of the Austrian 'Jacobins' supplied them with evidence nearer home. Anger and disappointment at the abandonment of enlightened despotism had led some of its adherents into 'subversive' paths. Enthusiasm for the levelling reforms of Joseph II had in most cases been the origin of the political radicalism of 1794. Some of the accused themselves emphasized this fact in the hope that it would serve as an excuse in the eyes of their judges. Thus we read in Jelline's defence: 'The Enlightened reforms of the Emperor Joseph kindled a blazing fire in me; I devoured the Enlightened political literature with insatiable avidity, and my opinions became more and more republican.'[1]

Could there be a more unequivocal confirmation of the long-standing prophecies of Cardinal Migazzi and the anti-Enlightenment party? Clearly it was high time not only to abandon further reform (that had been secured in 1792) but to turn back the clock and undo the dangerous work of enlightened despotism.

The laborious effort of dismantling the edifice of enlightened reform makes up the internal history of the Habsburg dominions in the decade following the Jacobin trials. The 'argument from the trials' was the decisive factor in bringing about the victory of the anti-Enlightenment party in nearly every field of government policy.

(i) *Amendment of the criminal law*

The reintroduction of capital punishment for high treason had its origin in one of the minor investigations into 'Jacobin' activities in 1794—that of four members of the Rovereto garrison, which ended when the major investigations were just beginning. Summing up this investigation, early in August 1794, the President of the Supreme Judiciary, Count Clary, concluded that the existing critical

[1] *Vertr. Akten*, F. 7, fol. 502.

situation of the monarchy made capital punishment for high treason essential, if views such as those expressed by the convicted soldiers were not to create a revolutionary danger; it was better for a few hundred to die than for thousands to run the risk of losing property and life.[1] Clary's view was supported by Count Kollowrat, and Francis sanctioned the setting up of a joint commission, representing the Supreme Judiciary, the Court Chancellery, and the Commission on Legislation, to draft an appropriate law.[2] After approval by the Council of State, the draft was entrusted to Sonnenfels for final editing. Though the latter was under explicit instruction to confine his comments and suggestions to matters of style, he submitted to the joint commission a number of substantial objections, the most important of which was to the provision by which the children of offenders were to be penalized through the total confiscation of the offender's estate. Sonnenfels's objection was upheld by a small majority in the joint commission, and though supported only by Count Zinzendorf in the Council of State, sustained by the Emperor.[3] The new law was promulgated in January 1795.

Apart from its main provision, it introduced a number of other important changes. Failure to report cases of high treason to the police or some other appropriate authority was to be punished by lifelong penal servitude. In the paragraph dealing with the offence of high treason, secret societies were for the first time officially associated with this concept. The last paragraph introduced an important new concept into the criminal law, that of 'impudent criticism' (*frecher Tadel*): 'He who purposely stirs up discontent against the government by impudent criticism in public, whether in speech, writing, or any other form, is to be regarded as a criminal offender against internal peace and to be sentenced to from five to ten years' imprisonment.'[4]

(ii) *Censorship surrendered to the police*

Clearly, this new criminal law was a far more effective

[1] Clary to Kollowrat, 11 Aug. 1794, *Hofkanzlei*, IV M 3, Tirol, 52 ex Sept. 1794.

[2] Au. Vortrag Kollowrats, 22 Aug. 1794; Ah. Handbillet an Kollowrat, 2 Nov. 1794, ibid. 3 ex Jan. 1795.

[3] Au. Note Vogels, 28 Dec. 1794, concerning 4350 ex 1794, *Kaiser Franz Akten*, F. 94.   [4] Ibid.

weapon for the suppression of freedom of speech, writing, and association than any new regulations dealing with censorship or freemasonry could have been. All the same, such new regulations were introduced to complete the repressive system. In June 1795 an order went out to close all surviving masonic lodges.[1] Existing censorship regulations were tightened up to eliminate loopholes, and were interpreted and applied with increasing severity.[2]

The continued appearance of prohibited or seditious literature despite the stricter regulations was a source of great anxiety to ministers, and by 1796 Clary had joined Pergen in urging that the entire censorship administration should be taken over by the Ministry of Police.

> Our Police safeguard our physical health, and I do not think that I am taking excessive liberties if I lay at Your Majesty's feet my humble suggestion that the Secret Police, this essential pillar of the Throne and of our general security, should be entrusted with the task of looking after the spiritual and moral welfare of our citizens, too.[3]

In 1801 Clary's humble suggestion, which was also one of Pergen's dearest ambitions, became the law of the land, and the Ministry of Police became the Ministry of Police and Censorship.[4] Its handling of the new task, however, did credit neither to itself nor to the country.

(iii) *Economic restrictionism*

Enlightened despotism fostered economic development because a strong state required the resources which only an expanding economy could provide. Questions of 'internal security' were not really considered in this connexion. However, by June 1794 Pergen had come to the firm conclusion that economic development, particularly if concentrated in the capital, was incompatible with the maintenance of internal security.[5] Economic questions were very far from being within the jurisdiction of his ministry, but Pergen felt

---

[1] Ah. Handbillet an Palffy u. Rottenhan, 9 June 1795, *Staatsratsprotokoll*, 1883 ex 1795.

[2] *Steierm. Landesarchiv, Gubernialakten*, F. 40, 4484 ex 1795.

[3] Au. Vortrag Clarys (Mossbach's draft), 23 Feb. 1796, *Vertr. Akten*, F. 152, fols. 138–41.   [4] Oberhummer, i. 176.

[5] Au. Note Pergens, 23 June 1794, *Polizeihofstelle*, 1794/1004.

compelled to point out that an expanding town population represented a constant source of danger to the stability of the State. He therefore urged that immediate steps be taken to reduce the swollen population of the capital, both by reversing the accepted economic policies which had attracted a 'wrong, unstable' type of person, and by expelling all foreigners who were not following a regular trade.

Pergen's note was submitted to the Court Chancellery. There it was decided after prolonged discussion, the details of which it would now be difficult to trace, to recommend action along the lines suggested by Pergen. The building of factories was to be restricted, especially in the capital. Magistrates were to revert to the policy of strictly limiting the number of journeymen entitled to become masters in their trade. Marriage was to be made more difficult for apprentices and journeymen in large towns. All foreigners not engaged in regular trade were to be expelled.

In the Council of State these drastic proposals were resisted only by Eger and Zinzendorf, both of whom believed in economic expansion and in *laissez-faire* as the best means of achieving it. Eger roundly condemned Pergen's thesis that an expanding economy and busy people represented a danger to internal security; frustration, unemployment, and poverty was in his opinion more likely to lead to such a danger.[1]

Ignoring this opposition, Francis sanctioned all the proposals of the Court Chancellery, which were then embodied in a decree dated 9 January 1795.[2] Apart from some temporary relaxations, it summed up the economic policy which the government tried to pursue up to 1848.[3] By embarking on this course, more than by anything else, the absolute monarchy in Austria signed its own death warrant. A state which sets its face against economic expansion at the behest of an over-anxious and self-important Ministry of Police is doomed, if only because the dreaded economic expansion cannot, in the long run, be prevented.

[1] Au. Note Vogels, 29 Dec. 1794, concerning 4072 ex 1794, *Kaiser Franz Akten*, F. 94.

[2] J. Slokar, *Geschichte der Österreichischen Industrie und ihrer Förderung unter Franz I* (1914: Vienna), p. 18.

[3] Ibid., pp. 21–126.

(iv) *Education and religion*

Joseph II's educational policies had long been a favourite target of the opponents of enlightened despotism. They strongly desired that education should once more be associated with the Catholic influence and traditions from which it had become divorced.[1] Plenty of arguments in support of this plea were found in the trials of 1794–5.

Pergen had already concluded from the investigation of the atheist cobblers and tailors that a new commission on education was urgently needed to revise the whole educational system. A note to this effect was referred to the Court Chancellery for consideration.[2]

While the question was still under discussion, powerful support for Pergen's demands came from Clary. The President of the Supreme Judiciary was setting down his own conclusions from the main trials, in which many graduates had been involved who had admittedly picked up their first radical ideas at the university. With passionate conviction Clary called for a new alliance between Church and State which would restore the Catholic religion to its former splendour and magnificence, and enable it to repair the grievous damage wrought on the minds of the Austrian people by the Enlightenment.[3]

A similar appeal came from the governor of the Tyrol, where 'Jacobin' activities had been discovered among students. And the solution suggested was the same—a reassertion of Catholic influence with regard to the choice of textbooks, the character of the curriculum, the selection of teachers, and the whole tenor of education generally.[4]

The case was stated in its most extreme form by the Palatin, whose views on government were undergoing a rapid and fundamental change as a result of Martinovics's revelations:

I am not convinced of the general usefulness of elementary schools ... for the peasants. In Hungary the education and enlightenment of

[1] Cf. Au. Note Kollowrats (draft), s.d. (*c.* Mar. 1790), *Nachlaß Kollowrat,* F. 13, No. 1169.   [2] Wolfsgruber, *Migazzi,* p. 824.
[3] Au. Vortrag Clarys, 17 July 1795, *Kaiser Franz Akten,* F. 80 (C).
[4] Au. Promemoria Waidmannsdorfs, 29 Sept. 1794, *Kaiser Franz Akten,* F. 85 (W).

the rural population seems to be a waste of effort, and is in any case liable to be dangerous and harmful in its consequences. Since it is the duty of the priests to instruct the peasants' children in . . . the duties of their station, it seems that in this country, where even small children are required to do . . . the lighter work in the fields, village schools are quite useless. . . .[1]

It would have required more boldness and self-confidence than Francis possessed to stand up to the combination of Pergen, Clary, Kollowrat, and the Palatin. The cause of enlightened education was hopelessly lost. Over two years' patient work by the Hungarian diet's Committee on Education was simply scrapped.[2] In Vienna, the new Commission on Education desired by Pergen was duly constituted under the significant title of *Studien-Revisionskommission*. Though its composition did not completely satisfy Cardinal Migazzi, its terms of reference were explicit enough. The Emperor wanted the new commission to work out an educational system which would produce 'well-behaved, religious and patriotic citizens', which, in his view, the existing system had failed to do. The presence on the commission of the Abbé Hofstätter, the leading intellectual of the anti-Enlightenment party, and of Hofrat Schilling, Pergen's faithful henchman, was sufficient guarantee that Francis and Migazzi would not be altogether dissatisfied with its labours.[3]

The records of the new Commission on Education still await detailed investigation. However, the general lines of its work are sufficiently clear. In 1806 we find Saurau himself complaining of the extent to which the clergy had recaptured control of the educational system.[4] But there was no return to a clerical monopoly in the old sense. Applications for teaching posts were soon to be sent for 'clearance' to the Ministry of Police.[5]

3. *In Defence of the Rule of Law*

Pergen's satisfaction with the new educational system was tempered by his anxiety about the 'subversive' influence still

[1] Memorandum, 16 Apr. 1795, Mályusz, No. 181, iii/9, p. 847.
[2] F. Eckhart, *A Short History of Hungary* (1931: London), pp. 145–7.
[3] Au. Vortrag Kollowrats, 8 Sept. 1795, *Kaiser Franz Akten*, F. 81 (K); Wolfsgruber, *Migazzi*, pp. 794–5.
[4] Bibl, *Der Zerfall Österreichs*, i. 146–7.   [5] Springer, i. 118.

being exercised by the teachers appointed under the old. As early as February 1793, after investigating a student riot in Prague, he had urged a general purge of teachers in schools and universities: 'Your Majesty should direct your attention to purifying the teaching profession throughout the hereditary provinces, and appoint to teaching posts only men whose attachment to monarchical government is beyond a shadow of doubt.'

Though Francis II had taken no action on Pergen's recommendation,[1] the demand for a purge of teachers and professors continued. There had been repeated protests from the Hungarian clergy and their supporters against Gottfried van Swieten's educational appointments in Hungary. One of the favourite targets of the clerical campaign was Professor Delling, who taught theology at Fünfkirchen according to Kantian principles, which were new and therefore unacceptable to the hierarchy.

In the spring of 1794 Delling's teaching was denounced to the Hungarian Court Chancellery on the basis of a manuscript handed to the authorities by one of his students. The Chancellery, wholly dominated by the Catholic party, found very dangerous implications in Kantian theology, and recommended Delling's dismissal, lest the young generation adopt principles whose consequences might well be detrimental to the security of the State.[2]

At the beginning of June 1794 the matter came before the Council of State. The perils of Kantian theology as described by the Hungarian Chancellery apparently so horrified Izdenczy and Eger that they gave their full approval to the proposed dismissal without for a moment considering its far-reaching implications.[3] Count Zinzendorf, on the other hand, had studied Kant, and could judge more coolly the real issues involved in the case. His opinion is worth quoting at length, for much was to follow from it:

I cannot help myself, but duty and conscience command me to state frankly that I can find in the report of the Chancellery nothing but passion, inconsequence, and the greatest injustice. Prof. Delling, whom

[1] Au. Note Pergens (? 12) Feb. 1793, and Ah. Resolution, *Pergen Akten*, x/A2, H22.
[2] Mályusz, p. 882.   [3] Ibid., pp. 882–3.

I have never seen in all my life, is being condemned without having been heard. No one has ascertained whether the manuscript so cunningly taken from him by one of his students, is really his work. He has been given no opportunity of making any statement concerning the passages of a piece of metaphysical writing which are supposed to be objectionable.[1]

As Francis was away at the front, the final decision rested with the Palatin, who was acting in Vienna on his behalf. In his resolution he both accepted and made explicit the underlying assumptions of Zinzendorf's position:

> Since considerations of that Justice which is due to everyone and the laws of the land require that no one, whoever it may be, should be condemned and punished without having been heard, and since the proposed suspension *ab officio* would indeed be a punishment, it will be necessary to order Prof. Delling . . . to make a statement concerning the accusations which have been brought against him and the meaning of the passages quoted by the Chancellery. . . . His statement will then be submitted to me together with the Chancellery's opinion on it. . . .[2]

This important decision was arrived at in the nick of time. For a new attempt at carrying through a purge without investigation was in the offing in Vienna, where the trial of the atheist cobblers and tailors had been concluded a short while before. In their plight, these men had willingly thrown the blame for their 'seduction' on the Josephinian preachers whose sermons had stimulated them to think about religious problems. Pergen could have desired no better illustration of the necessity of a purge among people in positions which enabled them to influence large numbers of their fellow citizens. His Note on the case, therefore, apart from calling for a new commission on education,[3] contained the further suggestion that all the preachers responsible for the cobblers' strange ideological journey to atheism should be immediately removed from their office.[4] The Council of State, as we have seen, referred the Note to the Court Chancellery for its opinion. There, the growth of democratic and radical ideas in recent years, the widespread internal disaffection since the outbreak of the war, and the extracts from the cobblers' and

[1] Mályusz, p. 883.
[2] Ah. Resolution, Ibid., No. 199, p. 883.
[3] *Supra*, p. 173.   [4] *Staatsratsprotokoll,* 1441 ex 1794.

tailors' statements which Pergen had attached to his Note had produced an outlook closely akin to that prevailing at the Ministry of Police. On 23 May 1794 the Court Chancellery sent a decree on its own authority to Cardinal Migazzi with orders to confine the incriminated Benedictine preachers without prior investigation, and to hold a consistorial investigation into the charges against the vicar of Penzing. The idea of a formal investigation into the charges against these men was rejected on the grounds that it would cause too much sensation, which was 'not advisable' under the circumstances, and that the confiscated writings of these men and their previous actions fully corroborated the cobblers' statements.[1]

The Chancellery's account of its dispositions reached the Council of State a few days after it had dealt with the case of Delling. Zinzendorf's stand for justice in the latter case, and the Palatin's resolution on it, must have impressed Eger deeply and given him the courage to make a similar stand in the case of the preachers:

[Has not the Chancellery begun] the trial *ab executione*? Is it permitted to punish a citizen, whatever his estate, without having heard him? Is it not punishment for a priest to be removed from his cure? . . . Why is there a desire to reduce Austrian justice which is held in such high esteem abroad, to an abominable pendant of a *Bastille* which has caused so much disaster? No one should be condemned unheard, that is a fundamental law; and there is less risk of danger in letting off someone who is guilty than in punishing someone . . . who is innocent. We are living at a time and under circumstances in which the purity, impartiality, and regularity of our justice must be regarded and venerated as the firmest pillar of the Throne.[2]

Prince Kaunitz, in one of the last opinions submitted by him before his death, gave the full weight of his support to Eger.

The Clergy must be honoured by the State and respected by the people. But it would in my opinion be very dangerous to concede them excessive influence and arbitrary powers, or to adapt our civil and police laws to ultramontane principles. . . . Such a course would bring

[1] *Erzbischöfl. Ordinariatsarchiv, Regesten,* No. 773.
[2] Votum Egers, concerning 1832 ex 1794 (copy), *Nachlaß Kollowrat,* F. 15, No. 1322.

the government into collision with the spirit of the times which cannot easily be changed. . . . I very much hope that small, shortsighted minds which have been thrown into utter confusion by the unexpected events of our time . . . will not succeed in leading the government astray by their numerical majority. . . . It is my conviction that justice is the securest foundation of States. . . .[1]

The Palatin drew the Emperor's attention to the flagrant irregularity of the Court Chancellery's action. It should have submitted an opinion on Pergen's Note. Instead it had acted of its own accord, without the necessary authorization, probably because it feared that the Emperor would never sanction the gross injustice which it considered necessary; nevertheless it had acted in the Emperor's name.[2] Both Kaunitz and the Palatin endorsed the draft resolution put forward by Eger, which reversed the Chancellery's orders and provided for the institution of a formal investigation into the charges against the preachers along the lines laid down by the law. Francis sanctioned the draft and upheld his resolution against repeated protests from Kollowrat and Migazzi, who had meanwhile actually proceeded with the arrest of the vicar of Penzing.[3] It was probably the indignant public reaction to this arrest which induced the Palatin to warn his brother that arbitrary arrests were no less a source of unrest than irreligion and political radicalism.[4]

The regular investigation which followed fully vindicated the Josephinian priests and acquitted them of any complicity in the offences for which the cobblers and tailors had been convicted. The investigating commission therefore ruled that they were entitled to resume their offices, but recommended their transference to equivalent positions elsewhere in order to avoid ill-feeling.[5] These recommendations were endorsed by the Council of State and sanctioned by the Emperor.[6]

One might have expected that the sensational reverse

---

[1] Votum Kaunitz', 14 June 1794, *Kaunitz Voten*, 1832 ex 1794.

[2] *Kaiser Franz Akten*, F. 91, fols. 81–82.

[3] Wolfsgruber, *Migazzi*, pp. 827–30.

[4] Votum des Palatin concerning 2355 ex 1794, 23 July 1794, *Kaiser Franz Akten*, F. 91.

[5] Au. Note Vogels, 7 Feb. 1796, concerning 4534 ex 1795, *Kaiser Franz Akten*, F. 95.   [6] *Staatsratsprotokoll*, 4534 ex 1795.

which was thus inflicted on Count Pergen by the Council of State would have silenced the advocates of purges without investigation. That, however, was not the case. One must remember that the Palatin's important ruling that no one must be condemned and punished unheard, and that dismissal from one's post constituted a punishment, was given before the more important of the Jacobin trials had even opened. The revelations which came out of these trials helped to make two important and influential converts to the views of Pergen and Kollowrat. One of these was none other than the Palatin himself, who wrote after studying the confessions of Martinovics:

[It seems] very necessary to keep a watchful eye on the professors, and to remove those who hold pernicious principles. . . . This could be done gradually, but in my humble opinion there ought not to be much delay, since the current trials against the traitors sufficiently illustrate the baneful effects of bad ways of teaching and bad professors.[1]

The second convert was Count Clary, President of the Supreme Judiciary. Clary held that the trials had above all demonstrated the inadequacy of the existing laws, even as amended by the Patent of January 1795, to deal with the internal revolutionary danger. It was essential to mete out punishment to all those who expressed opinions unfavourable to the Habsburg state and favourable to France. For those among them who were employed by the State, dismissal from office was the least punishment they could expect.[2]

Two such important conversions were bound to affect the struggle between the champions of the *Rechtsstaat* ideal and the exponents of the police state.

The Palatin's desertion proved fatal to the cause of Professor Delling. Though the investigation into his case failed to prove that he had ever denied the existence of God (as had been alleged), Delling's arguments for His existence failed to pass muster in the Palatin's eyes, now that the Jacobin trials were showing 'what sort of principles were being inculcated into the younger generation by bad professors'.[3]

---

[1] Memorandum, 16 Apr. 1795, Mályusz, No. 181, iii/9, p. 846.
[2] Au. Vortrag Clarys, 17 July 1795, *Kaiser Franz Akten*, F. 80 (C).
[3] Palatin to Francis, 9 Feb. 1795, Mályusz, No. 169, p. 778.

When the report of the Hungarian Court Chancellery on the investigation reached the Council of State, there were two votes for and two against the recommendation that Delling should be dismissed with one year's salary. Eger pointed out that there was no regulation or law whatever forbidding the teaching of Kantian philosophy, and that Delling had never been cautioned on the subject.[1] Zinzendorf exposed the philosophical incompetence of the Chancellery, and taunted with bitter irony the idea that someone should be dismissed from his teaching post because in Hungary the existence of God had to be proved *a priori*.[2] Both pleaded in vain, for Francis consulted the Palatin. To the latter, the risk that Delling's methodology might lead to scepticism and atheism among his hearers seemed too great since the political danger inherent in such attitudes had been demonstrated by the Jacobin trials.[3] And so Delling was dismissed with one year's salary.[4]

Clary had an opportunity of elaborating his views when he submitted the findings of the courts on a number of people who had been implicated by the accused in their evidence. It had been decided to interrogate these people *libero pede*,[5] and it had been found impossible to establish a prima facie case against any of them. Two of the suspects were in positions of influence: Strattmann, the Custodian of the Imperial Library, and Ratschky, a secretary in the Court Chancellery. Clary urged with great passion and conviction that these two men should be retired: the very fact that they had fallen under suspicion, as well as the character of their evidence—Strattmann admitted that he had been shocked by the condition of the French peasants in 1770—showed that they did not deserve the confidence the Emperor had put in them when making the appointments. Clary was compelled to admit, however, that he was in a minority and that the majority of Austria's Supreme Court recommended

[1] Mályusz, p. 886.   [2] Ibid., pp. 886–7.
[3] Au. Note des Palatin, 4 June 1795, Ibid., No. 199, p. 888.
[4] *Staatsratsprotokoll*, 1574 ex 1795.
[5] Au. Vortrag der Obersten Justizstelle, 4 Feb. 1795, *Vertr. Akten*, F. 4, fols. 3–16; presumably the names of these persons had not been mentioned in the preliminary investigations; otherwise they would have been interrogated by Saurau's commission.

merely a caution.[1] The Council of State endorsed the majority recommendation. Mindful, no doubt, of the Delling affair, Eger and Zinzendorf did not omit to draw attention to the character of Clary's argumentation, and condemned it as 'illogical and illegal'.[2] The Emperor decided in accordance with the majority.[3]

While this case was being decided in Vienna, suggestions for further dismissals came from Hungary. The Chief Public Prosecutor, Johann Németh, had drawn up a case against ten persons holding official (mainly teaching) positions, who appeared in the evidence of the Hungarian 'Jacobins' as purveyors of dangerous thoughts. It was not possible to prepare a legal case against them, since most of the required witnesses had been executed. The Lord Chief Justice of Hungary, therefore, supported by the new Palatin (Alexander Leopold had died as a result of an accident in July 1795), recommended that the ten should be dismissed without any financial compensation.[4]

Again, the matter came before the Council of State, where Eger now developed the late Palatin's thesis that dismissal from office without pension constituted a punishment usually inflicted only for definite and proven misconduct or crimes.[5] Zinzendorf subjected the prosecutor's evidence to a detailed and devastating criticism: if the suspects were guilty of the alleged offences, dismissal would be far too lenient a punishment; but if they were innocent, it would amount to the grossest injustice, and would needlessly deprive the Hungarian students of a number of very able teachers.[6] This time Reischach supported Zinzendorf's stand. Summing up, Hofrat Vogel (who usually managed to insert his own opinion into his summaries) reminded the Emperor of previous resolutions granting to suspects the protection of the law:

These Hungarian suspects have a right to the same treatment. Your Majesty is far too just to desire or to be able to punish anyone

---

[1] Au. Vortrag der Ob. Justizstelle, 16 Sept. 1795, *Vertr. Akten*, F. 12, fols. 650–79.
[2] Au. Note Vogels, 5 Oct. 1795, concerning 3441 ex 1795, *Kaiser Franz Akten*, F. 95.
[3] *Vertr. Akten*, F. 12, fol. 679.
[4] S. Domanovszky, *József nádor iratai*, i. 37.
[5] Ibid. i. 37–38.
[6] Ibid. 38–40.

whose guilt has not been established by due process of Law. Every man has a right to the protection of the Law. It is granted by the Sovereign to everyone alike, not as of grace, but as of duty, because the Sovereign must conform to the laws and protect the honour, property and good name of his subjects.[1]

Francis ordered that the Hungarian prosecutor must hold a regular investigation into the charges against the ten suspects before the question of their punishment, by dismissal or otherwise, could arise.[2]

Had Németh ever considered that a regular investigation would have yielded results, he would probably have undertaken it of his own accord. The reason for the proposal that the ten suspects should be dismissed from their posts was precisely the anticipated hopelessness of such an investigation. The new Palatin, Archduke Joseph (doubtless prompted by Németh himself), therefore tried to convince Francis that he had the right of dismissal without prior investigation.[3] But the proposals he now put forward were already considerably more moderate than Németh's earlier ones: the number of suspects to be dismissed was reduced from ten to five (including Professor Kreil and Count Török, the author of a well-known work on education), and they were to receive one year's salary.[4]

It was a notable victory for the champions of the law. But they were not satisfied with the extent of the concessions so far. Eger submitted that 'it would be more in keeping with Your Majesty's love of justice, if Your Majesty were to retire these five people in the ordinary way with the enjoyment of their pensions.'[5] Zinzendorf's words clinched the matter: 'The shortest, clearest, and most infallible political rule, which is based on religion, morality, good policy, and common sense, . . . is that justice is the strongest pillar of the Throne.'[6] In this conviction he endorsed Eger's opinion. On 19 October 1795 Francis resolved (despite the contrary opinions of Izdenczy and Reischach) that the five suspected

---

[1] Au. Note Vogels, 7 Sept. 1795, concerning 3086 ex 1795, *Kaiser Franz Akten*, F. 95.

[2] *Staatsratsprotokoll*, 3086 ex 1795.

[3] Au. Note des Palatin, 7 Oct. 1795, Domanovszky, No. 8, i. 43–48.

[4] Ibid. i. 48–50.   [5] Ibid. i. 52–53.

[6] Ibid. i. 53.

professors should be retired in the ordinary way with the full enjoyment of their pension.[1]

The present generation is not likely to underestimate the importance of these decisions, and should be aware of the political struggle and state of public opinion to which they were due. At the time, they prevented a large-scale political purge of civil servants, teachers, and professors. They made unthinkable the implementation of Pergen's proposal that the Ministry of Police should have the power of precautionary arrest for an indefinite period, which was still under official consideration.[2] The proposal had in any case been seriously criticized both in the Council of State[3] and by the Supreme Judiciary.[4]

The combative spirit of the partisans of legality even in the days of the Jacobin trials is well illustrated by Sonnenfels, who had once more been instructed to prepare a systematic collection of all 'political regulations' (*Polizeigesetze*).[5] True to his ideals, Sonnenfels submitted instead of the expected 'mechanical' collection a set of elaborately argued principles which amounted to a charter of civil rights against excessive police powers.[6]

As the fire of 1927 has wrought havoc with the relevant sources, it is difficult to trace the history of Sonnenfels's proposals. Rottenhan, who had replaced Kressel in the Court Chancellery in November 1792, was the first to receive them. He passed them on to his superior, Kollowrat, with the observation that Sonnenfels's principles had best be rejected 'unless one wishes to jeopardize public law and order for the sake of the approval of intellectuals'. He continued,

When peace has been restored, when public security is once more guaranteed by an army which can keep the restless spirit of reformers

---

[1] Ah. Handbillet an Pálffy, 19 Oct. 1795, *Staatsratsprotokoll*, 3582 ex 1795.

[2] *Staatsratsprotokoll*, 3644 ex 1794.

[3] Only the Palatin's *votum* survives in *Kaiser Franz Akten*, F. 91, fol. 420.

[4] The relevant documents seem to have perished in the fire of 1927, but the comments of Councillor Keeß were published in *Der Morgenbothe*, No. 1 (Vienna: 1809), pp. 202–11.

[5] *Staatsratsprotokoll*, 2363 ex 1794.

[6] Both surviving copies of Sonnenfels's *Ausarbeitung über die Polizeigesetze* are badly damaged and incomplete and do not supplement each other altogether. They are to be found in *Polizeihofstelle*, 1795/809, and *Hofkanzlei*, III A 3, Kart. 310. An introduction is to be found in *Pergen Akten*, xviii/A1, H27.

and fanatics in check, it will be time enough for philanthropists to renew their proposal to secure an impunity for subversive elements (*Ruhestörer*) which resembles the English constitution and their beloved *Habeas Corpus Act.*[1]

No doubt as a result of this kind of unfavourable comment, the Emperor instructed Sonnenfels not to concern himself with the organization and instructions of the police.[2] Despite this specific narrowing down of his terms of reference, Sonnenfels took it upon himself to protest against Saurau's practice of imposing a short term of imprisonment by way of 'political punishment' on those 'Jacobins' against whom insufficient evidence was found by the criminal court.[3] The result of his observations was a new general instruction which strictly limited the power of the police to inflict punishment on its own authority to those minor cases which did not fall within the competence of a court of law or any other public authority.[4]

Thus, Martini's stand on behalf of the accused was followed up by a persistent struggle on behalf of those directly or indirectly implicated by them. If a modern historian can write that in the Habsburg dominions 'the ideal of the *Rechtsstaat* eventually prevailed despite the political reaction after 1789',[5] it is a measure of the importance and achievement of this struggle.

4. *The End of Austrian 'Jacobinism'*

We must conclude with an estimate of the effects of the Jacobin trials on public opinion in Austria. Public opinion was uppermost in the mind of Pergen and Saurau throughout the trials. The greatest care was taken to give the verdicts the most effective type of publicity.[6]

The immediate effects were regarded as disappointing. Though a number of critical voices from among the intelli-

---

[1] Rottenhan to Kollowrat, 11 May 1795, *Hofkanzlei*, IV M 1, Kart. 1327.
[2] Ah. Resolution über Au. Note Kollowrats (herabgelangt März 1796), ibid.
[3] Au. Vortrag Sauraus, 24 June 1795, *Polizeihofstelle, Ältere Polizeiakten*, ii/2, H58.
[4] *Vertr. Akten*, F. 6, fol. 106.
[5] Valjavec, *Josephinismus* (1945: Munich), p. 127.
[6] Cf. Pergen to Clary, 10 Feb. 1795, *Vertr. Akten*, F. 152, fol. 253.

gentsia had been silenced,[1] public opinion generally showed no signs of becoming more ready to accept government policy uncritically. The wide gulf between government and people remained apparent, so much so that both Pergen and the Palatin were quite firmly convinced after the conclusion of the main trials that many more people would have to be arrested and tried before internal tranquillity could be regarded as assured: 'Although we have caught a lot of the culprits', the Palatin wrote, 'we have not really got to the bottom of this business yet.' And Pergen told Colloredo in August 1795 that while the arrests of the Jacobins had warded off the immediate danger of a conflagration, 'neither unbelief . . . nor wild democratic aspirations have been destroyed at the source: the itch to criticize even the best actions of the Monarch, and revolutionary leanings generally have not been suppressed.'[2]

The chief source of discontent, of course, was the government's obstinate continuation of the war. No amount of pompous publicity for the verdicts against 'black traitors' for their 'monstrous crimes' could persuade the public of the necessity or desirability of the war.[3] As in 1792 and 1793, public discontent would be loudest in expression and most formidable in extent whenever the fortune of war deserted Austrian arms and favoured the French. And after 1795 the French were winning nearly all the time. In Vienna the demand for peace was becoming so strong that the threat to the government from that source almost seemed to overshadow the blows inflicted by Bonaparte. Thugut wrote to Colloredo in July 1796,

Je crains toujours plus Vienne que toute la fureur de l'ennemi, et c'est de là que viendra notre ruine. Je me propose d'avoir demain une conférence avec M. de Saurau sur cet objet, car après tout, c'est la police surtout qui devrait aviser aux expédients de diriger l'opinion, particulièrement dans les lieux publics.[4]

---

[1] Bibl, *Der Zerfall Österreichs*, i. 73, 83. The *Österreichische Monatsschrift* ceased publication after its issue of June 1794.

[2] Palatin to Francis, 9 Mar. 1795, Mályusz, No. 172, p. 783; Pergen to Colloredo, 10 Aug. 1795, *Sammelbände*, F. 143.

[3] Cf. Au. Note Pergens, 20 Aug. 1796, *Pergen Akten*, x/B1, H72.

[4] Vivenot (ed.), *Vertrauliche Briefe des Freih. v. Thugut* (1872: Vienna), No. 469, i. 323.

The practical outcome of Thugut's conference with Saurau was an urgent appeal by the latter to Bishop Hohenwart to ensure that his clergy co-operated with the government in their endeavour to rouse some enthusiasm in the people for the war, and to get them to see the 'dangers' of peace.[1] Saurau himself took a leading part in these efforts by commissioning a national anthem from Haydn and organizing the 'Vienna Volunteer Corps'. But the French invaders met no popular resistance on Austrian soil in 1797. The desire for peace remained as strong as ever under French occupation.[2]

In other ways, however, the repressive measures introduced before and especially after the trials—and doubtless the trials themselves—succeeded in silencing the people and interrupting the development of their political consciousness which had taken such big strides as a result of the Josephinian reforms and the French Revolution. After the conclusion of the war, the number of those openly criticizing the government or expressing democratic opinions was counted only in handfuls in the various provinces.[3] By 1801 even the Ministry of Police reported that all was quiet and that there was no cause for anxiety:

The French Revolution had first been depicted in such attractive colours by writers and journalists . . . that young men were swept off their feet in admiration of it—young men who were not otherwise fundamentally ill-disposed. If the welfare of the State at that time inexorably demanded ruthless measures to prevent the spread of the pernicious disease, the firm application of these measures has had the desired effect—so much so that since then no more revolutionary movement was to be perceived in any part of the Monarchy. . . .

With these words Hofrat Schilling explained why the Ministry of Police had no objection to recommending a pardon for Schedel and Menz, who had been condemned to long terms of imprisonment in 1796.[4] The perilous legacy of

[1] Saurau to Hohenwart (draft), 27 July 1796, *Archiv für N. Öst., Präsidialakten,* 1796/164.
[2] Mayer, pp. 60–78.
[3] Au. Note Pergens, 27 Dec. 1797, *Kaiser Franz Akten,* F. 82 (P).
[4] *Vertr. Akten,* F. 6, fol. 413.

Josephinism and Revolution seemed to be effectively liquidated and internal tranquillity restored.

Pergen retired from the Ministry of Police in the following year. Probably he did not suspect that the silence which he had imposed might be the lull before the storm.

APPENDIX

Haus-, Hof- und Staatsarchiv Wien.
Kabinettsarchiv, Vertrauliche Akten, Fasz. alt 152, neu 107.

Allerunterthänigster Vortrag des zweyten Präsidentens bey der
obersten Justizstelle Freiherrn von Martini
Die Verhandlung des Kriminalprozesses wider die hier verhafteten
Staatsverbrecher betreffend

Eure Majestät.

Haben durch ein höchstes Handbillet vom 2. des laufenden Monats
dem ersten obersten Justizpräsidenten Grafen von Clary anzubefohlen
geruhet: daß zur Führung, und Erledigung des wider einige hier
verhaftete Staatsgefährliche Leute nun anzufangenden Kriminalprozesses zur Beschleunigung der Sache und zur engeren Verwahrung
des Geheimnisses ein judicium delegatum cum derogatione omnium
instantiarum unter seinem Vorsitz niedergesetzet, und dazu der
N.(ieder) Oe.(sterreichische) Appellazionspräsident Freyherr von
Löhr, dann sämmtliche Individuen der bereits aufgestellten Untersuchungshofkommission und nebst dem Freiherrn von Stupan, noch
ein Rath der obersten Justizstelle beygezogen werden solle.

Der von mir mehrmal abgelegte Pflichteid, und das mir gnädigst
anvertraute Amt eines zweyten Präsidenten bey der obersten Justizstelle, nicht weniger aber der warme Antheil, den ein jeder getreue
Unterthan, und um so mehr ein im Dienst schon ergrauter Staats-
beamte an dem wahren Ruhm seines gnädigsten Monarchens nehmen
muß, haben mich besonders in Abwesenheit des ersten Präsidenten
Grafen von Clary aufgefordert, Eurer Majestät diejenigen Bedenklichkeiten allerunterthänigst zu eröfnen, welche wegen Errichtung
dieses besonderen Halsgerichtsstandes mir aufgefallen sind. Ich erhielt
darüber den höchsten Auftrag, diese Bedenklichkeiten schriftlich
vorzulegen. Überhaupt muß ich allergehorsamst bemerken, daß die
Anstände, welche der Errichtung eines auf diese Art angeordneten
Kriminalgerichts im Wege stehen, sowohl (*a*) von Seite einiger dazu
bestimmten Beysitzer, als auch (*b*) von Seite der Inquisiten, vorzüglich
aber (*c*) in Rücksicht auf die Verfahrungsart selbst sich darbieten.
Überdieß (*d*) dürfte aus dieser Gerichtsart ein großes Aufsehen
entstehen, und gleichwohl (*e*) die Sache weder mehr befördert, noch
das Geheimniss strenger verwahret werden.

(A) Vermög des obangeführten Höchsten Handbillets soll das neue
Kriminalgericht erstens *aus den sämmentlichen Individuen* der dermaligen politischen Untersuchungshofkommission (diese sind zwey

Magistrats, und zwey Appellazionsräthe, zwey Polizeibeamte, ein Hofrath von der obersten Justizstelle, und der Präses Graf von Saurau) dann aus einem zweyten Hofrath der obersten Justizstelle, und den zweyen oberwähnten Präsidenten bestehen.

Diese Zahl von eilf Personen wäre an sich zur Schöpfung eines Kriminalurtheils um so mehr hinreichend, als *in der allgemeinen Kriminalgerichtsordnung* § 159 nur vier Beysitzer, und ein Präsidium erfordert werden. Es wird aber zu Ende des jetzt angezogenen 159.§ zugleich angeordnet: *daß als Beysitzer zu einer Kriminalberathschlagung Niemand beygezogen werden könne, als der bey dem Kriminalgerichte zum Richteramt eigends berufen, oder bey dem im Gerichtsorte bestehenden Magistrate als geprüfter Gerichtsmann angestellet ist.* Nun sind drey von denen der politischen Untersuchungshofkommission beywohnenden Personen mit den in dem Gesetze vorgeschriebenen Eigenschaften eines Kriminalrichters noch nicht versehen. Es müssten demnach auch diese politischen Beysitzer zum Kriminalgerichtsstuhl geeignet, und zu dem Ende in besondere Eidespflicht genommen; oder aber da diese ohnehin doppelt überzählig sind, gänzlich beseitiget, und auch andurch dem Kriminalgesetze ein Genügen geleistet werden; denn dieses schreibt in dem vierten Hauptstücke der Kriminalgerichtsordnung § 53 vor: daß bey erhobenen hinreichenden Innzichten der Inquisit von der politischen Stelle an die Kriminalbehörde abgeliefert werden müsse. Nun ist die dermalige Untersuchungshofkommission nur eine politische Behörde; es können daher die politischen Beysitzer, ohne dem Gesetze zu nahe zu tretten, nicht beybehalten, noch berechtiget werden die Inquisiten gleichsam an sich selbst abzuliefern. Welcher nicht ordentliche Fürgang Jedermann in die Augen fallen würde.

(B) Durch Beseitigung der politischen Beysitzer, welche das Kriminalrichteramt vielleicht selbst verbitten dürften, wäre zwar der erste Anstand gänzlich gehoben; es möchten aber die Inquisiten einen nicht ungegründeten Anlaß zu Beschwerden nehmen, wenn sie von dem ordentlichen Wege Rechtens abgezogen, und einer außerordentlichen Hofkommission übergeben werden sollten. Auch die größten Verbrecher sind befugt den Schutz des Gesetzes, welches auch die Strafe über sie verhängt, anzurufen, und die Prozedur nach der ordentlichen Gerichtsform zu fordern. Eine Forderung, die ein neues Gewicht erhält, wenn dem sichern Vernehmen nach sowohl die Militärpersonen, als die hungarischen Inquisiten an ihren gesetzmäßigen Gerichtsstand abgeliefert werden. Die Inquisiten mögen Mitschuldige seyn, oder nicht, so gehören doch alle unter die Staatsverbrecher; es scheinet daher kein Grund vorhanden zu seyn, um sie auf ungleiche Art zu behandeln. Es hat zwar seine volle Richtigkeit, dass der höchste Gesetzgeber in Nothfällen eine Ausnahme vom

Gesetze machen, und von der gewöhnlichen Ordnung abweichen könne und müsse: allein diese Abweichung setzt das daraus erwartete allgemeine Beste zum voraus, und läßt sich nicht dahin ausdehnen, daß andurch die Jemanden zustehenden Rechte ihm schlechterdings entzogen werden dürften. Bey dem standrechtlichen Verfahren werden auch alle nicht wesentliche Erfordernisse der Rechtspflege übergangen, allein die Zulassung eines solchen Standrechts ist nur ein Artikel des schon bestehenden allgemeinen Gesetzes. Durch einzelne Ausnahme, wenn keine Gefahr vorhanden ist, wird nur das Gesetz herabgewürdiget, Mißtrauen erweket, Gelegenheit zu Beschwerdeführungen gegeben und ein schlimmer Eindruck auf die Gemüther über die Gerechtigkeitspflege gemacht. Der allgemeine Wunsch ein baldiges abschrökendes Beyspiel zu sehen ist öfters die Wirkung der flüchtigen immer abwechselnden Neugierde; hat man diese einmal befriediget, so legt sich der Kitzel der Einbildungskraft, man denkt dem Hergange der Sache kaltblütig nach, und am Schlusse wird der, mit Hemmung des ordentlichen Rechtslaufes allzeit verbundene ungünstige Eindruk erwekt, und durch die Überlieferung gleichsam verewiget: hievon sind noch mehrere Beyspiele im frischen Andenken. Eine ganz andere Beschaffenheit hat es, wenn man den geraden Gang des Gesetzes fort wandelt, und sich keinen Absprung erlaubt, weil davon niemals ein fortdauernder übler Eindruck zu besorgen ist, und weil selbst der größte Bösewicht, wenn man ihm das bestehende allgemeine Gesetz vorhält, verstummen muß.

(C) Gesetzt aber auch, daß die Inquisiten auf das ihnen für mehrere Instanzen zustehende Recht Verzicht thun wollten, und es bey der Innhaltung aller übrigen Instanzen sein Bewenden haben sollte, so ergiebt sich doch noch ein anderes wichtiges Bedenken. Eure Majestät werden nämlich weit entfernt seyn, durch Einschränkung des Wirkungskreises der ordentlichen Instanzen auch die Wirkung der bestehenden Kriminalgesetze einhalten zu lassen. Man hat zwar auch in Gefäll, Erbsteuer, und Sicherheitssachen die derogationem omnium instantiarum Platz greifen lassen, doch ist diese Anstalt niemals auf die derogationem legum, oder auf die Entkräftung der Gesetze erstreket, vielmehr zu desto sicherer Vollziehung derselben hervorgesucht worden. Im gegenwärtigen Falle hingegen würden nicht allein die ordentlichen Justizbehörden, sondern auch die Gesetze selbst ihre Kraft verlieren müssen: den Beweis hievon liefern die §§ 170, 171, 174 und 193 der allgemeinen Kriminalgerichtsordnung. Nach dem 193. § wird den Inquisiten der Rekurs für zwey Fälle, und zwar für einen Fall zu der zweyten, und für andern Fall zu der dritten Instanz offen gelassen: sobald aber die Gerichtsbarkeit des untern mit der Gerichtsbarkeit des Obern, und sogar des obersten Gerichtsstandes würde vermenget werden, so kann man schon von der Rechtswohlthat des Rekurses nicht mehr Gebrauch machen, ein Recht dessen Verlust dem Verurtheilten nicht gleichgültig seyn kann. Dagegen möchte zwar eingewendet werden, daß bey mehreren schweren Verbrechen, und namentlich bey dem Hochverrath vor Bekanntmachung des Urtheils der Schluß der obersten Justizstelle abgewartet werden müsse: § 178 gegen derer Schlüsse aber kein weiterer Rekurs statt finden könne; allein sowohl in schweren als auch in schwersten Verbrechen ordnet das Gesetz § 170, und 174, daß der Kriminalprozess, wenn kein Standrecht eintritt, bey der ersten Instanz verhandelt, von ihr das Urtheil entworfen, sofort das Verfahren dem Obergericht vorgelegt, dort eingesehen, und geprüft und endlich auch von Seite der obersten Justizstelle, wenn die Sache auch dahin gelangen muß, das nämliche beobachtet werden soll.

Hieraus erhellt, daß in den Fällen, wo kein Rekurs statt hat, allemal dem Appelationsgericht, und manchmal auch dem obersten Justiztribunal obliege, *auf den Gang des Verfahrens die strengste Aufmerksamkeit zu wenden, die entdeckten Gebrechen zu heben, und die nöthigen Belehrungen zu ertheilen.* § 174.

Alle zur Beobachtung der guten Ordnung gehörigen Dinge, wie auch die zum Behuf der Inquisiten vorgeschriebenen Maaßregeln und Vorsichten können bey einer mit Übergehung aller Instanzen errichteten Hofkommission nicht mehr befolgt werden. Es fehlt schon an der wesentlichen Stufenfolge der Gerichtsstände. So gut auch eine in Kriminalsachen niedergesetzte außerordentlichte Hofkommission seyn mag, so bleibt doch solche ein einziges besonderes Halsgericht. Es würde alsdann keine Gerichtsbehörden mehr geben, welche den Gang des Verfahrens zu prüfen, oder die etwa unterlaufenden Gebrechen zu rügen befugt wäre, alle aus der drey Instanzen herausgehobene in einer Hofkommission vereinigten Personen, machen ja doch nur einen einzigen Körper aus: Niemand darf aber sein eigener Richter seyn, und es würde daher die wesentliche Kontrolle fehlen.

Obschon die Einsichten, und die Rechtschaffenheit der zur Kriminalhofkommission ernannten Beysitzer von Niemanden wird bezweifelt werden, so liegt es doch in der Natur der Sache, daß ein von einer Instanz allein geschöpfter Spruch nach der öffentlichen Meinung weniger Vertrauen einflößen werde, als wenn die Sache bey allen drey Instanzen erörtert, und entschieden worden wäre. In den Fällen, wo die zwey ersten Instanzen nur einig sind, so giebt doch die dritte Instanz der einen oder der andern das Übergewicht, und so sind immer zwey gleiche Schlüsse, welche die Sache entscheiden. Überdieß, wenn auch bey unerheblicher Streithändeln Niemanden der Weg der drey Instanzen verschlossen wird, möchte es dem Publikum schwer oder gar nicht begreiflich seyn, warum die Untersuchung und Entscheidung eines der wichtigsten Kriminalprozessen

nur allein einer Instanz anvertrauet worden sey. Überhaupt gewähret
die in dem Gesetze bestimmte ordentliche Verfahrungsart dem
Publikum weit mehr Beruhigung, als wenn man einen Rechtshandel
außer der hergebrachten Gerichtsordnung untersucht, und ent-
scheidet. Was die Kinder von ihrem Vater, aber das erwarten die
Unterthanen von ihrem Regenten, nämlich: ein weises, wohl über-
dachtes, nicht übereiltes Urtheil. Der Wunsch eines jeden gutden-
kenden Staatsbürgers ist, daß der Inquisit eher für unschuldig, als für
schuldig erkannt werde. Aus einer Gerichtsprocedur, welche nicht
nach den Vorschriften des Gesetzes vor sich gehet, pfleget aber
Grübeley und Tadelsucht zu entstehen.

(D) Aus diesem, oder doch ganz ähnlichen Gründen muß es
geschehen seyn, dass die in andern europäischen Reichen durch die
gallischen Empörungsseuche verursachten Ländererschütterungen,
und schwersten Missethaten nicht durch außerordentliche Kommis-
sionen, sondern durch die ordentlichen Behörden bestrafet worden sind.

Zu Neapel behielt bey Untersuchung der dasigen Staatsverschwö-
rungen nach den öffentlichen Nachrichten die sogenannte Vicaria
criminale und zu Turin der Senat seine ordentliche Gerichtsbarkeit,
und noch jüngsthin ist das Urtheil durch die Zeitungsblätter erschie-
nen, welches in Ansehung des Armfeldischen Hochverraths von dem
ordentlichen Hofgerichte zu Stokholm unterm 30. July dieses Jahrs
gefällt, und darauf von dem obersten Gerichte als letzter Instanz theils
bestättiget, theils auch verschärft worden ist. Das englische Kabinet
machte zwar den Antrag die auch in diesem Lande ausgebrochenen
Unruhen durch ausserordentliche Kommissärs untersuchen zu lassen,
es stellten aber die darüber einvernommenen sogenannten XII Groß-
gerichtshalter des Königsreichs die damit verbundenen Bedenklichkeiten vor; daher ist man von dem ersten Vorschlag gänzlich abge-
gangen. Bey uns wäre so was noch weniger nöthig, da das Laster des
Hochverrathes noch keine so tiefe Wurzeln gefaßt, noch auch in
irgend einer Provinz um sich gegriffen hat, wie in besagten Reichen.
Nirgends sind bey uns solche aufrührerische Thätlichkeiten ausge-
brochen, die allgemeine Volksstimmung ist immer für die Aufrecht-
haltung der öffentlichen Ruhe. Kluge und weise Gesetze, die nur aus
Menschenkenntniss, Staatenkunde und langer Erfahrung geschöpft
aber auch genau beobachtet werden müssen, sind die stärksten, und
sichersten Stützen des Throns. Gegen das Verbrechen des Aufruhrs,
und Tumults ist schon in den Gesetzen selbst das standrechtliche
Verfahren festgesetzet worden, und es wird auch demnächstens wider
die Staatsverbrecher die Todesstrafe verhängt, und kundgemacht
werden.

(E) Wenn aber auch ein Kriminalprozess durch eine einzige
Instanz geschwinder erlediget werden dürfte, so folgt noch nicht

daraus, daß die schon bestimmten ordentlichen Instanzen übergangen
werden können: der kürzere Weg ist nicht allemal der beste, wohl aber
ist in Ansehung der Gerichtspflege der gerade von dem Gesetze vorge-
zeichnete Weeg für jeden Fall der sicherste, und der behaglichste.
Nehme man den sehr möglichen Fall an: daß alle, oder mehrere oder
nur einer von den Inquisiten gegen die Aufstellung einer einzigen
ausserordentlichen Kriminalhofkommission eine Einwendung machen,
die Wohlthat des Gesetzes, die ihnen mehrere Instanzen gewähren,
anrufen, oder daß die Akten am Ende zu Handen des Staatsraths
gelangen sollten, und daß von diesem Eurer Majestät die Aufrecht-
haltung der ordentlichen Gerichtsprozedur eingerathen würde, so
ist es wohl vorzusehen, daß Höchstdieselbe die Bitte der Inquisiten
anhören und von dem Befunde des Staatsraths um so weniger abweichen würden, als fast bey allen bloß in Justizsache erstatteten
Vorträgen die oberste Justizstelle zur Amtshandlung lediglich ange-
wiesen wird. In diesen Umständen müßte die gerichtliche Untersuchung von neuem begonnen, oder eine besondere Revisionsstelle
erschaffen werden, wodurch dann eine ungleich größere Verzögerung
der Execution sich ergeben würde. Im Gegentheil, wenn die Sache
nach dem ordentlichen Verfahren, behandelt wird, Niemand dagegen
eine Einwendung machen kann.

Aber auch durch das ordentliche gerichtliche Verfahren dürfte der
Ausgang des Prozesses eben nicht sehr verschoben werden. Nach den
Gesetzen sind bey keiner Instanz mehr als 4 Beysitzer, und ein
Präsidium nothwendig; ein Präsidium, welches nur vier Stimmen zu
sammeln hat, braucht Zeuge der täglichen Erfahrung nur die Hälfte
weniger Zeit, als wenn die Umfrage auf zehn Beysitzer sich ausdehnen
muß.

Es läßt sich demnach die Aburtheilung der zu dem Militär,
oder hungarischen Gerichtsstande nicht gehörigen Inquisiten sehr
beschleunigen, weil

(1) die zur politischen Untersuchung bereits bis izt verwendete
Gerichtsmänner auch bey ihren Instanzen und zwar bey dem Kriminalgerichte des Magistrats zween, dann bey der Appellazion gleichfalls
zween, und einer von der obersten Justizstelle beybehalten, folglich
nur noch zween Räthe von der ersten Instanz eben so viele von der
zweiten, und drey von der dritten bestimmt werden dürften; mithin
das ganze Personale bey den drey Instanzen mit Innbegrif der Präsi-
dien, nämlich des Grafen von Clary und Freiherrn von Löhr dann
des einen Vizebürgermeisters nur aus 15 Personen zu bestehen hätte;
weil

(2) nicht nothwendig ist den Auszug der Akten dreymalen, nämlich bey jeder Instanz sondern nur allein bey der ersten verfertigen zu
lassen, mithin der zweyten, und dritten Instanz nur obliegen soll den

dahin gelangten Auszug genauest mit den Akten zusammenzuhalten, und allenfalls jenes, was zur Weesenheit abgängig scheinet, zu ergänzen; weil

(3) wohl thunlich seyn dürfte, da ohnehin die Hauptuntersuchung durch die dermalen bestehende Hofkommission schon gepflogen ist, daß einige Kriminalprozesse der diessortigen Inquisiten, wie es ohnehin mit den an das Militar, und an die hungarische Behörden Abgelieferten geschiehet, abgesondert, und für jeden ein besonderes Urtheil entworfen werde, da doch für jeden Inquisiten ein besonderes Verhörsprotokoll und besondere Akten vorhanden seyn müssen, weil

(4) auf solche Art nach Maaß, als das Urtheil für einige Verbrecher entworfen ist, solches an das Appellazionsgericht, sohin an die oberste Justizstelle nicht durch die Einreichungsprotokolle, sondern immer zu unmittelbaren Handen des Präsidiums einbegleitet, und dergestalten fortgefahren werden kann, daß da die erste Instanz die dritte Abtheilung vornimmt, von der Appellazion die zwote, und indessen von der obersten Justizstelle die erste vorgenommen werde; weil

(5) diese eigene Ausschüsse der drey Stellen sich öfters, als nur in den gewöhnlichen Tägen der Rathssitzungen versammeln, und ohne den Lauf der übrigen Geschäfte zu hemmen den vor Handen habenden Kriminalprozess ununterbrochen erledigen können.

Es kann übrigens keine Bedenklichkeit wider die Gerichtsbarkeit der hiesigen ersten Instanzen mit Grunde erreget werden, wenn auch der mir unbekannte Fall eintreffen sollte, daß ein oder der andere Inquisit dem hiesigen Kriminalgerichte entweder in Bezug auf die Art des begangenen Verbrechens oder der erfolgten Verhaft nicht unterstünde; denn schon vermög der bestehenden Gesetze gründet der Zusammenhang der Sache die Gerichtsbarkeit; die Inquisiten werden doch immer einem ordentlichen Gerichtsstande zugewiesen, und endlich in erforderlichen Fällen ist die oberste Justizstelle zur Anwendung einer solchen Delegation jederzeit berechtiget.

Was noch die strenge Verwahrung des Geheimnisses betrift; so ist nach dem obigen Antrag die Zahl der Richter ohnehin sehr eingeschränket, und man mag sie neuerdings ihres aufhabenden Eides der Verschwiegenheit nachdruksam erinnern. Finden diese angeführten Gründe und Vorschläge bey Eurer Majestät Eingang, so wäre der oberste Justizpräsident und die dermalige Untersuchungshofkommission hiernach anzuweisen.

Wien, den 15. Oktober 1794   MARTINI, m. p.

Allerhöchste Resolution

Ich trage dem Grafen von Saurau untereinst auf, und verständige davon auch den Oberst-Justizpräsidenten Grafen Clary, daß die unter seinem (des Grafen Saurau) Vorsitze des Hochverraths wegen politisch untersuchten Personen mit allen schriftlichen zur Sache gehörigen Verhandlungen, gesammelten Innzichten, Thatsachen, Verhörsprotokollen, Zeugenaussagen und so weiter sobald die erforderlichen Voruntersuchungen gänzlich werden zu Ende gebracht werden, dem hiesigen Criminalgerichte übergeben, und daselbst zwar so fördersam, als möglich, jedoch mit Beobachtung aller gesetzlich vorgeschriebenen Gerichtsförmlichkeiten processiret, und abgeurtheilt, sohin das Resultat an das hiesige Appellationsgericht der Ordnung nach gebracht, von diesem sofort das Ganze der obersten Justizstelle vorgelegt werden solle.

FRANZ, m. p.

BIBLIOGRAPHY AND SOURCES

I. ORIGINAL MANUSCRIPT SOURCES

(a) *Haus-, Hof- u. Staatsarchiv, Vienna*
Kabinettsarchiv:
  Staatsratsprotokoll, 1790–5.
  Kaunitz Voten, 1792–4.
  Protokolle u. Indices der Kabinettskanzlei, 1790–2.
  Kabinettsprotokoll, 1791–5.
  Handbillettenprotokol, 1792–5.
  Kaiser Franz Akten, FF. 8, 10, 10a, 10b, 78b–d, 80–85, 91, 92–97,
    119, 126, 149–63, 183, 184 (Alt).
  Vertrauliche Akten, FF. 1–33, 45, 56–64, 71, 152 (Alt).
  Kabinettskanzleiakten, Polizei-Vorträge, F. 1a.
  Nachlaß Kollowrat (Leopold), FF. 13–15.
Hausarchiv:
  Sammelbände, FF. 63, 97, 98, 143, 149, 162, 347, 348, 463.
Ungarische Akten:
  F. 261.
Staatskanzlei:
  Vorträge, F. 220.
  Noten an die Polizei, F. 1.
  Noten von der Polizei, F. 29.
  ad Polizei, F. 78.
  Notenwechsel mit der n. ö. Regierung, FF. 1–3.
  Noten an die Hofkanzlei, FF. 14–18.
  Noten von der Hofkanzlei, FF. 38–46.
  Noten von der Ungarischen Hofkanzlei, F. 7.
  Informationsbureau, Polizeiberichte, FF. 1–4.
  Interiora, Interzepte, F. 2.
  Große Correspondenz, FF. 405, 447.
  Diplomatische Correspondenz, Reich, FF. 233, 264a.
Staatenabteilungen:
  Schweiz, Berichte, F. 193.

(b) *Allgemeines Verwaltungsarchiv, Vienna*
Pergen Akten, vi–xxii.
Polizeihofstelle, 1793–5; Ältere Polizeiakten, ii/2.
Hofkanzlei, III A 3, III C 3, IV M 1–3 (1790–5).

(c) *Kriegsarchiv, Vienna*
Hofkriegsrat, 1794.

(d) *Archiv für Nieder-Österreich, Vienna*
Präsidialprotokoll, 1789–97.
Präsidialakten, 1789–97.

Polizei Oberdirektionsakten, 1789–97.
Nieder-Österreichische Regierung, Normalien, Geistliche Akten.
(*e*) *Steiermärkisches Landesarchiv, Graz*
Gubernialarchiv:
Miszellen, Kart. 223–5.
Gubernialakten, FF. 90–92.
Archiv der Stände:
Landtagsprotokoll, 1790–4.
Schuber 605, 606.
Nachlaß Saurau (Franz Joseph).
(*f*) *Ober-Österreichisches Landesarchiv, Linz*
Präsidialakten, 1790–5.
Polizeiakten, 1790–5.
(*g*) *Erzbischöfliches Ordinariatsarchiv, Vienna*
Regesten, Nos. 773, 789.
(*h*) *Archives Nationales, Paris*
Série AF ii. 57.
Régistres AF ii*, 221, 285; F 7*, 13.
(*i*) *Archives du Ministère des Affaires Étrangères, Paris*
Correspondance Politique:
Autriche, vols. 356–65.
Suisse, vols. 444, 446.
(*j*) *Public Record Office, London*
Foreign Office, 7, vols. 18–37.

2. ORIGINAL PRINTED SOURCES

(*a*) *Collections of documents, letters, &c.*
Ed. A. BEER, *Joseph II., Leopold II. und Kaunitz. Ihr Briefwechsel* (1873:
Vienna).
Ed. K. BENDA, *A magyar Jakobinusok iratai* (1952, 1957: Budapest: 3 vols.).
Ed. S. DOMANOVSZKY, *József nádor iratai*, i (1925: Budapest).
Ed. J. KROPATSCHEK, *Handbuch aller unter der Regierung Kaiser Josephs II.
. . . ergangenen Verordnungen und Gesetze in einer systematischen Ver-
bindung* (1784–90: Vienna: 18 vols.).
—— *Sammlung aller unter der Regierung des Kaisers Leopold II. . . . ergangenen
Verordnungen und Gesetze* (1792–4: Vienna: 5 vols.).
Ed. F. MAASS, *Der Josephinismus — Quellen zu seiner Geschichte in Österreich
1760–1790* (*Fontes Rerum Austriacarum*, 2. Abt., lxxi–lxxiii, 1951–6:
Vienna: 3 vols.).
Ed. E. MÁLYUSZ, *Sándor Lipót főherceg-nádor iratai, 1790–1795* (1926:
Budapest).
Ed. L. SCHIEDERMAIR, *Die Briefe Mozarts und seiner Familie* (1914: Munich:
4 vols.).
Ed. H. SCHLITTER, *Briefe der Erzherzogin Marie Christine, Statthalterin der
Niederlande an Leopold II.* (*Fontes Rerum Austriacarum*, 2. Abt., xlviii,
1. Halbband (1896: Vienna).

Ed. A. v. VIVENOT, *Quellen zur deutschen Kaiserpolitik Österreichs während der französischen Revolutionskriege*, i–iv (1873 ff.: Vienna).

—— *Vertrauliche Briefe des Freiherrn von Thugut* (1872: Vienna: 2 vols.).

Ed. F. WALTER, *Die österreichische Zentralverwaltung*, ii/4, 5 (*Veröffentlichungen der Kommission für neuere Geschichte Österreichs*, xxxvi, xliii (1951, 1956: Vienna).

Ed. G. WILHELM, *Briefe des Dichters Johann Baptist von Alxinger* (*Sitzungsberichte der Akademie der Wissenschaften in Wien*, cxl, 1899, II. Abh.).

Ed. A. WOLF, *Leopold II. und Marie Christine, Ihr Briefwechsel* (1867: Vienna).

(*b*) *Contemporary pamphlets, political literature, periodicals, &c.*

J. B. v. ALXINGER, *Alxingers sämtliche Gedichte* (1784: Leipzig).

—— *Bliomberis* (1791: Leipzig).

—— *Ueber Leopold den Zweyten* (1792: Berlin).

—— *Sämtliche Schriften* (1814: Vienna: 12 vols.).

ANONYMOUS, *Gedanken über die Justizverwaltung* (1789: Vienna).

—— *Die Kriegssteuer. Ein Schauspiel in 3 Aufzügen* (1789: Vienna).

—— *Freimüthige Betrachtungen eines philosophischen Weltbürgers über wichtige Gegenstände* (1793: s.l.).

Ed. C. D. BARTSCH, *Wiener Zeitung.*

A. BLUMAUER, *Sämtliche Werke* (1884: Vienna: 4 vols.).

L. FELBERER, *Widerlegung der Gedanken des Herrn Promovsky wider Herrn Siegfried Wieser* (1786: Vienna).

J. G. FOCK, *Gedächtnißrede auf den Höchstseligen Kaiser Leopold den Zweiten* (1792: Vienna).

Ed. G. GUGITZ, *Denkwürdigkeiten des Venezianers Lorenzo da Ponte* (1924: Dresden: 2 vols.).

F. A. HASLBERGER, *Salzburger Chronik*, ed. Martin, in *Mitteilungen für Salzburger Landeskunde*, lxii–lxix (1927–9).

F. HEGRAD, *Versuch einer kurzen Lebensgeschichte Kaiser Leopolds II. bis zu dessen Absterben* (1792: Prague).

L. A. HOFFMANN, *Babel. Fragmente über die jetzigen politischen Angelegenheiten in Ungarn* (1790: gedruckt im römischen Reiche).

—— *Ninive. Fortgesetzte Fragmente über die dermaligen Angelegenheiten in Ungarn* (1790: gedruckt im römischen Reiche).

—— *Patriotische Bemerkungen über die gegenwärtige Theuerung in Wien* (1791: Vienna).

Ed. L. A. HOFFMANN, *Wiener Zeitschrift* (1792–3).

Ed. ABBÉ HOFSTÄTTER, *Magazin für Kunst und Literatur* (1793–7).

F. X. HUBER, *Geschichte Josephs II.* (1790: Vienna).

—— *Beiträge zur Characteristik und Regierungsgeschichte Josephs II., Leopold II., und Franz' II.* (1800: Paris).

L. HÜBNER, *Lebensgeschichte Josephs II.* (1790: Salzburg: 2 vols.).

(J. v. IZDENCZY), *Gespräch zwischen einem österreichischen Patrioten und einem durch Ungarn reisenden Fremden* (1790: Vienna).

(I. v. Martinovics), *Testament Politique de l'Empereur Joseph II* (1791: Vienna).

—— *Oratio pro Leopoldo Secundo Rege ab Hungaris Proceribus et Nobilibus Accusato* (1792: Germania).

J. Molnár, *Politisch-Kirchliches Manch-Hermaeon* (1790: Leipzig).

J. Mrazek, *Rede an Österreichs Völker* (1792: Vienna).

J. Pezzl, *Charakteristik Josephs II.* (1790: Vienna).

(J. Richter), 'Warum wird Kaiser Joseph von seinem Volke nicht geliebt?' (1787: Vienna), in *Josephinische Curiosa*, i (1848: Vienna).

Ed. Schönholz, *Traditionen aus dem alten Österreich* (1914: Munich: 2 vols.).

Ed. J. Schreyvogel and others, *Österreichische Monatsschrift* (1793–4).

J. v. Sonnenfels, *Ueber die Liebe des Vaterlandes* (1785: Vienna).

—— *Uiber Wucher und Wuchergesetze* (1789: Vienna).

—— *Betrachtungen eines österreichischen Staatsbürgers an seinen Freund* (1793: Vienna).

—— *Handbuch der Inneren Staatsverwaltung* (1796: Vienna).

—— *Ueber öffentliche Sicherheit* (1817: Vienna).

Ed. F. v. Steinsberg and F. X. Huber, *Das politische Sieb* (1791–2).

K. Graf v. Zinzendorf, *Selbstbiographie*, ed. Pettenegg (1879: Vienna).

3. SECONDARY SOURCES

L. Abafi, *Geschichte der Freimaurerei in Österreich-Ungarn*, iv (1893: Budapest).

S. Adler, *Ungarn nach dem Tode Josephs II.* (1908: Vienna).

—— 'Die politische Gesetzgebung in ihren geschichtlichen Beziehungen zum Allgemeinen Bürgerlichen Gesetzbuche', in *Festschrift zur Jahrhundertfeier des Allgemeinen Bürgerlichen Gesetzbuches* (1911: Vienna).

K. Benda, 'Die ungarischen Jakobiner', in *Maximilien Robespierre 1758-1794. Beiträge zu seinem 200. Geburtstag*, ed. W. Markov (1958: Berlin).

E. Benedikt, *Kaiser Joseph II., 1741–1790* (1936: Vienna).

A. H. Benna, *Die Polizeihofstelle* (Unpubl. thesis, 1941: Vienna).

—— 'Organisierung und Personalstand der Polizeihofstelle (1793–1848)', in *Mitteilungen des österreichischen Staatsarchivs*, vi (1953), 197–239.

V. Bibl, 'Die nieder-österreichischen Stände und die französische Revolution', in *Jahrbuch für Landeskunde Nieder-Österreichs*, ii (1903).

—— 'Das Robotprovisorium für Nieder-Österreich vom 20. Juni 1796', in *Jahrbuch für Landeskunde Nieder-Österreichs*, Neue Folge, vii (1908), 235–75.

—— *Der Zerfall Österreichs*, i (1922: Vienna).

H. I. Bidermann, 'Die Verfassungskrise in der Steiermark zur Zeit der ersten französischen Revolution', in *Mitteilungen des Historischen Vereins für Steiermark*, xxi (1873), 15–105.

T. v. Borodajkevics, 'Die Kirche in Österreich', in *Österreichs Erbe und Sendung im deutschen Raum*, ed. Nadler-Srbik (1936: Vienna).

M. Darvai, 'Die politische Literatur in Ungarn bis 1825', in *Ungarische Revue*, ix (1889), 434–53.

J. Droz, *L'Allemagne et la Révolution Française* (1949: Paris).

F. Eckhart, *A short History of Hungary* (1931: London).

F. Engel-Janosi, 'Josephs II. Tod im Urteil seiner Zeitgenossen', in *Mitteilungen des Instituts für österreichische Geschichtsforschung*, xliv (1930), 324–46.

W. Ernst, 'Die Preissenkungsaktion Kaiser Josephs II.', in *Österreichische Volksstimme*, No. 301 (30 Dec. 1951), p. 5.

F. Fejtö, *Un Habsbourg Révolutionnaire — Joseph II* (1953: Paris).

A. Fournier, 'Joseph II. und der "geheime Dienst"', in *Historische Studien und Skizzen*, Dritte Reihe (1912: Vienna), pp. 1–16.

V. Fraknói, *Martinovics élete* (1921: Budapest).

C. Glossy, 'Schreyvogels Projekt einer Wochenschrift', in *Jahrbuch der Grillparzergesellschaft*, viii (1898), 304–24.

H. Gnau, *Die Zensur unter Joseph II.* (1911: Leipzig).

J. Godechot, *La Grande Nation* (1956: Paris: 2 vols.).

R. Gragger, *Preußen, Weimar und die ungarische Königskrone* (1923: Berlin).

A. J. Gross-Hoffinger, *Joseph II. als Regent und Mensch* (Neue Ausgabe: s.d.: Straßfurt).

C. Grünberg, *Die Bauernbefreiung und die Auflösung des grundherrlich-bäuerlichen Verhältnisses in Böhmen, Mähren und Schlesien* (1893–4: Leipzig: 2 vols.).

O. Hinze, 'Der österreichische und der preußische Beamtenstaat im 17. und 18. Jahrhundert', in *Historische Zeitschrift*, Neue Folge, 1 (1901), 401–44.

C. Hock u. H. I. Bidermann, *Der österreichische Staatsrat* (1879: Vienna).

G. Holzknecht, *Ursprung und Herkunft der Reformideen Kaiser Josephs II. auf kirchlichem Gebiet* (1914: Innsbruck).

F. Ilwof, *Die Grafen Attems* (1897: Graz).

A. Jäger, 'Das Eindringen des modernen kirchenfeindlichen Geistes in Österreich unter Karl VI. u. Maria Theresia', in *Zeitschrift für katholische Theologie*, ii (1878), 259–311.

R. J. Kerner, *Bohemia in the Eighteenth Century with special reference to the reign of Leopold II* (1932: New York).

I. Kont, *Étude sur l'Influence de la Littérature française en Hongrie* (1902: Paris).

W. C. Langsam, 'Emperor Francis II and the Austrian "Jacobins" 1792–1796', in *American Historical Review*, 1 (1945), 471–90.

—— *Francis the Good* (1951: New York).

G. Lefebvre, 'Le Despotisme éclairé', in *Annales historiques de la Révolution française*, xxi (1949), 97–115.

E. M. Link, *The Emancipation of the Austrian Peasant 1740–1798* (1949: New York).

R. Lorenz, *Volksbewaffnung und Staatsidee* (1926: Vienna).

H. Marczali, 'Die Verschwörung des Martinovics', in *Ungarische Revue*, i (1881), 11–29.

—— *Hungary in the Eighteenth Century* (1910: London).

W. Markov (Ed.), *Maximilien Robespierre, 1758–1794. Beiträge zu seinem 200. Geburtstag* (1958: Berlin).

F. M. MAYER, *Steiermark im Franzosenzeitalter* (1888: Graz).

A. MENZEL, 'Beiträge zur Geschichte der Staatslehre', in *Sitzungsberichte der Akademie der Wissenschaften in Wien*, ccx (1929), I. Abh.

P. v. MITROFANOV, *Joseph II. Seine politische und kulturelle Tätigkeit* (1910: Vienna).

P. MÜLLER, 'Der aufgeklärte Absolutismus in Österreich' in *Bulletin of the International Commission of Historical Sciences*, ix (1937).

H. OBERHUMMER, *Die Wiener Polizei* (1938: Vienna: 2 vols.).

A. POSCH, *Die kirchliche Aufklärung der Universität Graz* (1946: Graz).

K. PŘÍBRAM, *Geschichte der österreichischen Gewerbepolitik* (1907: Leipzig).

E. PROBST, 'Johann Baptist von Alxinger', in *Jahrbuch der Grillparzergesellschaft*, vii (1897) 171–202.

H. SCHLITTER, 'Zur Geschichte der französischen Politik Leopolds II', in *Fontes Rerum Austriacarum*, 2. Abt., xlviii/1 (1896).

J. SLOKAR, *Geschichte der österreichischen Industrie und ihrer Förderung unter Franz I.* (1914: Vienna).

A. SPRINGER, *Geschichte Österreichs seit dem Wiener Frieden*, i (1863: Leipzig).

S. TASSIER, 'Les Démocrates belges de 1789', in *Mémoires de l'Académie Royale de Belgique, Classes des Lettres et des Sciences morales et politiques*, xxviii (1930), fasc. 2.

F. VALJAVEC, *Der Josephinismus* (2nd ed.: 1945: Munich).

—— *Die Entstehung der politischen Strömungen in Deutschland, 1770–1815* (1951: Vienna).

H. v. VOLTELINI, 'Die naturrechtlichen Ideen und die Reformen des 18. Jahrhunderts', in *Historische Zeitschrift*, Dritte Folge, ix (1910), 65–104.

F. WALTER, 'Die Organisierung der staatlichen Polizei unter Kaiser Joseph II', in *Mitteilungen des Vereins für Geschichte der Stadt Wien*, vii (1927), 22–53.

E. WERTHEIMER, 'Baron Hompesch und Joseph II', in *Mitteilungen des Instituts für österreichische Geschichtsforschung*, Ergänzungsband VI (1901), 649–81.

E. WINTER, *Der Josephinismus und seine Geschichte* (1943: Prague).

C. WOLFSGRUBER, *Christoph Anton Cardinal Migazzi* (1890: Saulgau).

—— *Kaiser Franz II.* (1899: Vienna: 2 vols.).

—— *Kirchengeschichte Österreich-Ungarns* (1909: Vienna).

H. v. ZEISSBERG, 'Zwei Jahre belgischer Geschichte (1791, 1792)', 2 pts., in *Sitzungsberichte der Akademie der Wissenschaften in Wien*, cxxiii (1890), VII. Abh., and cxxiv (1891), XII. Abh.

E. V. ZENKER, *Geschichte der Wiener Journalistik von den Anfängen bis zum Jahre 1848* (1892: Vienna).

INDEX

Abaffy, Ferenc, 138.

absolutism, *see* despotism.

Ad Amicam Aurem, see Batthány, Alajos.

administrative changes, 2, 57, 75–76, 105, 106, 107, 111; in Hungary, 55, 64, 87, 111.

agitators, 37, 60, 61, 97, 118, 128–32, 146, 183–4.

agnosticism, *see* scepticism.

Alexander Leopold, Archduke, Palatin of Hungary 1790–5, 88, 106, 111, 142, 156, 160, 173–4, 176–81, 183, 185.

Alxinger, Johann Baptist v., 14, 25, 91 n., 112, 113; *Bliomberis*, 16 n.; *Prosaische Schriften*, 21 n.; *Ueber Leopold den Zweyten*, 91 n.

Amis du Bien Publique (Organization of the Vonckists), 77, 102.

arbitrary arrests, 40–41, 91, 93, 128–32, 147–8, 178, 183–4.

— rule, 21, 23, 25, 90–91, 93, 96, 100, 130, 157, 159, 162, 175–84; *see also* arbitrary arrests.

arbitration, 96, 122.

Arco, Count, 12.

aristocratic opposition, 3, 5–6, 9–11, 21 n., 25, 34, 36, 50–58, 84–90; in Belgium, 34, 83, 102, 111; in Hungary, 6, 10–12, 34–35, 50, 52–56, 71, 73, 86–88, 144–5; in Hungary, 6, 10–12, 34–35, 50, 52–56, 71, 73, 86–88, 144–5.

— privilege(s), 3, 5, 12–14, 21, 35, 51, 52 n., 53, 56–57, 67, 68, 70–73, 75, 77, 87, 112; *see also* Estates.

artisans, 29–30, 139, 150–1; *see also* *Schusterkomplott*.

Artois, Count d', 66–67.

Asia, 13.

atheism, see *Schusterkomplott*.

Attems, Count Ferdinand, 72–73, 81.

Attems, Countess, 81.

Auersperg, Count, Acting Governor of Lower Austria 1789–91, 46, 68.

Auersperg, Count Cajetan, 84.

Aufruf an alle Deutsche zu einem anti-aristokratischen Gleichheitsbund, *see* Riedel, Andreas.

Augarten, 150.

Babel, see Hoffmann, Leopold Alois.

Bacher, Secretary at the French embassy in Basle, 140.

Bahrdt, Karl Friedrich, 17, 41.

Balassa, Count Francis, Illyrian Court Chancellor, 73, 87.

Banat, 13.

Bannwarth, Ferdinand, Police Commissioner, 168.

Barsch, Polish *Chargé d'Affaires* in Paris, 140.

Bartsch, Conrad Dominik, editor of the *Wiener Zeitung*, 24, 35 n.

Basle, 140.

Bastille, 177.

Batthány, Alajos, 71, 136; *Ad Amicam Aurem*, 71, 136.

Bauern Zeitung, 47–48.

Bavaria, 49, 110.

Bavarian exchange project, 110.

Beaumarchais, 13; *Marriage of Figaro*, 13.

Beck, Captain, author of the *Eipel-dauerlied*, 136.

Beck, Christian August, political theorist, tutor of Joseph II, 20.

Beer, Franz Anton, Chief Director of Police (*Oberpolizeidirektor*), 39, 42, 43, 98, 117.

Belgian democrats, *see* Vonckists.

Belgium (Austrian Netherlands), 3 n., 34, 50, 52, 56, 71, 76–77, 83, 101–2, 110, 111, 116, 143.

Betrachtungen eines österreichischen Staatsbürgers an seinen Freund, see Sonnenfels, Joseph v.

Bibl, Viktor, historian, 156 n., 161 n.

Bichler, florist, see *Schusterkomplott*.

Billek, Leopold, auditor, 149, 155, 167.

Billek, Wasgottwill, Captain, 166.

Bischoffwerder, Colonel, Prussian emissary, 110.

bishops, 57.

Bliomberis, see Alxinger, Johann Baptist v.

Blumauer, Alois, 135, 148; *Beobach-tungen über Österreichs Aufklärung und Literatur*, 7 n.

PRINTED IN GREAT BRITAIN
AT THE UNIVERSITY PRESS, OXFORD
BY VIVIAN RIDLER
PRINTER TO THE UNIVERSITY

mm